LP
1, 42
N

Pop

Labour and the Press

From New Left to New Labour

SEAN TUNNEY

WITHDRAWN
from
STIRLING UNIVERSITY LIBRARY

sussex
ACADEMIC
PRESS

BRIGHTON • PORTLAND

0 | 01431 42

01/07

Copyright © 2007 Sean Tunney

The right of Sean Tunney to be identified as Author of this work has been asserted in
accordance with the Copyright, Designs and Patents Act 1988.

2 4 6 8 10 9 7 5 3 1

First published 2007 in Great Britain by
SUSSEX ACADEMIC PRESS
PO Box 139
Eastbourne BN24 9BP

and in the United States of America by
SUSSEX ACADEMIC PRESS
920 NE 58th Ave   Suite 300
Portland, Oregon 97213–3786

All rights reserved. Except for the quotation of short passages for the purposes of
criticism and review, no part of this publication may be reproduced, stored in a
retrieval system, or transmitted, in any form or by any means, electronic,
mechanical, photocopying, recording or otherwise, without the prior
permission of the publisher.

British Library Cataloguing in Publication Data
A CIP catalogue record for this book is available from the British Library.

Library of Congress Cataloging-in-Publication Data

Tunney, Sean.
   Labour and the press, 1972–2005 : from new left to new
   Labour / by Sean Tunney.
   p. cm.
   Includes bibliographical references and index.
   ISBN 1-84519-138-2 (h/c : alk. paper) —
   ISBN 1-84519-139-0 (p/b : alk. paper)
   1. Labour Party (Great Britain)—In mass media.
   2. Labour Party (Great Britain)—Public relations. 3. Press
   and politics—Great Britain. 4. Great Britain—Politics and
   government. I. Title.

   JN1129.L32T86 2007
   072—dc22

                                              2006020742

Typeset and designed by SAP, Brighton & Eastbourne
Printed by The Cromwell Press, Trowbridge, Wilts.
This book is printed on acid-free paper.

3597399400

WITHDRAWN from STIRLING UNIVERSITY LIBRARY

Labour Press
From New Left to New Labour

Contents

Preface

"Unless we can return to the principles of public service we will lose our claim to be the Fourth Estate. What right have we to speak in the public interest when, too often, we are motivated by personal gain?" (Rupert Murdoch, 1961)[1]

"A newspaper is an individual piece of private property which has public responsibilities expressing the views of those people who are running it." (National Publishers' Association chair Lord Goodman, 1976)[2]

"I make, and I seek, no excuses, and I express no bitterness, when I say that the Conservative-supporting press has enabled the Tory Party to win yet again when the Conservative Party could not have secured victory for itself on the basis of its record, its programme or its character." (Neil Kinnock, 1992)[3]

These quotations point to three difficulties with the press with which some opinion formers in the Labour Party grappled from 1972 onwards; the year when the party commenced with its first full-scale internal discussion on the mass media. First, in contrast to a significant proportion of the broadcast media, the national press is mainly owned by wealthy individual private interests, but is also expected to perform a collective democratic function — providing the diversity of news and opinion required in a democracy. Second, the press's private ownership has been concentrated in the hands of only a few companies and individuals, over which, in contrast to broadcast regulation, there is little public influence through representatives — and readers have little control. Third, a local difficulty for Labour was that it faced a British press that was predominantly hostile to it for much of the period under discussion (even if Kinnock's claim about its decisive influence over the 1992 election is more debatable). The discussions, debates and answers to these three difficulties are the subject of this book.

I look at how the Labour Party, in developing its policy after 1972, addressed the effect of British press ownership and control on political democracy. It is clear there were important problems with Labour's strategies from the 1970s into the early 1980s. Such difficulties explain why there were disagreements in the party over implementing policies. But they do not provide a sufficient explanation as to why the policies were gradually abandoned. There are many examples across British public life where, in the slow process of policy implementation, difficulties have been ironed out.[4] With regard to the press, media theorist and former Labour activist James Curran cites the example of the Scandinavian government newspaper schemes where this has been the case.[5]

To explain why the Labour Party's newspaper policies were not implemented, the book will place the shift in those policies within the context of how general party strategy altered and how those responsible for decisions about press policy also changed. Broadly speaking, groups and individuals, tending to be on the left of the party or at least more radical in approach, attempted to provide answers to the three problems identified, which were stifled by forces that were more often on the right of the party. As has been revealed in relation to broadcasting policy, the left/right divide punctuated policy debates and ended up marginalizing attempts to find solutions.[6]

In addition, I shall argue that there was an inherent tension within Labour's seemingly similar policies designed both to ensure that Labour could be more fairly represented in the press and to diversify and democratize newspaper ownership. This came to a head when, under Neil Kinnock, Labour switched its emphasis away from providing solutions to the problems of bias through structural changes to the press market towards reinvigorating a political marketing strategy with the existing newspapers. In order to tackle bias, policies for structural change came to be considered redundant and dealing with concentration of ownership became a positive hindrance. I shall consider how the attempt to market Labour, along with the effect of swimming with the tide of economic globalisation, came to dominate press policy, to the exclusion of initiatives to diversify the press. It illuminates the emphasis New Labour has placed on political communications and the press.

To set the context, Chapter 1 will first consider why it is important to analyse Labour's press ownership policy. It will assess aspects of the first two difficulties with British newspaper ownership that earlier Labour policy attempted to address. Finally, it will look at various models for ownership and control of the press relevant to Labour's ideas, before outlining the structure of the rest of the book.

Acknowledgements

I would like to thank Professors John Callaghan and Mark Phythian, Mike Haynes and Wolverhampton University; Professors Julian Petley and James Curran, Eric Shaw, Granville Williams, Jonathan Hardy, Matthew Taylor, Stephen Smith, Jeremy Tonkin, Ruth and, especially, Jane Thomas for their help and support; and all those who kindly agreed to be interviewed. For Jane, Daniel and Erin and in memory of my parents.

Abbreviations

AES	Alternative Economic Strategy
BECTU	Broadcasting Entertainment Cinematograph and Theatre Union
BMIG	British Media Industry Group
CLPD	Campaign for Labour Party Democracy
CPBF	Campaign for Press and Broadcasting Freedom
CPF	Campaign for Press Freedom
DCMS	Department of Culture, Media and Sport
DTI	Department of Trade and Industry
FCG	Free Communications Group
GLC	Greater London Council
GLEB	Greater London Enterprise Board
IBA	Independent Broadcasting Authority
IPA	Independent Press Authority
IWC	Institute for Workers' Control
LCC	Labour Co-ordinating Committee
NATSOPA	National Society of Operative Printers, Graphical and Media Personnel
NEB	National Enterprise Board
NEC	Labour's National Executive Committee
NGA	National Graphical Association
NPA	Newspaper Publishers Association
NPC	National Printing Corporation
NPF	National Policy Forum
NUJ	National Union of Journalists
OFCOM	Office of Communications
OFT	Office of Fair Trading
OPA	Open Press Authority
SCA	Shadow Communications Agency
SOGAT	Society of Graphical and Allied Trades
TUC	Trades Union Congress

Labour in Government

Labour in government/ opposition		Labour leader	Elections
Government	1966–1970	Harold Wilson	1966
Opposition	1970–1974	Harold Wilson	1970
Government	1974–1976	Harold Wilson	1974 × 2
Government	1976–1979	James Callaghan	1979
Opposition	1979–1983	Michael Foot	1983
Opposition	1983–1992	Neil Kinnock	1987, 1992
Opposition	1992–1994	John Smith	
Opposition	1994–1997	Tony Blair	
Government	1997–present	Tony Blair	1997, 2001, 2005

1

Introduction
Labour's Problems with the Press

Why the Press?

Why should policy on the national press and its ownership still be regarded as an important area of study? After all, it is assumed that most British people now receive the news and information about politics predominantly from the broadcast media rather than newspapers.

As we shall see, the press has had a particular importance in the period covered in this book from 1972 onwards. Unlike other parts of the mass media, it has not been under pressure to achieve "balance" in its output. Thus it has had the scope to be more obviously politically weighted in its coverage. It was precisely for this reason that it attracted the attention of the Labour movement as a whole, which perceived the press as predominantly partial in its reporting.

The press also affects the broadcast media. The study of media influence on voters is contentious and inconclusive.[1] Nevertheless, some writers have tentatively suggested that television could have some long-term influence on voter behaviour.[2] Equally, studies of the 1980s and early 1990s, the period in which the press was particularly blamed for Labour's defeats, have pointed to the influence on news values that the Conservative press had on broadcasters. It was perceived that there were areas where the press focused and the broadcasters followed.[3] In defining the news agenda for broadcasters, the press played a significant part.

What is more, those in the Labour Party interested in the media regarded press coverage as hugely significant. In the 1970s, when the focus was on ownership, all national newspapers were considered important. Later, as Neil Kinnock's leadership concentrated more on press and media management, Labour strategists focused increasingly on contacts in the "quality press", whose output, it was believed, affected the political agenda of what was perceived to be the more influential broadcast media. Latterly, Labour strategists have focused more on managing tabloid press output, following Neil Kinnock's experience in the 1992 election. Thus some studies have indicated the continuing significance of the press on British political communications and, more importantly, so has the Labour Party.

During this period, when considering the national press, the Labour Party focused its attention on the mass circulation dailies and Sunday newspapers covering Britain. So does this book.

There are a number of ways to consider Labour Party policy on press ownership. Some analyses of media ownership and regulation policy make changes in national and international regulatory law their broader canvas.[4] Other work has considered it in the context of British government media and newspaper policy more generally.[5] To some extent, it has also been situated within social democratic policy internationally.[6] This book's emphasis is different in that it is mainly written from the perspective of modern Labour Party history. It considers press ownership policy within the context of power relations in the Labour Party and changes in party policy more generally. Its context is modern political history rather than just media history.

However, one needs to specify what is meant by Labour Party policy, as there is scope for rival interpretations. And even the idea of there being a single Labour Party policy has been implicitly contested.[7] At various points, the policy of the party, the leadership, and, at times, the Labour government have seemed to be separate things. And press reporting has helped to blur this question further.

Following Labour Party historian Lewis Minkin, this book regards the Labour Party's conference as pivotal.[8] It defines party policy as that decided by the conference. When one set of actors – usually the leadership – designates the party's policy differently, it will be made clear.

Much of the information on which the book is based comes from internal Labour Party sources. These include the minutes of Labour's National Executive Committee (NEC) and the submitted internal policy papers collated by Labour's research department, the minutes of the Parliamentary Labour Party and Shadow Cabinet, Labour Party and trade union annual conference transcripts, Hansard records of parliamentary debates, public inquiries, such as the Royal Commission on the Press, Green and White Papers and government bills. In addition, the author interviewed senior Labour Party figures involved with press ownership policy, former press policy advisers, civil servants involved with political communications and media management, working journalists, media union officials and media academics and activists involved in Labour press policy formulation.

Importantly, gaining access to Neil Kinnock's personal papers provided valuable, previously unpublished information about the party's internal discussions regarding press ownership and media management policy. These internal party sources illuminated many of the decisions made, but they also provide new insights into the relationship between the party leadership and the press owners. The next step is to consider the first two difficulties identified in the preface, which concern, first, the democratic functioning of the press in the context of private ownership and, secondly, the issue of public control over the press – given this private ownership.

The Press and Political Democracy

The first two difficulties outlined above posed a problem for British democracy – one that Labour policy in the earlier period that we are considering grappled with. Labour thinkers and activists considered that democracy did not have the press that it needed to function adequately.

The German philosopher Jürgen Habermas has developed an influential notion used by theorists to consider democratic communication. In his idea of a "public sphere" we get an outline, however abstract, idealized and historically questionable, of the press needed. One function of the press is to provide a space where discussion and differences in political debate can be aired (an important idea in relation to the first difficulty set out above). The newspapers can be explicitly ideological, providing "lines" and viewpoints, making it possible for there to be rational-critical public debate of political issues.[9]

It follows that, along with entertaining and informing, newspapers need to provide a platform for different politicians and interest groups to make plain their complaints and concerns – offering a dialogue for diverse views and political viewpoints.[10] Thus, titles need not be free from "bias" or necessarily be balanced. A public sphere requires a lively range of views.[11] Democracy requires diversity and pluralism in the press. There should be a number of differing political positions; otherwise, groups may be deprived of the right to receive and impart information.

But democracy also necessitates representation. In political terms, the interests of democracy are served when a range of viewpoints are represented. It has been suggested that democracy requires there to be an allocation of newspaper and media resources for the persuasion of views that is roughly the same as the distribution of opinions in society[12] – a point to be considered in the chapters that follow. At the very least, parties should have forums where their ideas are published. Culturally, newspapers need to represent, and report on, minorities and marginal voices. Citizens and voters require a diversity of ideas and opinions in order to exercise citizenship effectively and participate in the public sphere.[13] The press and media operate to provide opportunities for citizens to learn and become involved.[14]

This notion of representation has its problems.[15] More particularly, it was entangled in the Labour Party with a concern to have Labour's viewpoint represented in the press – a key subject of this book. What is important to register, however, is that political democracy requires, at the least, press and media plurality to provide wide and diverse representation. It has other requirements too. And these will be addressed in due course.

Does Ownership Matter?

If we are to consider Labour policy on ownership, press diversity and concentration, then we need to consider the relationship between them. The connection between concentration of ownership and diversity of press content is not simple. There is surprisingly scant research evidence on the effects of concentration.[16] It has been disputed that ownership diversity aids political democracy.[17] There are those who argue that concentration brings diversity of content and little danger to democracy.[18] Research into the Canadian press, for example, has questioned the idea that diminished competition leads to less information diversity.[19] However, research in the USA has shown that papers in more competitive markets have been superior to monopoly titles.[20]

Theoretically, it can be argued that concentration means that companies can take advantage of their size to use their resources more effectively; it allows a greater range of output to be provided and loss-making titles to be subsidized. Also, some consider that companies have to be large to survive and compete internationally in a world seen to be dominated by economic globalization. Only such companies can maintain their independence from interest groups.[21] However, as media economist Gillian Doyle indicates, few of these assertions are automatically true. The savings made as a result of concentration need to be invested in diverse titles for the advantages to be realized.[22] Moreover, the point on independence can be turned on its head to suggest that press conglomerates should be accountable to diverse interest groups, an idea to be considered later.

Moreover, a series of influential texts concerning the huge US media market has argued that media ownership concentration is deleterious to political democracy.[23] Media concentration leads to fewer information sources. Output becomes increasingly uniform. The dominance of the large press corporations can drive out smaller companies. This supremacy is strengthened by the dual nature of the newspaper market, where advertising revenue can add to the domination of certain titles.[24] This too is considered in more detail later.

As concentration increases, so does power and political influence. In capitalist economies, the result has been increased dominance by business interests.[25] What is of major concern is that concentrated ownership leads to the political viewpoints and values of the dominant media owners, managers and companies being represented, in preference to other positions. The press can be used as a vehicle for owners, managers and editors.

Alternative, opposing political ideas can be squeezed out of the frame. Research into the media in western Europe has confirmed that direct and indirect editorial interference is not confined to Britain.[26] Indeed, one effect that Peter Humphreys' research on the European media identifies is that owners and managers can use their media to influence public policy, either for commercial or for political reasons.[27] The political ascent of Silvio Berlusconi has been a notable illustration of a phenomenon relevant to the book's analysis of the evolution of New Labour's policy. Recent research has pointed to dominant media corporations' use of political influence to relax regulatory obstacles to expansion.

Whether or not it can be proved in all instances that media companies want some political opinions or types of cultural output to dominate, the risk exists. And the greater the concentration, the greater the risk of abuse. It is true that other factors – such as the size and wealth of the market, or the extent to which newspaper companies share resources, such as news-gathering through agencies – are important factors in gauging diversity of content. The extent that diversity of content is affected by cross-media ownership, which we will consider in a moment, is partly dependent on whether consolidation promotes this same joint use of resources. Nevertheless, as Gillian Doyle specifies, although diverse press ownership does not guarantee diversity of political content, it is a prerequisite of it.[28] Without diverse ownership, political democracy is compromised.

Ownership and Control – Are they Linked?

In order to consider Labour Party policy on press ownership and control we also need to consider the relationship between the two. The foregoing discussion assumes that ownership and control are linked. But are they? Pluralists have questioned this. Similarly, Colin Seymour-Ure, for example, argues that the relationship between ownership and control has become more complex than when the old-style press barons dominated. Chief executives of British newspapers in the recent past have not been extensive capital owners and individual owners have not exercised control.[29] The notion that professional managerial control had become divorced from ownership was well known in the Labour Party, advanced by the post-war revisionists and, particularly, Labour Foreign Secretary Tony Crosland. Crosland had argued that such managers had different interests from the profit-seeking owners of old. Capitalism, in this sense, was dead.[30] What Crosland identified was described in one famous account as *The Managerial Revolution*, which saw managers as a separate class from the "capitalists proper", not dependent on private ownership.[31]

However, this idea was in its turn effectively challenged. Economist Paul Mattick, for one, argued that in large corporations the diffusion of share ownership meant that for numerous smaller shareholders, ownership and control were indeed separate. But as a consequence, less stockholding was needed for control over a corporation. Larger minority shareholders could combine with managers and directors, who were usually shareholders also, to control the companies. Managers might have autonomous interests in areas such as the distribution of profits. But the concerns of large shareholders were the same as those of managers if the company was to thrive in a competitive economy.[32] Later research was sceptical of the broader claims of writers such as Mattick. Nonetheless, it confirmed that company directors tended to own significant shareholdings and that they also had similar class origins to those major shareowners who maintained "participation in strategic control".[33]

Thus, across industry, control has been dispersed between senior management and owners, who share the same profit-seeking motives. With press companies, however, there is the age-old tension between profit and political power, with powerful shareholders and managers facing the same dilemma as the press barons of old. Commercial considerations were always there, along with political ones. It is still true that even the most politically dictatorial of owners have to consider profit and loss in a capitalist market. Any political motives would have to be fused with powerful capitalist instincts. Many writers have quoted Lord Beaverbrook telling the 1947 Royal Commission on the Press that he ran his papers for "propaganda and for no other purpose". But he went on to tell the commissioners that: "No paper is any good for propaganda unless it has a thoroughly good financial position."[34] So in fusing these motives managers have acted like owners on a day-to-day basis; examples on Fleet Street include Lord Stevens, Lord Matthews and, more recently, Lord Hollick.[35]

Secondly, it has been argued that editors have assumed greater control since the 1980s. However, importantly, the owners and chief executives have the power to hire and fire. They choose the editors and senior managers. They set the financial parameters of individual newspapers and make the final "bottom line" decisions, which determine whether a newspaper lives on or dies. The editors operate in the light of these "bottom line" diktats, as the last full-scale British inquiry into the press was told.[36] For the newspaper moguls, such as Rupert Murdoch and Conrad Black, Jeremy Tunstall's research shows that in fact, they have built "their acquisitions around their personal management". Their managers have been important in how their companies operate. But they themselves have intervened personally and relied on regular contact with managers and editors.[37]

Tunstall's survey notes that some editors have seen their control increase. But in such cases they have become "editor managers" and "entrepreneurial editors" – more integrated with the commercial management of the titles. So the prototype "entrepreneurial editor" David English, editor and then editor-in-chief of the *Daily Mail*, was on the board, and later chair, of Associated Newspapers. And David Montgomery was also a managing director for part of his time as *Today* editor. Kelvin Mackenzie at *The Sun* and Andrew Neil at *The Sunday Times* were given increased editorial power by Murdoch after showing their profit-making ability on their respective titles. Both were "vigorous editorial promoters of Murdoch and News International interests".[38]

Thus editors have not necessarily become divorced from the owners and chief executives. Despite Tunstall's description of Neil's and Mackenzie's power as "untrammelled", Neil himself has chronicled his regular discussions with Murdoch and emphasized the mogul's political influence on *The Sun*.[39] Similarly, Tunstall cites the clearest example of the rise of editorial power on a "quality" newspaper as that of Max Hastings on the *Daily Telegraph*. Yet, Hastings himself has written of the regular criticism to which his proprietor Lord Black subjected him. Hastings states that during his time at the *Telegraph* he "never held the view that I could expect editorial freedom to be absolute".[40] Tunstall himself also notes that the entrepreneurial archetype, David English, talked on the telephone every day with Lord Rothermere.[41]

Thus, although control is now diffused among "entrepreneurial editors" and senior managers on British national newspapers, these figures still tend broadly to share the motives of the leading shareholder owners. In this sense, while individual reporters, feature writers, sub-editors and, particularly, columnists have varying degrees of autonomy over their own work, for newspapers overall, ownership and control have the potential to be closely related and often are. And the demands of business and the market act as a crucial influence. The most important exception with regard to ownership is *The Guardian*, where there was a history of editorial sovereignty. Ownership has been in the hands of the Scott Trust, which at times has had a journalist on its board, although not as a staff representative.[42] The question of editorial and senior journalist autonomy on the Mirror Group newspapers is examined in Chapter 5.

The British National Newspaper Market

So political democracy requires press pluralism and pluralism requires diverse ownership and control. If we are to consider the Labour Party's policy on the press, we need to know to what extent the British national newspapers provide pluralism. It could be argued that the British newspaper market has been able to deliver a relatively diverse output, considered overall (although less so if we consider it as a segmented market, as we shall see in a moment).[43] It has also been suggested that the press market's vitality is indicated by the increase in the number of pages produced and the creation of new titles as others have folded.[44] However, the number of newspapers has considerably decreased.

An important consideration for Labour was that launching a new title is extremely expensive. It is also a risky business.[45] The introduction of new technology and the defeat of the British print workers have not resolved this.[46]

Group	Title	Net UK Circulation	Share
News International	*The Sun*	3,168,739	35%
	The Times	567,179	
Daily Mail and General Trust	*The Daily Mail*	2,293,654	21%
Trinity Mirror	*Daily Mirror*	1,607,213	15%
Northern & Shell	*Daily Express*	810,758	14%
	Daily Star	710,658	
Press Holdings Limited	*The Daily Telegraph*	876,691	8%
Guardian Media Group	*The Guardian*	350,304	3%
Independent News & Media	*The Independent*	221,089	2.5%
Pearson	*Financial Times*	135,035	one per cent
Total		10,741,320	> 99%

Table 1.1 British national daily newspaper ownership by UK circulation

Moreover, ownership is not diverse. One method of assessing whether a market is an oligopoly is to apply a concentration ratio in order to assess, in the case of the media market, the audience or readership share of the top four or five companies.[47] Press concentration has been a feature of media ownership both in western Europe and in the world's main superpower, the USA.[48] But the concentration ratio of the UK national press is among the highest in western Europe.[49] The top four companies account for well over 80 per cent of UK circulation and the top five have more than 90 per cent of the total.[50] Concentration has increased significantly since the last Royal Commission on the Press reported in 1977, when there were concerns that there were nine nationals – each with a separate owner.[51] There are important economic reasons for such a development.[52] There is clearly an economic incentive for each newspaper to increase its share of the market in the absence of government restrictions.[53] This area of ownership legislation has been a key topic in Labour thought on the press. Without these restrictions on market share, the press market-place is likely to be an example of market failure, as the range of companies involved is limited. And, by implication from what we have noted, it is also an instance of democratic deficit.

Cross-Ownership and Synergy

Aside from direct concentration, Labour Party battles have also been conducted more recently over another strategy in which press companies have engaged. This is "diagonal" concentration, where companies diversify across different media in cross-media expansion or where non-media companies expand into the press or other media markets.[54] An example that Labour was particularly concerned with was newspaper expansion into television broadcasting ownership.

There can be a number of motives for cross-media expansion. Economies of scope can be achieved if two dissimilar products share some component, making it cheaper for them to be produced or marketed by the same company. There is immense potential for economies of scope both within newspaper ownership and through cross-ownership. Publishers of a range of titles can combine in such areas as advertising sales. A product created for one market – for instance, a newspaper feature – can be repackaged for use in a television report. Such expansion can lead to efficiency gains for business.[55] Again, companies justify expansion in terms of the need to be competitive in a global market. However, as Ben Bagdikian, among others, argues, synergies provided by cross-ownership can reduce the range of content and diverse ideas as material from one corporate source gets recycled into different forms.[56]

How much synergy takes place in the British press context is more open to debate. Cross-media ownership can achieve synergies.[57] The immediacy of press news, however, means it is open to only some forms of repackaging.[58] The only repackaging available for yesterday's news is as tomorrow's fish and chip wrapping (and even that use has all but disappeared). Yet one area where recycling can happen is between the press and other news media, where immediacy is at a premium and a similar political slant can be reproduced. Thus political influence can be reinforced.

Aside from the question of political influence, newspaper companies have viewed broadcasting as a medium with a more stable economic future, providing more long-term profit opportunities.[59] The main economic advantage of cross-ownership has been the opportunity to cross-promote products between different media. However, here there is also a potential for conflict with editorial integrity, as the press sacrifices its potential for impartiality in order to seek intra-corporate promotion. This consideration will become important when we look at the justifications given for relaxing cross-ownership legislation under Tony Blair's government. We shall analyse whether such policies have in fact been aimed at the maximization of profits rather than political plurality, at economic advantage rather than expanding democratic discourse.

Advertising and Labour Representation

Another important feature of the newspaper market, in relation to questions of political democracy and Labour representation, is the effect of advertising. Newspaper finances are atypical within business. Like other media, newspapers operate in two markets simultaneously. Readers consume the newspapers in one market and are sold to advertisers in another. Advertising is the main source of revenue for many newspapers. This leads to an important division in the national press market. Although fewer in number, the wealthier have greater demand for newspapers. But, importantly, there is also a far greater pressure for supply, as there is competition among publishers to provide high-income readers to advertisers. In 1998, the top 21 per cent by income had more titles aimed at them than the bottom 50 per cent. The "quality" titles aimed at the wealthier gain a much larger percentage of their income from advertising, especially luxury goods and classifieds. The mass-circulation press, by contrast, raises a great deal of its revenue simply from its cover price.[60]

One consequence of this phenomenon – which has been termed "bifurcation"[61] – is that it is possible for "quality" titles to be competitive with a much lower circulation than the "populars". Thus, while News International closed *Today* as a loss-maker, the paper in fact had a circulation larger than three of the surviving "quality" titles. For the tabloids, in other words, there is a pressure for huge sales.[62] There has been an attempt to sustain a mid-market sector among the nationals, making for a tripartite market. However, as Colin Sparks argues, the trend of the market as a whole has been towards bifurcation.[63]

Bifurcation has a significant implication for democracy. Less wealthy readers do not simply have to pay a larger percentage of their disposable income to obtain their newspaper of choice. They are also completely excluded from having the same range of press aimed at them as their richer counterparts. It has been claimed that the newspaper market, without as powerful an industry regulator, has been more effective than television at providing output aimed at diverse interest groups.[64] However, as Sparks notes, it is only in the élite newspaper market that there is any degree of ownership diversity. In the rest of the market, which is much larger, there is not the same plurality.[65]

If democracy is dependent on receiving a range of information from different sources, then the result is a marked inequality in democracy based on income. It pays to have high quality journalism for the business community – hence the historically good quality journalism in the *Financial Times*, for instance. There is an important space in the "quality press" for information, debate and discussion on politics and economics. There are not the same pressures in the tabloid sector. In the "populars" there is less space for such debate because of the compulsion to deliver a huge readership. The market demand is to fill the paper with accessible popular topics, such as celebrity and sport, rather than informed discussion on current affairs.[66] There is also a compulsion on "quality" papers to seek affluent readers, even in the case of *The Guardian*, which does not have to report to shareholders or a proprietor. The bias against low-income readers also affects the US press, for instance.[67] But the UK press is unusual in the extent to which bifurcation is focused on the national dailies.

Equally importantly, in each segment there are smaller circulation titles, which lose out in the economies of scale. They have to produce a paper similar to those of their rivals but, because of both sales and advertising, the market leaders will raise significantly more revenue. Furthermore, market leaders can typically charge more for advertising, as the *Daily Telegraph* did in the early 1990s,[68] making it more difficult for new competitors to enter the press market.[69] But it also provides for further concentration with the "circulation spiral", where advertisers are attracted to the more successful newspapers in a mutually reinforcing spiral of success.

Thus, the question of advertising is key. It heavily influenced Labour Party discussions on newspaper diversity and the promotion of the party in the press during the early period considered here. For many, the effect of advertising was to bias the press against Labour representation, militating against the interests of the Labour Party or the Labour movement – that is, Labour and the trade unions. At that time, the party and the Labour movement were seen as synonymous in this context. As it was the poorer readers who tended to vote Labour and to be union members, it was the Labour movement that was less well served by a press so dominated by advertising. The most notable victim of this advertising effect was the last title with direct connections with the Labour movement, the *Daily Herald*.[70]

In addition, we have seen that democracy requires press diversity and the representation of different viewpoints. Narrow newspaper ownership in theory hampers diversity. Representation requires that a major party, such as the Labour Party, has its views articulated in the press. However, despite the impact of advertising, press coverage under Tony Blair showed that Labour could be represented without the problem of ownership being tackled.

Thus, although it appeared to those concerned that the demand for Labour to be promoted in the press (the third difficulty identified in the preface) was synonymous with the demand for diversity of ownership (the second difficulty), subsequent events showed this was not the case. Such a possibility was not at all apparent to those involved, who covered a broad spectrum and placed differing degrees of emphasis on the issue of Labour promotion as opposed to that of diversity. It will be argued that one division in Labour Party policy in the period from the 1970s can be seen in terms of the underlying tension between these two demands. But there was also another, related concern.

The Press, Political Democracy and Participation

We have already seen that political democracy in Britain has a problem. With regard to the concentration ratio, the British national press does not have the diverse ownership required of it. However, as an influential UNESCO report concluded as far back as 25 years ago, democratization also requires that citizens (both those working in the media and newspaper readers) participate in decisions made in and over the mass-circulation press.[71] The recent rise of Internet citizen journalists indicates the hunger of some ordinary citizens to participate in the reporting of news.[72] As one noted democratic theorist has argued, democracy has to do with political equality, of which access to the media is a part. And, in order to guarantee that access for equality, there must be some control by citizens.[73] There needs to be democratization *of* the media, as well as democratization *through* the media.[74] This is not such a strange idea. It follows on naturally from the notion of representation.

How can representation of different interests and political positions be achieved? The answer can be only briefly outlined in this book. (A discussion of the theory of media representation is also outside the scope of this work.) Merely calling for diverse political and cultural representation in the press, while ignoring the nature of the individual or organization providing that representation, is to take a narrow view of the issue. Such a call is for representation without democratic control over that representation. It is to demand representative democracy without the democracy. As the UNESCO report made clear, citizen groups need both access to and participation in media systems – a right to communicate by citizens, dialogue rather than top-down monologue.[75] As Ingunn Hagen notes, communication implies a two-way process.[76] This is the sort of two-way dialogue and interaction that citizen journalists are demanding of "big media" on the Internet.[77] And indeed, the quest for a two-way dialogue has latterly been explored even by Labour's former communication supremo, Alastair Campbell – on a website owned by the largest single media company in the world, AOL Time Warner.[78] But to facilitate a representative interaction on both "sides" requires something more than that commercial newspapers facilitate citizen blogs as an adjunct to their Internet sites.

Democratic representation requires that citizens have some control over the newspapers' output. The logic of calling for political representation without such democratic control is that it would be acceptable for News International to own all the UK national press, as long as its newspapers representatively articulated the views of the different major parties. Of course, News International did switch its support from the Conservatives to "over-represent" the Labour Party in the period being considered – a key motif of this work – but the broader problem of representation remains, nevertheless. Political democracy requires democratization of the press.

Models for Ownership and Control

Now that we have considered briefly some requirements of political democracy, it is possible to examine how Labour fared in providing blueprints for a press policy that would attempt to deal with the three problems identified earlier: of ownership diversity, representation and democratic control. To do this, it is important to map the press and media models that have been put forward, so we can reflect in the book's conclusion on the ideas that have influenced Labour Party thinking since the 1970s. An effective review of the models on offer for providing a diverse press has been given elsewhere, so we shall not consider this question in depth here.[79] Instead we will concentrate on mapping the models specifically designed to provide democratic ownership and control of the press and media.

A Classical Liberal Pluralist Model

Liberal pluralists believe the market can provide fairly complete diversity. It enables anyone to publish any opinion they want. Independence from state control means that the press can operate as an effective watchdog. Classical liberal pluralists view that there is no democratic deficit as citizens already control newspapers – through the market. While it is consistent with such a position to call for some minimal anti-monopoly constraints, any attempts at further state interference are explicitly undemocratic. Liberal pluralists adapt the traditional "fourth estate" argument by suggesting that, through the market, the press reflects the views of its consumers and therefore can act as a legitimate public mouthpiece.[80]

However, there are problems with such an argument. The British press market, as we have seen, is not diverse: ownership is concentrated. Entering the market is very costly.[81] Also, proximity to business and the "bottom-line" mentality can act as deterrents to expensive investigative reporting, particularly that concerning corporations.[82]

Moreover, the idea of the market as a democratic device assumes that the exclusive élite of press owners and controllers automatically subordinates its own views to provide an information service demanded by the consumers, in order to sell its product. However, as we have already seen, some former editors have chronicled how proprietors have taken an active role in influencing their titles. Also companies have wider business interests, which would be served by cross-promotion, and can use their newspapers to lobby for commercial legislation that readers have not demanded.[83]

In any case, the market itself is a relatively blunt instrument for expressing individual wants and desires. Choices are limited to a pre-existing range. Supply creates its own demand as much as the other way round. One recent survey of the US media considered that markets do not give people what they want but give them more of "what they want within the range of what is most profitable to produce and/or in the political interests of the producers".[84] Readers have limited ability, via the market, to influence media content.[85] One cannot identify one's preferences for particular parts of the "bundle" that make up newspapers. It is because of the market's flaws as a democratic tool that marketing research is used to discern consumers' unquenched desires, as we shall see in Chapter 6. Moreover, importantly, the free market's view of "one dollar, one vote" provides for plutocracy, not democracy. People voted neither for Rupert Murdoch nor for Lord Black.[86] This problem of inequity is particularly visible in the press market. As indicated earlier, it is heavily shaped and structured by advertisers, stripping poorer readers of the possibility of exercising their own preferences, even if they are prepared to spend the same cash buying a paper as their richer counterparts.

Nevertheless, any attempt to influence press ownership legislation faces the historically prevalent liberal pluralist notion in Britain that freedom of the press means ownership freedom from any government control.[87] Yet, as Curran identifies, the key contradiction at the heart of British media regulation is that it has been assumed that the press should be organized as a free market while broadcasting is to be publicly regulated. As a result, policies regarded as harmful for the press have been propagated as valuable for broadcasting.[88]

The Public Service Model

To extend this latter theme, the public service model also attempts to answer contradictions inherent in the liberal pluralists' position by applying the broadcast model to newspaper ownership and separating the press from business and advertiser domination. Although, as we shall see, it provides the potential for diversity, it does not guarantee it. The interventionist models for the press flowing from the public service model were associated with left social democrats within the Labour Party.[89] These people concentrated their arguments as much on attempting to provide balance and increasing representation as on developing press ownership diversity.

The public service model regards communication as operating as a decommodified "public good", based on universal access and democratic equality.[90] Here democratic control is primarily exercised by the state on behalf of the people, who elect representatives. In this sense the public service model shares élitist conceptions with the liberal pluralist model. Its advocates suggest that the public service model requires the media to be separate from the state.[91] However, this independence is by no means automatic. The emphasis is on state regulation as the form of control.[92]

Those in the Labour Party who wanted to adopt the public service model for the press supported extensive state involvement.[93] As a consequence they faced again the difficulty of state control.[94] Even in less radical versions of the public service model there is the danger of state censorship and dominance over appointments and funding. State regulation can be used for party political advantage. It runs the danger of paternalistic élitism.[95] In particular, like the liberal pluralist model, it can exclude democratic accountability in terms of the involvement of press workers and newspaper readers.

The New Left: Radical and Neo-Marxist Alternatives

This last point has been the subject of a series of new left recommendations for democratic ownership and control of the press and media. One such recommendation comes from a neo-Marxist new left source. Raymond Williams's proposals were for the state to fund independent self-managed institutions providing newspapers run by "the only people capable of guaranteeing [press] freedom: the working journalists themselves".[96]

A problem with Williams's system is the idea that democracy equals pure producer democracy – that journalists should have sole ownership and control over production. While Tom Baistow's solution of putting editors into the dominant position would be more autocratic, sole journalist control can also be viewed as élitist and implicitly undemocratic. Such a system would at least require further checks and balances.[97] There would need to be some role for civil groups and political parties, as well as readers – those groups that democracy requires be represented in newspapers.[98]

Theorists of participatory democracy argue that representation is not sufficient for democracy. Citizens need to be involved in other spheres, including the press and media, as we saw earlier. The strength of participatory democracy, as one advocate indicates, when considering both political and media democracy, is that "it relies on the ability of citizens to make informed decisions rather than choose between élites to make decisions for them".[99] An important new left thinker who has advocated participatory democracy is Carole Pateman, who argues that it is precisely through involvement that citizens "learn" democracy.[100]

A direct attempt to address the problem of providing the diversity that liberal pluralists desire, but which the market on its own has shown to be incapable of providing, comes with James Curran's social market or democratic media model.[101] Other examples of this form of interventionism have been successfully applied in other European, and particularly Scandinavian countries, as we shall see in Chapter 2. (Indeed, Curran has more recently rather cheekily reappropriated "third way" rhetoric effectively to reassociate the term with its earlier Scandinavian conception.)[102] For the press, intervention has taken the form of attempts to redistribute advertising revenue and subsidies to provide for new start-ups to diversify the newspaper market. This model can be more clearly considered as providing diversity for democracy, rather than democratic control.

Nevertheless, Curran has more recently developed a version of this model, which borrows from the European initiatives, with a plethora of different forms of control and ownership. In doing so, he provides one answer to the problem of journalist domination over broader citizen control. A sector where there could be journalist newsroom democracy would be just one component of the system. It would have a public service core and a "civic media section" for parties, interest groups and social movements to be supported. In addition, there would be a private enterprise sector in which the editorial independence of journalists could be protected. It would also contain a social market sector of minority media, which could include organizations with consumer or community representation. Also included would be self-managed enterprises, which would allow for some journalist control, and a "professional media sector", where there could be staff control. Thus there would be a combination of areas with newsroom democracy and others with community representation.[103]

Curran's system is mainly designed for broadcasting and publishing, and it would need to be adapted for the press. Furthermore, "independence from the state" needs to be more clearly defined. Such a model may be seen as idealistic in the context of assumptions about the role of the state and democratic involvement in present-day Britain.[104] It certainly requires some clarity about the economic and political structure that would be associated with it. However, such a notion has the merit of going beyond mere journalistic democracy and party representation to consider broader community representation. While the model may appear Utopian, it borrows mainly from existing European media systems, suggesting that it is at least possible.

No model of the press required for political democracy is entirely free from problems. However, some strands of the alternative systems can be highlighted, which fuse aspects from the social democratic and radical democratic traditions, among others. A democratic model of ownership and control would need to represent a diverse range of opinions, including those of minorities. Such a model would need to avoid market domination and censorship as well as paternalistic, bureaucratic and authoritarian state control. It would therefore require some form of democratic influence on, and participation in, the running of the media industries both by the workers in those enterprises and by the wider community.

The Structure of the Book

This chapter has explored some of the problems for political democracy with the British press. It has also considered some of the media models outlined to deal with such problems. The rest of the book will set out how the Labour Party dealt with these questions. While many worry about the power of the press, fewer are aware of the political alternatives that have been considered. Some in the Labour Party were prepared to debate these alternatives and put forward proposals on how to regulate newspaper power for the common good.

Chapter 2 will assess the period from 1972 until Labour entered government in 1974. It will explore the rise of the National Executive Committee study groups and their influence on policy creation, the models for a plural and democratic media considered by *The People and the Media* report, which will inform later chapters, and the publication's effect on Labour Party policy.

Chapter 3 explores press ownership policy creation and debate within the Labour Party during the 1974–9 government. It will explore the distancing between the government and the party on the question of democratic media ownership, as evidenced by the different attitudes of each to the 1977 Royal Commission on the Press. It will also explore other influences on party policy during that period, including the pressure for Labour representation.

The turbulent period from 1979 to 1983 will be considered in Chapter 4. Themes analysed here will include the role and policies of Labour's media study group, as part of demands for "leadership accountability" in the Labour Party. The study group's influence on the 1983 manifesto is also considered.

Chapters 5 and 6 analyse the changes in policy on ownership and control during the Kinnock and Smith years. Chapter 6 particularly explores the relationships between these changes and shifts in party media presentation, associated with the renewed emphasis on marketing and press management, as a bid for Labour representation. These two chapters will also explore changes in the party regarding the sources of policy creation and the decreasing emphasis on policies aimed at structural alteration of the press. The short-lived changes heralded by Smith in both policy creation and media relations are also briefly assessed in Chapter 6.

Chapter 7 concentrates on Tony Blair's reign as leader of the party. It is argued that, with the general shift towards a pro-market agenda in all areas, the increased emphasis on press management strategy to provide representation led to a further downplaying of newspaper policies that would provide for political democracy. The book's final chapter further explores the 2003 Communications Act as a culmination of the development of Labour policy, and analyses the development of Labour policy in relation to the various press and media policy models identified in this first chapter.

2

The People and the Press
Party Debates up to 1974

In the previous chapter we looked at the argument that political democracy is enhanced by diverse press ownership and by broader involvement from journalists and the public in newspapers' editorial decisions. In 1967, however, Labour Prime Minister Harold Wilson firmly rejected calls for government action to preserve diversity in press ownership. He told that year's Granada Television Awards that "there would be the most appalling risks in government intervention". Implicit in his comment was a concern about Labour representation – how the newspapers would treat the Labour Party: "It is not only a question of what would be done but of what some might think was being done."[1] Nevertheless, by 1974 the party had produced a document which explicitly identified the "need for intervention". It advocated a "radical restructuring" of the press market to aid diversity and to provide journalists with some involvement in decisions about the work that they produced.[2] What had happened in the interim to bring about this change?

At the root of it was the fact that a rising Labour left had combined with representatives of a resurgent trade union movement and sections of a more hesitant right to push for structural press reform, in the face of a reluctant Labour Party leadership. However, there was also an underlying tension between the demands for press diversity and the desire of the Labour movement (both the party and the unions) to be positively represented in newspapers – demands that at the time seemed synonymous.

The tension within the party between the concern for press diversity and anxiety over how Labour was represented was not new. Wilson's interest in the press promoting the party had influenced the 1965 Monopolies and Mergers Act, later incorporated into the 1973 Fair Trading Act, which governed newspaper takeovers for the rest of the millennium. The 1965 act defied the previous British tradition that rejected specific laws for the press. However, the Labour government resisted implementing the tougher rules on takeovers that the 1962 Royal Commission on the Press had recommended, and the legislation had little effect as far as arresting concentration of ownership was concerned.[3]

Instead, Wilson's desire for Labour to be reported positively in the press had an impact on the proposals for press diversity and how they operated. According to the 1965 act, titles with a circulation of more than half a million needed to be investigated by the Monopolies and Mergers Commission, if mergers were proposed. But the Wilson administration gave the Secretary of State discretion to allow newspaper takeovers when it was thought that otherwise titles would fail financially.[4] The government deliberately worded this discretionary loophole clause vaguely so that Wilson could interfere to preserve Labour support and discourage the party's enemies from monopolizing the press. In the event, however, the party could not rely on its supporters to buy up titles, so Wilson seems to have encouraged leading contenders to acquire newspapers with the hope of some reciprocal gratitude at the time of the next election.[5] Jeremy Tunstall cites the cases of *The Times* in 1966-7 and *The Sun* in 1969, where Labour governments agreed to buy-ups where there were political motives for approval.[6] The Labour Cabinet was divided over whether to oppose a planned merger of IPC and Reed, which would supposedly have meant the end of the then Labour-supporting *Sun*. However, tellingly, Wilson regarded action against the company that also owned the *Daily Mirror* as political suicide.[7] For him, positive representation of the Labour Party in the press was more important than guaranteeing diversity of newspaper ownership. But in any case pressure to transform Labour's press diversity policy arose as a result of changes within the party.

New Pressures on Labour:
The Labour New Left and Union Radicalization

By the late 1960s the political and economic settlement upon which the West had based its development after World War II was being threatened. Instead there arose a challenge to the Keynesian policy of demand management, which the Labour Party had increasingly relied on, to the exclusion of public ownership.[8] There was also an explosion of industrial militancy, as hostility to the Labour government's policy of wage restraint grew.[9]

The Labour government was ejected from office in 1970. While the ensuing crisis of Keynesian economics prompted a reaction from the new right, leading eventually to Thatcherism, it also led to an advance by the Labour new left. The core figures of the early British new left had originally come together in 1956.[10] With media theorist Raymond Williams at the forefront, the new left was concerned from the outset with issues regarding the press and media. While some of its original supporters refused to become involved in the Labour Party, others sought to open up a mainstream space for the expression of counter-cultural libertarian ideas by actively engaging in the organized political process and joining the party. This new left current helped fill the political and economic policy vacuum created by the crisis of Keynesianism and the failure of the Wilson government.[11]

While some of the Labour right had looked to the Scandinavian system and resisted further nationalization of the economy, the response of the Labour new left to the economic crisis was to demand a national enterprise board. Their argument echoed the critique of oligopolization outlined in Chapter 1. The British economy, they argued, was now dominated by oligopolistic concentration. Faced with multinational domination, Keynesian solutions were thus largely ineffectual.[12] This analysis provided the left with a critique of what became known as "globalization" years before the Labour right adopted the term. It also gave a renewed impetus to critiques of press monopolization.

Yet the Labour new left, influenced by the participative possibilities of the late 1960s, was also fixated on democratizing the state and civil society. As a prelude to this process of democratization it wanted to transform the party and to make the party conference sovereign. Extending political democracy through press reform was part of the same process. The figurehead of this new movement was Tony Benn.

The Labour new left also saw that at the root of the problem of state control experienced by "Old Labour", to use the modern terminology, was the lack of industrial democracy. Leading Labour new left economist Stuart Holland, for example, advocated greater democracy within industry as a counterbalance to a potentially overweening state.[13] Discussions on how to involve those working on newspapers in having a say over what they produced were part of this debate.

Support for employee control had enjoyed a renaissance both outside the party and within it and was bolstered by a series of industrial "work-ins", which provided some evidence that employees were capable of managing their own enterprises, with outside help.[14] Yet while the demand for employee democracy became official party policy, the commitments made in Labour documents remained mostly vague. The Labour left was not clear where workers' autonomy ended and state involvement began.[15]

The rise of the Labour new left was further strengthened by the continued growth of union militancy. A new left-wing trade union leadership supported the introduction of some measure of employee democracy and challenged the doctrine of "social democratic centralism" – that is, the unions' support for Labour leadership control over the party. An opening was thus also created for the dissenting new left activists, who took over local parties as control by old-style cliques collapsed.[16]

One of the early successes of the new left upsurge was in helping to revitalize and reorganize the party's research work. From the 1960s onwards the left used its increasing presence on the National Executive Committee (NEC) as a power base. After 1970 the NEC's subcommittees became part of the policy-making process and the left concentrated its energy on these eighty-plus committees.[17] Outside co-optees, including academics, had equal status with MPs on these committees, also known as study groups. They were chaired by NEC members, rather than members of the Shadow Cabinet. One co-opted academic, Stuart Holland, was the main architect of the left's economic strategy.[18] As we shall see, it was a new left academic, James Curran, who would have a crucial influence on press policy throughout the 1970s and into the 1980s.

The Communications Study Group

The communications study group was established in May 1972 and was primarily concerned with the press. It built on the interest in press and media policy among academics that had blossomed in the 1960s. Members of a party study group on advertising, which had reported in 1971, had already raised concerns about press oligopolization. However, they had counselled against extensive intervention. Nevertheless, their report recommended that "drastic action" might be needed in the future.[19] Demands for just this sort of response came from some involved in the communications study group.

The communications study group was set up to guide policy creation, albeit only indirectly: its report was never voted on by the party. However, it was significant in influencing later policy development, and, perhaps more importantly, it prefigured a host of debates that were to percolate through the party for years afterwards.

Like other study groups, its membership included MPs and senior trade unionists and sympathetic academics, but it also incorporated journalists.[20] The study group was initiated by Labour's research secretary, Terry Pitt. James Curran describes the political character of the people Pitt brought together as generally supportive of the Labour leadership.[21] Yet a pointer to the direction it was going to take was that the man who was becoming the figurehead of the movement to transform the party, Tony Benn, chaired it for most of its existence.

What the Labour new left faced was a battle with Harold Wilson and the right in the party, who preferred to work with the existing press to seek a fairer press for Labour. The leadership, as considered further in Chapter 3, were reluctant to implement any policies that would challenge the existing press. But the new left were also engaged, in the study group, in a more covert contest with some of the traditional left, particularly those in the trade unions, who thought that encouraging diversity in the newspaper market was more a matter of providing a voice for the Labour movement than of encouraging a potentially dangerous politically diverse press.

Labour Representation in the Press

Press representation was much on the minds of Labour activists in the early 1970s. According to James Curran, the concern to develop a Labour movement press and a left press "was always the subtext" of those on the study group.[22] Another study group member, the *Labour Weekly* journalist Martin Linton, remembers that "the issue of what we could do about it was one everyone wanted to explore".[23] The division was over whether to call for a broader range of titles, including a left press, or to be more forthright in voicing the demand for Labour movement papers.[24]

Old left trade unionists were among those in the party who had become ever more hostile to what they regarded as a sustained press assault on the increasingly militant unions. The general secretary of the National Union of Journalists (NUJ), Ken Morgan, described the TUC annual congress as conducting an "annual swipe at the media" at this time.[25] And press union representatives themselves were dealing out the blows. Richard Briginshaw, general secretary of the National Society of Operative Printers, Graphical and Media Personnel (NATSOPA), in 1972, was typically forthright. For him the "ultimate interest" of the newspapers was "to bash the unions and make them the scapegoats for every political, financial and economic ill the country suffers".[26] The response of the 1971 TUC congress had been to resolve to set up machinery to monitor the unions' treatment in the media.[27]

At the study group's first meeting a majority of trade unionists saw newspaper anti-union bias as the most pressing problem to be tackled.[28] One participant who was particularly concerned about representation, Martin Linton, put the point succinctly. He rejected the idea of universal subsidies to the press as merely "feeding the mouth that bites you".[29] Such subsidies, he suggested, would only help the more profitable and predominantly anti-Labour movement press. Nevertheless, such a viewpoint did not go unchallenged. The future Arts Minister, MP Hugh Jenkins, argued that the general approach to the press and media should put diversity uppermost, not aiming to "encourage socialist media but to create a framework within which such media can and will emerge".[30]

Outside the study group, it was argued more distinctly that the main aim of any new ownership legislation would be to promote a Labour movement press – with press diversity being a secondary concern. This was a unifying theme of both Labour right and left.[31] *Labour Weekly*, a newspaper that had been set up by the Labour Party in 1971, was running a campaign called "The Case for a Labour Press", which sought to push for newspapers directly linked to the Labour and trade union movement, similar to those in Norway and Sweden. It reported that the primary effect of the communications study group's policies would be to increase the number of Labour-supporting titles.[32]

Moreover, Linton himself argued for such a "Labour press" on the basis that, unlike the then Labour-supporting *Sun* and *Daily Mirror*, such new newspapers would be a campaigning tool for Labour. Reflecting a view which would influence discussions on Labour representation in newspapers by the means of political communications management in the 1990s, he argued that the press was involved in agenda-setting – "it does not pick the winner but it picks the battlefield". A Labour press would help shift politics on to a more radical agenda, with a more left-wing consensus, as was the case in Norway and Sweden.[33] It is far from clear, though, that the basis of the Scandinavian social democratic consensus was its press.

A Press for Democracy

Few on the study group, however, had so exclusive a commitment to Labour representation in the press. Another major concern for various members was how to provide policies to diversify press ownership, which they saw as essential to enhancing political democracy.

The background paper, produced for the study group's first meeting, had identified dissatisfaction with the press on precisely this count. It identified many of the same issues listed in Chapter 1 as affecting political democracy. That is, newspaper ownership was becoming more concentrated, the number of newspapers was shrinking and advertising spending was leading to bifurcation.[34] These concerns were articulated by the study group's most influential contributor, James Curran.

The study group identified concentration of newspaper ownership as a main issue to be discussed at its first meeting – notwithstanding the senior trade unionists' concerns.[35] At its second meeting the discussion divided on how much state involvement was needed to provide press plurality, a debate that set the tone for subsequent gatherings.[36] The different views can be reduced to four basic positions of group members on how to advance diversity – some of them linked to demands for Labour representation in the press. We will look at these in turn below, and return to a discussion of the merits of some of the various schemes in Chapter 3.

Plural Views: Diversity and Plurality

The State Solution

One influential member of the study group, Geoffrey Goodman, argued that the market on its own could not provide the kind of press necessary to enhance democracy and that the state should intervene directly.[37] With the print union NATSOPA he therefore called for a National Printing Corporation (NPC).

The corporation he envisaged would provide state aid to less profitable newspapers. According to the proposed plan, the NPC would buy printing plant – at a minimum, the presses and assets of newspapers set to merge or close – and it would contract out newspaper production. Indeed, some on the study group envisaged the NPC as operating in a similar way to the contract system that commercial terrestrial television broadcasters were subject to, in a public service-style model, as considered in Chapter 1.[38]

One supporter of the plan, the Labour press advocate Martin Linton, saw that to deal with the "two problems – of access and finance" the NPC should subsidize new publications and those existing titles with smaller circulations. Subsidies and contract renewal would be dependent on the papers' readerships. If a newspaper failed to rise above a certain circulation, its contract would not be renewed. If it achieved a particularly high circulation, its subsidy would be cut.[39]

However, this scheme was a costly way of addressing a problem of press print capacity shortage that did not exist.[40] Also, it did not deal with a major barrier to entering the newspaper market. New entrants did not just face the obstacle of high production costs, which the NPC would effectively subsidize, the effect of advertising also presented a difficulty. But the NPC did not address the problem of bifurcation.

Another difficulty was that the NPC was open to government control. By deciding between different leases, it would be exercising an explicitly political judgement. It is accepted that newspapers, unlike British broadcasters, explicitly editorialize. Thus, by choosing one title for subsidy over another, the corporation would be shifting the newspaper industry's whole political alignment. It was unclear who should make such political choices, using public money. The NUJ opposed the scheme for this reason.[41] The representation of the party was also an issue here. There would be a potential pressure to support those newspapers favourable to Labour. This problem re-emerged when other public service models were considered after 1979, as we shall see in Chapter 4.

Newsprint Subsidy and an Advertising Tax

An interventionist alternative to the NPC scheme was an across-the-board control of the price of newsprint; that is, the paper on which newspapers are printed. This scheme, by which a central agency would sell newsprint at a subsidized rate – similar to the way newsprint had been distributed during World War II – was advocated by the NUJ. A TUC report thought that it would stop newspapers going out of business, thus reducing diversity, and it would encourage new entrants deterred by the cost of newsprint.[42] However, such a scheme would either be costly (and subsidize also the most profitable companies) or be ineffectual.

As an alternative, many on the study group preferred a tax on advertising to apply to all the media, to provide a newsprint subsidy that would target less profitable publications. This redistributive tax would seek to tackle the problem of bifurcation. It commanded broad support among those interested in media reform, not all of whom were on the new left, including some whose interest was primarily in Labour movement representation in the press. One key member of the study group, Eric Moonman, in an example of "policy transfer", looked to other European states, particularly the Scandinavian countries, for inspiration.[43] As we shall see, in this and the following chapters, some of the policies Labour considered were adaptations of those enacted by other nation states. Policy transfer, or as Richard Rose tends to describe it, "lesson-drawing", describes a feature of state policy-making.[44] Similarly we can adapt this description to consider Labour Party policy development.

In Moonman's scheme, subsidies would have to be based on technical and financial, rather than cultural or political, grounds. The aid, again, would be reduced as more profits were made. Supported publications had to be in genuine need, to be technically efficient and to be primarily composed of news and opinion, as opposed to entertainment. Papers that were part of a group would receive a reduced subsidy.[45]

In addition, the advocates of the subsidy called for a separate launch fund for new publications, which would have to fulfil the same criteria as those seeking the newsprint subsidy. A board, independent of the state, which included a broader range of representatives, would oversee this.[46]

However, a key question was how such a scheme would be funded. There were objections to reducing funding as paper sales increased because publishers wanting to save money could deliberately cut off distribution to more costly areas – and those deprived of their newspapers would simply blame the Labour government.[47] Another suggestion was to allocate on the basis of the ratio between advertising and editorial content – Moonman's preferred option.[48] Some of the scheme's provisions were also open to the objection that its criteria – such as its stipulation concerning news and opinion – were subjective.[49] Nevertheless, similar schemes determined by objective criteria have operated successfully elsewhere in Europe.

Use of Government Advertising

The third strategy suggested as a means to advance press diversity was to spread government advertising – such as that for jobs and to advertise services of nationalized industries – across the press, as the Norwegian government has successfully done. Press qualifying for a newsprint subsidy would also have advertising placed with it from government, nationalized industry and local government.[50] Such a scheme posed the threat of increased state political patronage, however, with state bodies interfering to strengthen Labour movement press representation, though this has not happened in Norway.[51]

Box 2.1: Labour's Schemes Abroad

Were any of the schemes considered in the Labour Party practical? Many of the schemes were policy transfers from other parts of Europe. In the 1990s most major western European nations, with the exception of Germany and the UK, provided subsidies to the press in order to aid press diversity.[52] Among the more successful schemes for sustaining plurality were those set up in Sweden and Norway.

No simple comparison can be made between these schemes and those called for in the Labour Party.[53] Nevertheless, they provide an indication of how some of the Labour proposals could work successfully in practice.[54]

Sweden's main direct subsidy, first introduced in 1972, has been selective.[55] Like the proposals made by Moonman, here subsidies are financed by a cross-media advertising tax paid to those papers in a weaker market position. Also in a similar way to proposals discussed by the British Labour Party, the subsidies have paid for a proportion of the aided papers' newsprint.[56] A Press Subsidies Council distributes the money.[57]

The Swedish subsidy system has been successful in using similar methods to achieve aims comparable to those sought by Labour Party activists with the policies the party adopted in the 1970s. Concentration of ownership in Sweden has by no means approached the British level.[58] In tandem with recent anti-monopoly laws, subsidies have played a "key role" in saving newspapers.[59] Moreover, despite fears to the contrary, diversity has been achieved without the state politically interfering in the press or impeding its role as a public watchdog.[60]

Norwegian governments have also implemented a press subsidy system that appears to be both practical and effective. One reason why it cannot be directly compared with many Labour solutions is that the state has provided the subsidies centrally. Nevertheless, Norwegian subsidies have similarities to Labour Party proposals.

In a manner analogous to the policy suggestions made in *The People and the Media* that we shall consider later in this chapter, and subsequent Labour Party proposals, some subsidies are targeted. In the Norwegian system they have been channelled to those papers that are the second largest in their particular market, known as "No. 2s". Again, in a familiar fashion to the later proposals agreed in the Labour Party, direct subsidies are also made to publications that represent special interests.[61] In addition, a state advertising system, distributed to all newspapers, similar to the scheme set out in *The People and the Media* and in later party policy, has also been successful.[62] While state bodies have necessarily played a significant role in allocating funds, rules have also been introduced at the same time to prohibit interference in editorial policy.

The Norwegian subsidy system, together with the country's more recent media concentration legislation, has been effective in providing for diversity. The Norwegian system has maintained a large number of newspapers and a high level of readership.[63] Whereas subsidies have accounted for only 2 per cent of total press income, they have ensured the survival of many "No. 2" publications – slowing down concentration of ownership.[64] While subsidies have become less important in preserving Norway's Labour movement press,[65] they have promoted broader political and cultural diversity. One powerful example was the creation of the national daily *Klassekampen*, a left title that has provided a broadly alternative viewpoint and has often been critical of the Norwegian government, despite its funding.[66]

The Advertising Revenue Board and Curran's Solution

Conflict between advocates of the different methods of encouraging diversity in press ownership came to a head in March 1973, in a debate between Moonman and Curran.[67] Both saw scope for some "arm's-length" state intervention but dismissed the explicitly statist National Printing Corporation. The debate was over how much state control was needed to achieve a more diverse press.

One answer to the problem of bifurcation and diversity was provided by an Advertising Revenue Board or, in Curran's variant, a Media Advertising Corporation. Hugh Jenkins initially advocated this idea on the study group, and Curran vigorously supported it.[68] Again it was a policy transfer from the Scandinavian systems related to social market notions, as referred to in Chapter 1. Yet it was more explicitly state interventionist than the Scandinavian schemes, reflecting what was perceived as the more concentrated nature of the British national press. It can also be argued that it was a product of new left enthusiasm for greater state involvement, as a key part of the advertising function would effectively be nationalized.[69]

The advertising corporation would collect all revenue for press publications directly from advertisers and in many variants would even fix advertising rates and sell advertising.[70] It would directly redistribute funds predominantly back to publishers, in proportion to circulation. The revenue would thus be distributed on the basis of the number of readers – not, as with advertisers, on the composition of the readership. In this payment there would be provided an incentive to encourage the most effective promotion of advertising space. Such a scheme would reduce the economic distortion of advertising. The advertising value of each consumer would become the same, thus undermining the bias against lower-income readership publications.[71]

In addition, the corporation would keep a proportion of funds both to subsidize newsprint costs in inverse proportion to a title's circulation and to provide a launch fund for new publications. The newsprint subsidy would offset the problem that, without it, the overall scheme could close some of the broadsheet titles because their effective subsidy by advertising would end. It would also start to cancel out the advantages that accrued from economies of scale, which we looked at in Chapter 1. Although there was far greater state involvement in this proposal than in the European schemes on which it was based, Curran argued that his suggestion had little potential for political manipulation and censorship.[72]

Curran's extensive work heavily influenced the study group. In March 1973 it settled for a Media Advertising Corporation, where redistribution was based on circulation. However, not everything went Curran's way. Tony Benn, from the chair, still called for more discussion on a public service concept of the press, with a printing corporation, echoing the commercial broadcasting model, which Curran had explicitly dismissed.[73]

Broadening Newspaper Decision-making

The other major area of policy considered by the study group, as we saw at the beginning of this chapter, concerned demands for journalists, as producers, and others to be involved in deciding what newspapers produced. Employees' involvement in newspapers raised particular questions, however, because of the power of media influence, the apparent inviolability of the liberal classical notion of press freedom, and the relationship between press employees and wider community involvement.

At the forefront of the demands for journalist participation was the short-lived Free Communications Group (FCG), with its journal *The Open Secret*.[74] It had worked with NUJ chapels in increasing involvement in decision-making.

Encouraging employee participation became NUJ policy in 1972.[75] Several newspapers had forged agreements with the union, allowing increased consultation on policy and staffing matters. Indeed, when one prominent editor, Charles Wintour, wrote a book on the national press in 1972, he felt the issue sufficiently important to merit two chapters.[76] The NUJ participated in helping shape changes made on the *Daily Express* in 1973 – the first time this had happened in Fleet Street.[77] And by 1974 *The Times* and the *Daily Mirror* were having monthly consultative meetings with journalists.[78] (Other collective decision-making structures for those working on the *Mirror* are discussed in Chapter 5.)

The FCG's aims were broader than just these initiatives, however. The first pamphlet in its *In Place of Management* series identified an array of demands to be negotiated with newspaper companies. These ranged from a call for collective news team-working, through consultation and the sharing of editorial and managerial control, culminating in demands to share ownership with management.[79] Inspiration came from the French newspaper *Le Monde*, which had "led astray" many British journalists, as the hostile commentator Wintour put it.[80]

Box 2.2: Journalistic Influence in Europe

Across Europe there are legal sanctions to provide for a measure of influence and protection for journalists – related to schemes considered in British Labour Party discussions.

- In Germany, journalists have been given some voice on editorial policy.
- In the Netherlands, similar statutes exist in collective labour agreements.
- In Austria, journalists have "freedom of opinion" so they can refuse to involve themselves in work that conflicts with their own personal views.
- In Sweden, journalists can refuse to write stories that offend a code of conduct, although this right is based on collective negotiation, not law.
- In France, journalists are given severance pay if they resign or are sacked when a publication's ownership changes.

Greater participation has been limited to a few individual newspapers, such as the French newspapers *Le Monde* and *Libération*, which have been part-owned and controlled by their employees.[81]

From the outset the study group considered involving journalists in press decision-making. A background paper flagged up the possibility that the study group could consider the creation of structures for both self-management of new press titles and participation in existing ones.[82]

Despite its involvement in practical initiatives, the NUJ leadership wanted only limited journalist participation – reflecting the views of the Labour right. Asked to summarize its position at the start of 1973, the study group was told that the NUJ leadership considered that press freedom rested "upon theoretical individual proprietorship", whose effects could be mitigated by barring the owners from influencing editorial policy. The union's research officer, George Viner, considered that the newspaper proprietors could be persuaded to agree to such a policy as they would "not want to be cast in the villainous role of manipulators of public opinion".[83] Viner accepted that existing TUC proposals for supervisory boards, which would have some powers of veto over management, should include the newspaper industry, but he thought that broader control "could be calamitous in the newspaper industry".[84]

Yet the union's view was not the only sway on Labour Party thinking on the study group. More influential was the demand by Geoffrey Goodman and other journalists in the group that newspaper employees should be involved in decisions over what their papers produced.[85] And it was the approach outlined by the experienced journalist Neal Ascherson, from the FCG, which the group explicitly agreed to, during the meeting at which it decided on Curran's press diversity proposals.[86]

While the NUJ leadership had made a distinction between journalists' participation and power-sharing, Ascherson argued for the same range of demands as those outlined by the FCG. Proposals for newsroom democracy ranged from the right of access to company information through staff control of broad editorial strategy – where the editor was in charge of day-to-day decisions – to the launch of press co-operatives. Reflecting the debates outlined in Chapter 1, Ascherson was among those on the study group and in the party who wanted not just journalist involvement but broader public involvement in newspaper decision-making. He saw the need for other employees to be included also, with journalists as majority owners in staff co-operatives. But he went further, and supported the idea of increasing the public's involvement in decisions as to what some newspapers printed. He envisaged that outside interests, including readers, could have a non-controlling stake in newly launched co-ops.[87]

Tony Benn, as the study group's chair, was also committed to the idea of the public having some say in what was written in the papers. In April 1972, typically entering the lions' den, he made the demand for broader involvement in the press to a conference of the Guild of British Newspaper Editors. However, Benn's speech here was not reported in anything like the same detail as remarks that had a similar implication, which he made in his chair's address at the end of the 1972 Labour Party conference, and which were strongly condemned in the press.[88] Benn subsequently drew up a paper for the Shadow Cabinet that encouraged participation by both press employees and the broader public.

However Benn's demands were constrained by his concern for the

Labour movement to be represented, to reduce anti-Labour movement bias – he wanted to strengthen union power and to provide only limited involvement from readers. He visualized the election of newspaper worker committees, which would adjudicate on complaints from the public about examples of bias. Such a body would have no powers beyond the ability to make a report, but gradually a body of opinion would be built up that Benn envisaged would influence future news production.[89]

The study group did not consider Benn's scheme. Instead, although the Newspaper Publishers Association (NPA) was "fanatically hostile" to broadening journalist participation in newspapers as a threat to press freedom, the study group supported Ascherson's approach.[90]

The Way Forward for the Communications Study Group: Delays, Divisions and Decisions

It had originally been intended that the report of the communications study group would be published as an opposition Green Paper by the end of 1972. However, this underestimated the contentious nature of the discussions and the scale of the task involved. Nevertheless, *Labour's Programme for Britain 1973* gave important pointers to the party's position on the press. It explicitly adopted a new left position, advocating diversity in press ownership and regarding journalist involvement as "essential" in aiding press independence.[91] The study group delayed making decisions repeatedly, and divisions emerged between the right and left as to what strategy to adopt. This indecision was to continue to dog Labour press policy-makers after 1974. MP Christopher Mayhew launched a rearguard action to scupper any policy on journalist control of the press, although he was in a minority.[92] The other division was about whether to adopt a public service model, supported by Benn, or a strongly interventionist social market model to bring press diversity. Again at the root of the debate was the tension over Labour movement representation in the press. Benn argued that the Labour Party should set up a commission to govern the media and oversee a printing corporation within a public service framework. Yet a majority considered that setting up a politically appointed body to regulate the press and media would be open to political influence, including, potentially, by Labour and the unions.[93] As it was, the study group eventually placed its emphasis on a social market model. However, with the delay, despite what had been written in *Labour's Programme for Britain 1973*, the February 1974 election manifesto included no input from the study group and omitted any mention of press or media policy.[94]

The People and the Media:
Diversity More Than Representation

The eventual production in 1974 of the study group's report, *The People and the Media*, was Labour's first-ever public document dealing with the press and media. Again it is important to remember that the discussion paper represented the position of the study group, not Labour Party policy.[95]

Reflecting the study group's new left emphasis, the report made its case for intervening to extend plurality of ownership and was less concerned with explicitly promoting a Labour movement press. It focused less on the relationship between the government and the press than on the responsibilities of the press to the public.[96]

The concern with Labour representation in the press was also evident. *The People and the Media* argued that press bias, particularly against the unions, was heightened by ownership concentration. Nevertheless it was "the tight pattern of ownership" rather than the bias that was emphasized.[97] Political democracy required a diverse press as a guarantor of free expression, not just to inform but also "to express the views and interests of different sections of the community".[98]

The proposed solution again highlighted the tension between a public service model and a social market one. Despite the objections of Curran and others, early in the report it was articulated that the media should be entrenched within the public service model and public funding framework. The report supported the setting up of a state-funded Communications Council, which would oversee "the operation, development and interrelation" of the media, including the press. However, its role did not appear as all-embracing as the body envisaged by Benn. Its main task would be to oversee a right of reply (discussed in later chapters below). It would also review and publicize the operation of the press. In addition, although the final report's draft had rejected calls for a National Printing Corporation, the actual published report left this possibility open, albeit only tentatively.[99]

Despite its seeming adherence to public service principles, however, the overall emphasis of *The People and the Media* was towards an interventionist social market model. It identified advertising and bifurcation as a key threat to diversity, and the group agreed to the setting up of the Advertising Revenue Board to deal with these problems. The board would administer all advertising revenue. Advertisers would still be free to choose which press and media to advertise in, and newspapers could still take as much of whatever advertising they wanted. The board would hold back some surplus revenue to launch new titles.[100] Newspapers receiving funding would again need to reach a certain circulation before all subsidies were made available. In addition, as with Curran's proposals, the report called for newsprint subsidies to provide extra financial support. Yet *The People and the Media* also advocated diversifying the advertising of all "government and semi-government bodies" to include all smaller publications, despite Curran's fears.[101]

The report also called for journalist input in decision-making, although it was less explicit than Ascherson had been. It endorsed community involvement in newspaper decisions in general terms. Press workers would have a chance to participate in decisions at all levels and to influence the general emphasis of the product with which they were involved.[102] Any publication that received public financing would need to operate some form of participation, although the report made no specific recommendations.[103]

Subsequent critics have pointed to the prediction in *The People and the Media* that, without action, there would only be two or three newspapers by the 1980s. Researchers who influenced early New Labour thinking have used this apocalyptic crystal ball-gazing to criticize what they see as all "Old Labour" work on the press and media.[104] It is important to remember that, while there are more than three national newspapers in Britain, the national press landscape is dominated by just three companies, as we saw in Chapter 1. The Labour pamphlet's authors could counter that their claim was more well-founded than the widely held later predictions that introducing new technology and curbing union influence would see a broad range of new entrants provide a genuinely diverse press.

At the time *The People and the Media* faced major opposition from the newspaper industry, and the Labour leadership distanced itself from the proposals. Anger within the newspaper industry centred on plans for an Advertising Revenue Board (see Chapter 3). One notable later attack came from Dennis Hamilton, the former chair of Times Newspapers. Hamilton was concerned that the revenue board's position as a prop of the press would compromise the role of newspapers as a public watchdog. He saw that the board gave the state a dominant responsibility, which it was incapable of adequately fulfilling because it did not have the knowledge and ability of press entrepreneurs to respond to readers' concerns.[105] However, as was noted, the revenue board's funding criteria were politically neutral. The liberal pluralist fears Hamilton harboured were also levelled against the analogous Scandinavian schemes. Also, as we saw in Chapter 1, his claim that the market could operate as an effective watchdog can be questioned.

Where Hamilton's critique was potentially more telling was that the board scheme was complicated and lacked sufficient political support across the Labour Party. It could well have been the case, as Curran has more recently accepted, that an advertising levy would have been more widely supported.[106]

Nevertheless, any form of state intervention would probably have been opposed by the newspaper businesses. Intervention would have had to challenge the historically prevalent liberal pluralist notion in Britain that freedom of the press means ownership free from any government control. Frederick von Hayek had provided a classic critique of extensive market intervention earlier in the twentieth century (which would later influence Thatcherism), echoes of which were heard in Hamilton's criticisms of the revenue board scheme, with regard to the role of entrepreneurs. Hayek rejected the idea that a central collective authority could centralize individuals' knowledge and be aware of all the factors involved in a decision, as required by Labour's plans.[107]

Instead, it was with the operation of the market that the major component of knowledge was developed – the fleeting "knowledge of time and circumstance", developed through entrepreneurial competition.[108] This knowledge was decentralized and dispersed, and it was co-ordinated by the market. In the case of the press, competition meant that entrepreneurs were informed of what readers wanted from their newspapers, through the market. State intervention, such as that envisaged by those in the Labour Party, would be detrimental.

However, Hayek saw the market as based on individual entrepreneurs, as did Hamilton, and realized that monopolization undermined this. The precise problem that Labour's plans wanted to address was that there was a concentration of ownership in few hands – there was an oligopoly. The "invisible hand" had not produced decentralization. Critics have therefore questioned how Hayek's decentralized knowledge operates in this situation.[109] Supporters of Labour's plans could argue that, contrary to Hamilton, intervention to challenge the oligopoly was therefore needed, to diversify the market.

The distance between the proposals of the communications study group and the position of the leadership was reflected in the fact that the study group proposals failed to be included in the second 1974 election manifesto in October – having been too delayed to influence the first. A joint meeting of the Cabinet and the NEC in June 1974 discussed a draft manifesto that made some restricted commitments, calling for the press and media to be "shielded from political and commercial pressures". The press and media were also to be encouraged to become "more responsive to the needs of the community so that they can play an active part in strengthening our democracy".[110] Yet the October 1974 manifesto, like the February one, made no specific mention of press and media policy.[111] Indeed, the party's press and broadcast spokesperson, John Grant, later distanced the leadership from *The People and the Media* after Wilson returned to office. He wrote to *The Times* stating that it was a discussion document and "in no sense was it government policy".[112]

So the development of discussions in the Labour Party's study groups showed a marked shift from the views outlined by Wilson, cited at the start of this chapter. Yet the way the debates in the party had moved on by the time of the two 1974 elections was not reflected in leadership statements or party policy.

However, the communications study group's proposals formed the basis of the Labour Party's submission to the third Royal Commission on the Press, which had been set up by Wilson soon after he became Prime Minister.[113] In its report, the study group had welcomed this commission, although it had been set up independently of the group's work. The study group report's first draft confidently predicted that "it is unlikely that the commission will reach a conclusion radically different from our own".[114] However, as Chapter 3 explains, this prediction proved to be more a case of wishful thinking than an effective assessment of the commission's direction or the Labour leadership's view.

3

The Party, the Government, the Commission and its Minority

Labour from 1974 to 1979

In the first year of the new Labour government the party and key figures in the administration appeared to be agreed – the newspaper industry had a problem. Labour shared the view that there was a powerful pressure towards press concentration that was "socially undesirable"; that there was press bias against the left; and that the fate of individual newspapers should not be "determined by market forces".[1] Implicit in this assessment was the belief that diversifying the press played an important role in enhancing democracy, aiding debate and identifying alternative agendas for discussion.

However, there was less consensus within the party about how to deal with the problem of press diversity and about the prime motive behind what was being demanded. Those who had pushed for the proposals in *The People and the Media* wanted diversity of ownership and broader involvement in press decisions. Those who spearheaded Labour's submission to the Royal Commission on the Press, which the Wilson government set up in 1974, were also happy to see such an outcome, but their main motivation was to provide for an official Labour movement press. For them, as for the minority of the commission, supported by the party, Labour representation in the press was at the heart of the need for structural change – a concern shared by Harold Wilson. Nevertheless, while traditional Labour marketing techniques were out of vogue, Wilson was primarily concerned to increase Labour's support in the newspapers by courting press owners, a strategy that eventually ruled out structural reform.

The Labour Government and the New Left

On coming into office in 1974, the Labour government refused to implement the new left policies in the manifesto. The new left were subject to "containment and marginalization", as one account starkly puts it.[2] Tony Benn led attempts to provide the newly established National Enterprise Board (NEB) with powers to have a substantial stake in profitable companies. But Wilson confined the body to bailing out lame-duck companies and reduced planning agreements to voluntary codes, which private industry could ignore. Critics saw that the NEB was likely to fail before it started.[3]

Instead, while the left was denounced, what critics have regarded as the dog days of the Labour government saw the disintegration of Labour revisionism. An IMF loan and subsequent public spending cuts, together with the government's reluctant embrace of monetarism, saw the demise of Keynesianism. Various interpretations have been given for the shift in Labour's economic policy.[4] Whichever is accepted, writers have argued that the Labour government's determination to tackle inflation led it to turn its back on the party programme and stray from the goals of traditional social democracy.[5] By the time the Labour government considered the proposals from the royal commission, Labour was also battling to preserve itself as a minority government. Its attempt to sustain its strategy by means of a social contract with the unions was failing, as members balked at continued pay restraint for seemingly little reward. Labour policy on employee democracy – to ensure that companies provided their workforce with more information and to encourage extending joint decision-making within companies – had not been fully elaborated before Labour went into office and was not developed in government.[6] Instead, the proposals from the commission the government set up to consider industrial democracy, the Bullock Inquiry, already watered down from those of the TUC, were further diluted by the Labour administration's 1978 White Paper. Legislation was delayed until after the following election, which Labour lost.[7] By the time it went into opposition, it had done little to deal with the British press.

Party Plans

Yet in 1975 the party wanted change. That year Labour's conference passed a groundbreaking motion. The proposal reflected party thinking at the time so closely that even those who opposed parts of it did not do so openly, but merely questioned the thinking behind the segments they found objectionable. The resolution welcomed the publication of *The People and the Media*. It directed itself to the Labour government and called for an Advertising Revenue Board, a differential newsprint subsidy, a launch subsidy and a National Printing Corporation, overseen by a reconstituted and representative Press Council.[8]

By agreeing to this resolution, the party backed the main demands of the communications study group and, if anything, exceeded them. As before, the Scandinavian social market systems, by then being developed, heavily influenced these proposals for ownership diversity. There were major differences, however, between the problems facing the Scandinavian press and those facing its British counterpart. These were used to justify going beyond the north European schemes.

The 1975 conference motion also integrated the two motivations behind Labour policy – it considered diversity both as an aid to the functioning of political democracy and as way of bolstering Labour representation in the press. By considering expression as a "democratic right", the conference reflected the concern to provide newspapers that aided the functioning of democracy. However, as we shall see, the party did not go on to consider explicitly the issue of democracy. Instead, speakers in the conference debate again highlighted what they considered as newspaper bias and the need to improve the Labour movement's representation in the press – issues that would concern Labour supporters.

The party also agreed on the need for broader participation in the control and ownership of the press. The motion again solely concentrated on the press industry's workforce. It stipulated that any newsprint and launch subsidy would be dependent on there being a form of employee participation. The motion's proposer made the same awkward substitution of the press workers for all citizens that had been made before – and one that would be later made again.[9]

The Royal Commission on the Press

The 1975 conference motion was an additional pressure on the Labour government. But by this stage, at least, the government provided some indication that it was itself already considering these concerns, if not the solutions put forward. Within months of being elected in February 1974, it had announced that it was setting up a Royal Commission on the Press.[10] In a Commons debate in the weeks following the announcement, Trade Minister Peter Shore, charged with overseeing the newspaper industry, recognized the existence of bifurcation and argued that there was a powerful pressure towards concentration of newspaper ownership.[11] The latter, he considered, "might be judged correct by purely economic criteria", but "would almost certainly be socially undesirable".[12] And the same debate saw the Prime Minister, Harold Wilson, question the classical liberal conception of press freedom.[13] He argued that journalists operated self-censorship when faced with press business diktat.[14] However, during his period in office, Wilson proved reluctant to legislate when faced with the "deep questions of newspaper economics as well as press freedom".[15]

Wilson and Labour's representation in the press

Wilson's primary concern in dealing with the press was with Labour's coverage. Though hesitant, he was, at the beginning of his second term in office, at least prepared to consider structural change as one possible remedy. There was a tension here with policies to diversify ownership, but there was also a further tension within the interest in press representation. Wilson faced a dilemma. How could any structural change be achieved to improve Labour's representation without further alienating the existing press from a Labour government?

As Prime Minister, Wilson had come to share the wider Labour antipathy towards the press, following the eclipse of a personal honeymoon with the papers that had started in the 1960s. The setting up of the royal commission was, in part, a reaction to the newspapers' role in two controversies involving Marcia Williams and Ted Short, the latter of which was later shown to be part of a "dirty tricks" campaign, which the press recycled.[16] Wilson also considered that the newspapers only ever articulated the positions of those opposing Labour on issues such as the party's debate on membership of the EEC.[17] The broader concern in the Labour Party with newspaper representation had been fuelled by the February 1974 election, which saw the bulk of Fleet Street support the Conservatives. Only the *Daily Mirror*, in the words of one Labour MP, "reflected the aspirations of the people".[18]

Nevertheless, at least publicly – for it is true that he was known for tailoring his words to fit his audience – Wilson's decision to set up the royal commission was in response to Labour backbench fears over press concentration and cross-ownership. These had been heightened by the closure of the Scottish *Express* newspapers, where jobs had been lost and, as Wilson acknowledged, the readers' choice of newspapers had been narrowed.[19]

Nonetheless, Wilson's unease over cross-ownership concerned the fact that it threatened to jeopardize Labour representation in the press. He suggested that, without "outside interests", it would be much more difficult for a title to survive financially. However, the problem with these interests was that they could bias a newspaper's coverage. His concern was that, if Labour's nationalization plans threatened a newspaper company's wider interests, then the effect would be to prejudice the company against the party.[20]

Wilson's ambivalence towards the royal commission reflected the twin pressures he faced – the demands from the party for structural change and the concern not to alienate the press. Advising him was the intellectual driving force behind Labour's communications study group, James Curran. Curran redrafted the initial inquiry terms, and Downing Street appointed the original chair, the radical judge Mr Justice Finer, following Curran's advice. (However, Finer died within months of being appointed and his successor, Oliver McGregor, was more conservative in outlook.[21]) Wilson did express some interest in "economic intervention that would encourage the founding of new papers".[22] In the end, however, he justi- fied his Labour critics' fears that he saw the commission as a way of diffusing concerns rather than addressing them.[23] And he told Conservatives that he shared their worries over subsidies.[24] As the then *Labour Weekly* journalist and now loyalist Labour MP Martin Linton put it: "Wilson could see that if anything he threatened to do to the press would immediately provoke hostility, he would reckon it wasn't worth doing. It would be simply like pulling the tiger's tail."[25]

Linton's account is borne out by Wilson's own evidence to the commis- sion. His "remarkable document" detailed the newspaper smears over Short and Williams.[26] But what is significant is that, instead of wanting to tackle the question of press ownership head-on, Wilson identified the problem more narrowly as one of how journalists operated. His solution was to tighten the laws on privacy, contempt and defamation. The onus was on press companies themselves to control more effectively – to put "their own house in order".[27]

The Labour Party's Submission to the Royal Commission

The party's submission to the commission also reflected the concerns with improving how the broader Labour movement was represented in the press. However, its recommendations centred on structural change of the press market. Those selected from the NEC to represent the party were likely to be particularly anxious to address newspaper coverage. The five representatives included Lena Jeger, who headed the party's Press and Publicity Committee, which was directly concerned with this coverage. Another was Donald Ross, who edited *Labour Weekly*, which promoted the party and had called for a Labour press. The others were two research department officials and Eric Moonman. Thus, only one person from the study group, and none of the majority that backed the new left proposals, was involved in this key delegation.

The party representatives thus prioritized legislation to create the conditions for a newspaper that would do for the Labour movement "what *The Times* does for the establishment". They recognized the issue of bifur- cation. They assumed that such a paper would have a higher proportion of lower-income readers than the existing broadsheets. The party officials argued that it would be financially impossible to produce a daily Labour movement newspaper relying on a similar number of readers as the *Daily Telegraph* had because it would not be able to charge similar advertising rates.[28] For this reason they argued that there needed to be redistribution of advertising through government intervention. Their concern was also linked with creating a press that aided political democracy, however – so that "every section of the community has an equal opportunity to express its views and interests".[29] The NEC representatives provided similar solutions to those the party would agree to later that year. There would be an Advertising Revenue Board, financing new launches and a differential newsprint subsidy, and the universalizing of government advertising.[30] A National Printing Corporation was also mooted, which the representatives saw as a way of providing for the expected shortfall in printing capacity that would come with the establishment of the new newspapers they envisaged.[31]

These proposals showed a clear difference of approach between the party and the Labour government. However, there was a problem for the Labour campaigners. The NEC's proposals were not actual party policy when they were put forward, because they were submitted before the party's conference in 1975. Instead, the submission was based on some, but not all, of the ideas contained in *The People and the Media*, which the NEC also submitted separately, "without commitment".[32] Nevertheless, by the time the party's representatives spoke to the commission, the 1975 conference policy had been passed. By then, party and government policy were already at odds.

Not surprisingly, this seeming ambiguity was a source of some confusion to the royal commission. The commission concluded from the NEC's evidence that it was not firmly committed to the Advertising Revenue Board proposals and wished the commission would consider other alternatives.[33] This blunted the impact of Labour's demands. Also, by focusing on creating a space for a Labour movement press, Labour's demands had an element of "special pleading". However, there were other barriers facing the party's plans too, since the unions, though wanting structural change in the press market, were divided over strategy. The main opposition, however, came from the press businesses and editors.

Reaction to Labour's Plans

The Advertising Revenue Board

In response to Labour's proposals for an Advertising Revenue Board, the press owners and editors closed ranks. The Newspaper Publishers Association[34] was backed by the Guild of British Newspaper Editors in questioning whether the board would deter some publications from raising circulation or the number of pages they produced.[35] The role of a board in fixing advertising rates, they suggested, would hinder competition and "subsidise inefficiency".[36]

The publishers argued that advertising redistribution would not help economic viability, since one of the major economic problems was not advertising revenue but "overmanning", which could be solved with new technology.[37] The press businesses rejected a key assumption of bifurcation behind both the revenue board and any advertising tax proposal. They argued that a disproportionate amount of advertising was not spent on attracting those with high income. They noted, for instance, that many "quality" newspapers had lower social class readers.[38] Finally, the publishers and the advertising industry saw that the board would imperil editorial independence. Editors would sway their views towards those of the board in order to stay in business.[39]

Labour supporters of the advertising board could respond that the objections took a narrowly market-driven view of efficiency and ignored the arguments justifying press diversity on the basis that it was needed for information and to facilitate debate, required in a democracy. Thus, it could be argued that the cost to the community of the negative externalities that have come with market provision – the lack of press choice – was greater than that of some marginal increase in inefficiency. In addition, the charge of inefficiency is similar to one that had been levelled against the Scandinavian subsidy systems and which has been found to be largely unproven (see Chapter 2). If such an argument had been made about market-led provision of the arts in Britain, for example, then the Arts Council would have been disbanded.

As for the charge that the Advertising Revenue Board did not address the real problem of "overmanning", advocates could retort that the board proposals neither helped nor hindered the ability to deal with staffing levels and did not automatically preclude the introduction of new technology within the press. Instead, the board would make some publications more viable at the expense of others. The claim that "overmanning" provided the primary obstacle to diversity has not been borne out by the subsequent failure of new technology to broaden the range of titles extensively.

Further, advocates of Labour's scheme could point to the role that bifurcation has played in the British press and the fact that a large proportion of advertising revenue has been targeted at high-income readers, as we saw in Chapter 1. And as for the claim that the broadsheets had some C/D/E social class readers, this in itself is not surprising. The more important aspect is whether these papers attract a larger percentage of A/B readers, which they do.[40] If it were otherwise, then what would be the attraction to advertisers in paying premium rates to newspapers that had a lower circulation than their tabloid counterparts?

Newsprint Subsidies, Launch Funds and an Advertising Tax

However, the press companies were expressing a more broadly held concern about the amount of state intervention that the Advertising Revenue Board would involve. There was wider support, though, for providing the differential subsidies that the Labour Party also proposed, when these were separated from the more interventionist Advertising Revenue Board plan. In addition, experience from other countries has shown that, with advertising tax and levy schemes, the fear of editorial independence being compromised has been dispelled. Also, these schemes have been shown to be completely financially viable.

So should the Labour Party have rejected the complicated Advertising Revenue Board plan and taken a leaf directly out of the Scandinavian book and proposed a cross-media advertising tax to provide a differential subsidy and a launch fund? The idea of a tax on advertising has been a controversial one in Britain, since it was one of the taxes used to attempt to stifle the radical press in the nineteenth century. Yet one influential supporter of a revenue board, Curran, now admits that a modern tax to pay for subsidies would probably have got the support of the right wing of the Labour Party and, as it was supported by the TUC, might thus have stood more chance of being agreed to by the government.[41]

Some press companies dramatically suggested that they were so hostile to subsidies, however, that they might "prefer that their papers should close rather than that they should run the risk of the freedom of those papers being limited".[42] The press companies also rejected launch funds. They considered that if a group wanted to start a newspaper with a different political stance, the existence of a customer base would have been enough to ensure the paper's success. They "would in no way resent a newcomer which aimed to give, what it believed to be, a different political emphasis".[43]

Yet supporters of launch funds could cite bifurcation and the high barriers to newspaper market entry discussed in Chapter 1 to refute these claims. The existing publishers' assessment that a new title would not be "resented" ignored the possibility that this newcomer might highlight what it believed were the biases and shortcomings of the other newspapers' content, something that might not be received too well. Moreover, it would be competing for the readers of the existing publications and therefore would be treated by them as a competitor.

In addition, the press businesses and advertisers opposed universal advertising by the government, the former calling it a "dictatorial" and expensive intrusion into the operation of advertising agencies.[44] The companies thus ignored which organization was the agencies' paymasters in this situation and thus had the ultimate power over where advertising was placed. Nevertheless, it should be noted that Labour's plans for universal advertising overlooked a dilemma. Its plans, together with increased diversity, could have led to the state advertising in far-right papers, which Labour supporters would be likely to deem racist, and in such soft porn publications as the *Daily Sport*, which would be likely to offend a range of supporters.

Broadening Democratic Involvement

Chapter 1 looked at the argument that one of the requirements of a press to provide for political democracy is that it should be subject to some form of democratic participation and involvement. As with the proposals in *The People and the Media*, however, the Labour Party did not heavily emphasize the question of democracy within the press in its submission to the commission. Key activists considered that this was not achievable in the short term.[45] They did not refer to the democratic arguments when they spoke to the commission, and in their written proposals they referred only briefly to the involvement of press workers and not at all to the role of readers and citizens.[46] The party representatives' proposals were hazy when specifically referring to the press – the launch fund would be available only to trust-based newspapers, such as *The Guardian*, for example, and the proposals on democracy that related to industry as a whole would also apply to newspapers.[47]

But the publishers rejected any further involvement by press employees in newsroom democracy. They used liberal pluralist notions to defend their right to have a privileged role in public debate based on private ownership.[48] The NPA accepted that a newspaper's management controlled many areas, including the editor's budget, staffing levels, salaries, the number and type of specialist reporters employed and the percentage of editorial space. Indeed, the newspaper companies' representatives admitted that: "These inhibitions might be said, of course, to prove the validity of the radical proposition that press freedom is a chimera under a free enterprise system." But they argued that the same was true under a state-run structure, as was the case at the time in eastern Europe.[49]

What the Labour new left policy was attempting in this instance, however, was to ameliorate management domination by handing some influence over to those in the enterprises, rather than the state. Indeed, supporters of industrial democracy could argue that their plans went beyond state or market control to address some of the problems associated with both.

The State, the Market and Press Employees

Press employers and, latterly, the royal commission rejected Labour's proposals because they believed state intervention could not effectively replace the market. We looked earlier at the basis of this claim in the work of Hayek. Proponents of employee democracy believe Hayek's thinking provides an insight that helps justify their answers to problems of both state and market control. This is relevant to press policy.

The kernel of Hayek's thought – the belief that not all knowledge can be centralized – is part of the reason for his popularity. Yet the implication is that knowledge in enterprises comes in only one of two ways. It is either developed through competition and is thus narrowly based. Or Hayek implicitly assumes that only entrepreneurs can codify all of the knowledge developed by workers, which runs counter to his general view that all knowledge cannot be centralized.[50] If proponents of broadening democracy consider Labour's press plans in this light, then they could argue that if Labour did not explicitly involve newspaper workers, they would, at the very least, be ignoring this huge resource of knowledge. The application of this knowledge would provide a check and balance on statist solutions.[51] Equally, one argument for increasing democratic participation in private press operations is that, without it, the creative knowledge of all those in the industry is not harnessed as effectively as it could be. The successful participation of outside software writers and ordinary citizens in the development of open-source software is a more recent example of a similar idea.[52]

Industrial democracy is only one method of securing participative democratic control of the press. A notable democratic theorist, writing at about the same time as the royal commission was taking submissions, isolated three criteria by which any democratic system can be judged: the extent to which all constituent groups are involved in decision-making; the degree to which decisions are open to democratic control; and how far ordinary citizens are involved in administration.[53] The emphasis on industrial and newsroom democracy excludes other constituent groups, such as the wider community, who consume the press or are affected by it, for instance. The more recent impact of the citizen journalist has once again highlighted the role of the community in the press. Following this argument about constituent groups, citizens would need to be involved in decision-making. Readers and other citizens may have different concerns from those of journalists and printers.[54]

A discussion of mechanisms for extensive community control is outside the scope of this book. (See Chapter 1 for some of the debates on democratic participation.) Nevertheless, it is worth pointing out that the operation of democratic control in the press is replete with difficulties. Writers have pointed to problems with participatory democracy in decision-making, which could be applied to democratic involvement in newspapers. Not the least of these is the size and complexity of society: any simple extrapolation from how participatory democracy operated in ancient Athens to present-day situations would be inappropriate. It may well be that many decisions facing workforce representatives and readers, regarding such topics as marketing for example, would be too complex to be made by anyone other than experts. It is sometimes said that direct democracy is better suited to making "either/or" decisions than to multiple-choice selections, which are perhaps better handled by non-mandated representatives.[55] Thus, advocates of democracy would need to limit the level of participation by the citizenry who wished to take an active interest in newspaper control. However, citizens might decide on long-term broad policy issues based on proposals formulated by elected representatives on boards of newspapers. And even before the use of the Internet became ubiquitous, writers were noticing that new technology had made a re-examination of different forms of participatory democracy possible.[56]

These were some of the relevant issues of democratic theory. The Labour government, meanwhile, was grappling with the practice of widening democracy in the press. Its involvement in the issue of the closed shop highlighted the problems of identifying broadening press democracy solely with democracy in the newsroom. And its experiment in broadening democracy in the newspaper industry in practice did nothing to strengthen the case for widening democratic control over the press.

The Scottish Daily News

One of the reasons for the establishment of the Royal Commission on the Press was the closure of the Scottish *Express* titles. When the newspaper folded, the Labour government came under pressure to support plans – in the interests of press diversity – for a newspaper to rise from the ashes as a workers' co-operative.[57]

While there were divisions from the start within its senior ranks, the Labour government responded to the request for aid and backed the co-operative *Scottish Daily News* to the tune of £1.75 million – half the estimated launch costs – with money from the Department of Industry and the NEB, presided over by Tony Benn.[58] The rest of the launch money came from workers' own redundancy payments, public subscription and the publisher and former MP Robert Maxwell.[59] For the first two months the *News* provided some hope to those who considered that many British newspapers were dominated by autocratic management. But after this short interlude Maxwell took over as chief executive, and the experiment effectively died. The paper limped on, but within months it had ceased publication.[60]

There were a number of reasons for its failure. The Labour government was divided on backing the venture, with right-wing ministers reluctant to back co-operative initiatives.[61] They refused to cover a financial shortfall, which would have meant Maxwell's money would not have been needed.[62] As a result, the publisher came to dominate the inexperienced co-operative and, after financial difficulties, adopted control. He subsequently ignored works' council decisions, ending democratic involvement.[63]

However, government reluctance and Maxwell's participation were not the only reasons for the newspaper's failure. Like many of the NEB's funding recipients, help went to a failed enterprise. The best journalists had flown to more solvent titles. Those left produced a "miserable" title – "a really cheap, nasty, tabloid rag", according to one employee.[64] Events, in other words, bore out the conclusion of an independent report commissioned in the wake of the Scottish *Express* titles' closure, that it was not feasible to launch a new paper, because its circulation would be too small.[65] There was also a poor take-up of advertising. Yet advertisers later admitted that they were reluctant to advise the *News* on this area, where management experience was lacking.[66]

What the *Daily News* episode indicated was that newspaper co-operatives required more than just financial support; they needed advice and training. Such ventures also needed safeguards. It was also essential that there was a properly costed scheme, with an independent assessment of whether a market existed for the publication before going ahead. As it was, one prominent advocate of broadening newspaper participation noted that the failure of the *Scottish Daily News* "unquestionably set back the cause of internal democracy, spreading disillusion among both politicians and press workers".[67]

The Closed Shop and the Charter

The Labour government also involved itself in the press democracy debate in the saga over its repeal of the ban on closed shops – that is, where all employees (including journalists) are obliged to join a union. The government was responding to huge union pressure from the movement in repealing the law.[68] Joint opposition to the ban brought the unions and government closer, and the repeal became part of the social contract.[69]

Yet the government faced concerted pressure from press businesses and editors, "united in a way" not "seen before", articulated in hostile press coverage.[70] The fact that Fleet Street contained both closed shops and workplaces where there was 100 per cent union membership, by agreement, mattered little.[71] Some on the right of the Labour Party also expressed profound misgivings. All opponents were particularly hostile to the journalists' union, the NUJ, which took more radical positions on this and other issues from 1974, and which changed its position on closed shops more than once in the course of the debate.[72]

There were a number of objections to the original 1974 Trades Union and Labour Relations Act, but three stand out. First, the Labour government was accused of strengthening the power of journalists in order to influence newspaper editorial policy. The anxiety was that editors would be forced into the NUJ and would have to abide by the chapel agreements.[73] Opponents saw it as "only a short step to [the] election of editors by chapels".[74] Eric Moonman and some ministers were among those in the Labour Party who were concerned about editorial interference.[75] Yet, the senior minister piloting the law, former NUJ activist and editor Michael

Foot, slyly questioned this view with typical wit, by quoting the nineteenth-century essayist William Hazlitt. As Secretary of State for Employment, Foot suggested that the main threat to editors came from newspapers owners, who were now concerned over others muscling into their territory. "William Hazlitt said that regicide was quite a respectable affair as long as it was only done by kings and queens but it was when the common people took a hand that a different view was taken of it. The same principle seems to be applicable to the alarm now spread."[76]

Following a right—left tussle the NUJ, in fact, rescinded its position that editors should be compelled to be part of the closed shop and agreed to give assurances that it would not attempt to instruct editors on editorial policy matters.[77] Under heavy pressure the union drew back from demanding a measure of journalist participation in editorial policy. Instead, the publishers' campaign succeeded in equating journalistic involvement in editorial decision-making with control by the NUJ's headquarters.[78]

A second objection, again shared by a number of Labour backbenchers, including Moonman, along with the newspaper companies, editors, Conservatives and Liberals, was that the closed shop could prevent outside contributors from having "free access" to the press.[79] Nevertheless, double standards were applied here. A previous president of the Guild of Newspaper Editors, Frank Owens, in a remarkable contribution, told the royal commission that everyone should be allowed to have access to the press.[80] Yet one Labour MP pointed out that what was being asserted was not actually free admission but the entitlement of editors to determine who had the right of entry.[81]

The Labour government responded by insisting that the NUJ leadership did not wish to use closed shops in order to exclude such contributions. Ministers indicated that the requirement that all journalists join the union had operated in much of Fleet Street without such exclusion and, indeed, could not be used in this way.[82] Yet the policy left open the possibility that outside contributions could be restricted. The difficult area of sports journalist contributors indicated this. Here, indeed, the union did campaign for the restriction of non-union sporting stars' copy.[83]

The fact that journalists arguing for broader participation could deny wider access to outside contributors provided a problem for proponents of employee control. It pointed to a real dilemma. It illustrated the potential problems with the lack of clarity in Labour Party thinking. Labour's proposals on democratic involvement in newspapers were mostly restricted to those involved in the industry. They were ambiguous on the relationship of these plans to broader citizen participation. The legislation had the potential both to advance employee democracy and concomitantly to set back community involvement, because journalists could advocate restricting access to contributors.

There was a third objection to the act. As Moonman viewed it, "perhaps

[the] most important" concern was that the Labour government was damaging Labour's representation in the newspapers by challenging the press. Putting the newspapers' backs up was self-defeating: "The Labour Party does not benefit from antagonism towards the press."[84] This was becoming a more powerful consideration again.

Nonetheless, the government's view of the legislation was that it was neutral. It merely meant there was neither an inducement to provide a closed shop nor a deterrent against such a course, if agreed by both management and unions. It saw that, rather than legislating, both unions and management should be encouraged to produce a binding charter on press freedom, as was being discussed by both sides.[85] What followed again signalled the hostility of the press businesses and editors to any attempt to interfere with their right to control their titles.

Negotiations over this charter foundered. In an early draft the editors demanded that employers should be able to check the political affiliations of journalists before employing them.[86] Talks broke down when the representatives of press companies and editors took the view that such a charter could only be agreed if journalists were barred from creating closed shops.[87]

It was after this that the royal commission stepped into the breach. Its plan for a charter provided the newspaper companies with a problem. The proposals appeared even-handed and were far from advocating widespread journalistic control. Indeed, they were meant to preserve editorial autonomy over both outside contributions and union involvement. However, the commissioners' first recommendation was that a journalist should be free "to act, write, and speak in accordance with conscience without being inhibited by the threat of expulsion or other disciplinary action by his union or his employer".[88] In other words, in a policy transfer from other European countries, journalists would have a "freedom of conscience clause" that prevented them from being dictated to by those in superior positions over the political and moral line they took. Commissioners also recommended that journalists be involved in the appointment of editors, although they did not indicate how they thought this would be achieved.[89]

The response of the publishers, in the words of Curran, was to go "ballistic, because the whole thing had boomeranged. It boomeranged in that very British way when a discussion is taken in a way that hadn't been intended." The press companies were hostile to the charter clause, which implicitly challenged the view that press freedom was to be simply equated with employer control.[90]

Facing this pressure, the Labour government rejected the charter. Calls for broader involvement in press decision-making therefore received a setback. The Labour government had dipped its toe in these waters, by advancing the closed shop legislation, and had witnessed an illustration of the potential problems with the party's proposals and the hostility of those in control of the press to any attempt to inhibit that control.

The Royal Commission Findings and the Minority Report

In their overall findings the majority of the commissioners sided with the critics of the party's proposals to the commission. Although the majority accepted the notion that the press was a "special case", which was essential for the maintenance of democracy, they rejected extensive intervention.[91] While, as we have suggested, such intervention would have needed to be backed up by safeguards, Curran suggests that the rejection of intervention in the newspaper market prefigured the onset of Thatcherism.[92] The Labour Party chair, speaking for the party, as opposed to the parliamentary leadership, denounced the report as "bland and complacent".[93]

However, the commission was not unanimous in its findings. Two of its members, David Basnett and Geoffrey Goodman, produced a Minority Report, which the Labour Party latterly promoted.[94] Basnett and Goodman called for more interventionism. They were shocked by what they also saw as the complacent approach of the other commissioners in the face of increasing concentration of ownership.[95] For the Labour government adviser Goodman and the union leader Basnett this concern was again linked, nevertheless, to the idea of press bias against Labour and the unions. The answer was to restructure the market so that an official Labour movement press could flourish (an idea that Goodman had already promoted).[96]

The Labour Party and the commission dissenters, however, differed on the ways to achieve the restructuring. The minority reintroduced the call for a commercially viable National Printing Corporation (NPC), as a back-up if a shortfall in printing capacity demanded it, and a state-financed launch fund to provide assistance to new titles – a proposal which had recently been backed by the TUC.[97]

This was a hybrid solution. The use of a commercially viable print works was part of a social market proposal. Yet the emphasis on a print corporation and the rhetoric of using "the template of the BBC", as Goodman has recently described it, was in the public service tradition.[98]

Rather than a solution that would restructure the market by directly impacting on advertising, such as that proposed by the Labour Party to the commission, Basnett and Goodman felt that funding should be provided by the government. They accepted that bifurcation was a block on diversity.[99] However, they considered that the solution was not to alter the advertising market but to use the NPC to make it possible for newspapers to be printed, because existing businesses might not offer their surplus printing capacity to new entrants.[100]

The Labour Party general secretary, Ron Hayward, considered that the Minority Report's proposals did not go as far as those of the party.[101] But Goodman and Basnett were more specific than the party on widening decision-making in the press, even if their proposals were still not fully formed. They envisaged that the National Printing Corporation's unionized employees, many of whom would be printers, would make up half of its governing board. The board would have no power over which papers it published – the only grounds for refusal being financial viability – answering legitimate fears on this point.

The report's authors advocated new staff-led press co-operatives and, unlike Labour's proposals, suggested some wider citizen involvement "possibly with consumer/reader representation on a board", an idea they did not explore in detail.[102] The report thus went beyond statist solutions to address what were seen as the problems of the market, recommending some measure of broader popular control in effect as a potential check and balance.

Press companies and the majority of the commission opposed the Minority Report's proposals because the state would be involved in selecting which papers received launch funding and access to printing facilities.[103] Yet, as we saw earlier, targeted subsidies in European states have not necessarily led to direct government interference. It would not be surprising, nevertheless, if the newspaper businesses did not welcome the possibility of new titles encroaching on their existing market share.

However, critics could argue that one difficulty with the proposals was that the key barrier to increased diversity was not the lack of commercially priced print facilities. It was the operation of advertising, as we saw in Chapter 1, which the Minority Report's authors did not address because they felt "the strength of the advertising lobby was such that you simply weren't going to get very far with that".[104] There was already excess capacity in the printing industry, as sceptics such as the printers' union, the NGA, the editors' representatives and the Advertising Association all told the royal commission – and the commission agreed.[105] Critics could suggest that the concern not to confront advertising businesses limited the effectiveness of the proposals.

The Labour Government

The Minority Report was widely supported in the Labour movement.[106] After all, it was very similar to the position advocated by the TUC, and the Labour Party was promoting it. But the Labour government did not back it or the recommendations made by its own party.

By 1977, when the royal commission reported its findings, James Callaghan had succeeded Wilson as Prime Minister. It is now clear that members of the Cabinet held secret meetings with the authors of the Minority Report. Those involved – Roy Hattersley, Peter Shore and Michael Meacher – were prepared to set up a ministerial committee to discuss the minority recommendations. According to Goodman: "There was a real possibility, and I'm not exaggerating, given the kind of reception that we received." However, the politicians were concerned about "a huge outcry from the Conservative press", as was the new Labour leader.[107]

Before he died, Lord Callaghan cast doubt over whether any scheme that involved giving financial assistance to the press would have been "ever a runner" under his administration. The press businesses and editors, as well as the royal commission, did not support such proposals.[108] And as the head of his policy unit, Bernard (now Lord) Donoughue, also said, the minority Labour government's parliamentary position was too precarious for such radical reform to be tackled: "without a Commons majority, it was prudent not to open another front".[109] In addition, Callaghan regarded proposals for state assistance to the press as simply unworkable.[110]

The government also had in front of it the commission's recommendations. The commissioners recommended tightening up monopoly and mergers law, making it less susceptible to the sort of political interference Wilson had engaged in to encourage Labour representation in the press.[111] As we have seen, they also called for protection for journalists from editorial and press business interference and for journalists' involvement in the election of editors.

Yet the Labour government shelved these demands. After taking a year to respond, Trade Minister Michael Meacher told Parliament that the question of the press charter was still being dealt with. In addition, Meacher merely noted: "The other recommendations are under consideration."[112] With these words the Labour government dismissed years of commission deliberations.

The 1979 Manifesto

The Labour election manifesto of 1979 was short, and the section on the media much shorter. There was nothing specifically about the press. For the media as a whole, all the British people were told about Labour's plans was that: "Our aim is to safeguard freedom of expression; to encourage diversity; and to guard both against the dangers of government and commercial control."[113] The proposals for diversity had been reduced to a wish. All mention of government intervention and of internal press democracy was avoided.

Why was this? One answer was that discussion on the media in the NEC's Home Policy Committee after Callaghan assumed office had tended to concentrate on broadcasting. This was in the absence of a communications study group. As far as the press was concerned, all eyes were focused on the royal commission. The do-little response from the Labour government provoked little reaction from the NEC's study groups until after Labour returned to opposition in 1979.

Of overriding importance, however, was that policy agreed by the party conferences on a whole range of issues had not made it into the manifesto. The policy was drawn up by the NEC, based on submissions from groups such as the communications study group, and then went to conference to be voted on. Clause V of Labour's constitution stipulated that the NEC and Cabinet or Shadow Cabinet would jointly draw up the manifesto from this.[114]

In 1976 the NEC presented *Labour's Programme for Britain*, which was agreed by the party's conference and was meant to be the basis for the election manifesto. The 1976 programme did not have an extensive section on the press, yet it succinctly reiterated Labour's conference policy commitments.[115] For two years before the 1979 election, the election subcommittees of the Cabinet and the NEC had been meeting, and drafts had already been worked out. The media was one of the areas discussed, according to the head of the party's research department at the time.[116] Yet the day after the government's defeat in a vote of confidence, which made an election inevitable, officials at No. 10 revealed their own draft manifesto, which became the basis of discussions.[117]

Callaghan dominated the Clause V drafting committee and insisted that the less radical No. 10 proposals should prevail.[118] He, in effect, employed a veto, which the left protested had no basis in the party's constitution.[119] Policies previously agreed by party conferences were jettisoned or ignored.[120] In axing the radical commitments and cutting the word-length, the party diluted its commitment to press reform.

There was thus a clear division between the position of the Labour Party and that of its government that continued from the first few months of the 1974 administration. The party's plans to facilitate diversity in the press, influenced by Scandinavian social democratic and social market practice, were rejected by its leadership. By 1979 the manifesto had little in the way of positive commitments either for press diversity or for broader democratic involvement.

However, if the plans had been successfully implemented by the Labour government, along with making a Labour press more achievable, they might have gone some way to enriching democratic life in Britain. Nevertheless, while many objections to the plans can be debated, their attempt to go beyond the Scandinavian social market paradigm meant that there was a potential over-reliance on a supposedly all-knowing state, without checks and balances. The proposals on the roles of both journalists and the wider community as a possible check and balance were hazy.

The involvement of the Labour government in instituting the closed shop legislation highlighted this gap in Labour's plans. It was shown that greater industrial democracy had the potential to act as a barrier to increased public participation and access.

By the time that the Callaghan government received the royal commission report, which called for limited journalistic involvement, and the Minority Report, which went much further, the tide was turning. The corporatist era, which had seen the development of the Bullock Inquiry on industrial democracy – where such ideas as employees sharing control were considered, if not acted on – was ending.[121] Again the proposals for democracy across all industry faced intense employer opposition and divisions within the Labour movement.[122] It is not surprising that plans to broaden participation in the press died too.

Nevertheless, as we shall see in Chapter 4, as Labour went into opposition following the 1979 election defeat, two themes highlighted here would be re-addressed. Labour campaigners would consider representation in a new light, just as they would develop new ideas aimed at providing a press that was more representative of the political range of opinions in society. Also the role of citizens' participation in the press and workplace democracy would come further to the forefront as campaigns for the "right of reply" gained momentum.

4

Flow and Ebb
Labour from 1979 to 1983

Change swept through every area of the Labour Party between 1979 and 1983. Press policy was no exception. In 1979 Labour made no specific promise to act on the press. Yet the 1983 manifesto gave a solid commitment to diversify newspaper ownership, the like of which had never been seen in a Labour election programme. This attempt by Labour's new left to reverse its failure to include the party's conference policy on press reform in the 1979 manifesto should be seen within the context of wider developments in the party.

Party Policy from 1979 to 1983

By 1979 a battle was brewing. A swath of party activists felt the party wasn't being listened to by its leadership. Clause V had failed to reflect party policies, including those on the press. With their ranks swelled by new recruits who did not share the deference to the party leadership of the past, the activists demanded increased accountability. As the party's general secretary starkly put it, reflecting the left's feeling of betrayal, activists wanted ministers to "act in our interests".[1] The high-profile talisman in this clash was again Tony Benn. The Campaign for Labour Party Democracy (CLPD), which had been formed in 1973 to ensure that conference decisions were put into practice, championed the demand to give the NEC power to determine the manifesto.

Along with the left-dominated NEC, the CLPD was more successful in achieving its related proposals for electing the party's leader and on ensuring that MPs had to be reselected before every general election.[2] Pre-empting the first of these moves, James Callaghan resigned in 1980, to be replaced by Michael Foot.[3] Although Foot came from the left, he had opposed the Bennite new left project and its associated constitutional demands.[4]

As part of the organizational reforms, Labour revamped the NEC's policy-making consultation mechanism to encourage wider discussion in the party. This new procedure was cumbersome and affected press policy development. The conference set up new subcommittees, such as a revamped communications study group, renamed the media study group, which would then discuss and publish its report within two years. Branches and constituency parties were encouraged to respond to the NEC, but could not take formal decisions. On the basis of the responses, the NEC would draw up a draft statement, which would be submitted to conference for approval.[5]

The upsurge of calls for democratic accountability was also linked to the new left's demands for state intervention and economic control. The demise of Keynesian welfarism as Labour's governing ideology had found the party's right-wing temporarily bereft of ideas and demoralized. As the leadership's organizational control over the party disintegrated after 1979, it lost its powers to veto NEC policies on important issues such as economic intervention.[6]

Again activists tied party democratic accountability to the wider debate on democratizing the state. While their influence at this time should not be overstated, two new left extra-party groupings, vying for ideological influence on the Labour left, were concerned with these questions and also the role of the British press. One was a grouping that was known by the title of the British Communist Party journal it produced, *Marxism Today* (see Chapter 5). Another was called the Institute for Workers' Control.

After it had retreated from Keynesianism, the social democratic right also retreated from the ideological debate both at the conference and on the NEC. Instead, it saw the press as a weapon in its counter-offensive – using its contacts to discredit the left.[7] This both brought the right closer to some newspapers and emphasized the potential and importance of improving Labour's representation through the existing press.

The left's challenge within the national party reached its zenith with Benn's narrow defeat in his bid to become deputy leader at the 1981 conference. The subsequent pressure from the left-leaning NEC for constitutional reform prompted a backlash from the TUC leadership. While publicly supporting the left's policies, it started to challenge the new left's organizational influence. Buoyed by this, the right also started reorganizing. They removed Benn and cohorts such as Frank Allaun from key NEC committees, although not the media study group.[8]

By 1983 the tide had turned again on policies for employee democracy and interventionism, in an abrupt shift from what had been laid out in *Labour's Programme 1982*, which had been based on the left's Alternative Economic Strategy (AES). The 1983 manifesto represented a compromise between Keynesianism and Bennite interventionism, which still influenced the document, despite the right's new dominance of the NEC.[9] The left's influence on the manifesto was partly a product of the previous four years. In addition, according to the then right-winger Roy Hattersley, the new head of the pivotal home policy subcommittee, John Golding, recognized that Labour was heading for a large defeat. He thought it best for the 1983 manifesto to be associated with some left-wing ideas, so that the left would be identified with that result.[10]

The left's success in changing Labour's constitution had convinced some on the social democratic right that they should split from the party. They were not prepared to see constituency members determine policy. This schism was to cost the party dearly in electoral support, as many Labour voters switched to the new party, the SDP. The assault on the left and the battles over the constitution had distracted Labour from the task of being elected.[11] As it was, facing a Liberal–SDP Alliance, as well as a Conservative Party bolstered by the Falklands adventure of 1982, the party ended up polling only 28 per cent in the 1983 election, a mere 2 per cent more than the Alliance.

The 1979 Party Conference and the Media Study Group

The 1979 conference, following the party's election defeat that year, reflected the fixation with democratic accountability, giving discussions on the press and the media added impetus. Delegates again agreed on the need for newspaper ownership reform, which, as was explained, was now explicitly coupled with party democracy. By fusing previous recommendations and combining policy transfer with innovation, the conference motion certainly fudged some of the long-running debates, but it also put forward one of the more radical European social democratic press policies. Alongside calls to aid diversity, with a fund for new publications, an Advertising Revenue Board and a National Printing Corporation, the successful motion called for producer press co-operatives, demanded a national debate on alternatives for democratic control of the press and insisted on a right of reply, as well as discussing calls for a Labour movement newspaper. It also set in train the procedure in 1980 for reassembling what was thereafter known as the media study group, to consider these proposals.[12] Following the frustration with the findings of the Royal Commission on the Press, the study group's explicit aim was to prove that public intervention in the press was possible, both practically and politically.[13] Chaired by the MP Frank Allaun, the study group included left MPs such as Benn, Michael Meacher and Stuart Holland.[14] A minority, including Philip Whitehead and Austin Mitchell, were not of the left.[15] Trade unionists involved included, from the NUJ, Ivor Gaber, who was later to become an academic, and Brendan Barber, who would much later become TUC general secretary. Academics who participated included James Curran and Greg Philo. Journalists were also involved, such as Tom Baistow and Geoffrey Goodman, as well as Chris Mullin from *Tribune* and Harold Frayman from *Labour Weekly*.[16]

Diversity and Labour Representation

Balance beyond Diversity: The Independent Press Authority

A more specific reason why press and media reform was on the agenda after 1979 was that the Labour movement again felt itself under attack. That year's election had seen *The Sun* join the ranks of the "anti-Labour chorus", treating Callaghan's middle-of-the-road programme as "a reworking of the Communist Manifesto", as one commentator put it.[17] An indication of Labour's attitude to this was that, according to Tony Benn, the biggest cheer during his speech to a 1980 special party conference came when he quoted from the Glasgow University Media Group's work on media bias against the unions.[18] Also, in 1980 the TUC published the pamphlet *Behind the Headlines*, which argued that newspaper bias against the Labour movement was a key factor in the 1979 election result.[19]

The response of party thinkers to this perceived hostility took an interesting turn. As we saw, Labour Party policy had so far treated diversity of press ownership and Labour representation in the newspapers as practically synonymous. If you considered one, you would be considering the other. However, we have seen that this obscured important differences. If Labour's schemes for diversity of press ownership were aimed at merely providing greater political parity in the press, then they were rather blunt instruments. Introducing schemes to modify the advertising market would certainly have made a Labour movement press more possible, but it would not have guaranteed greater political equivalence. Increasing diversity of ownership could have led to a greater number of right-of-centre newspapers being created, for instance. Such schemes for diversity were unlikely to have a predictable political effect.

Such was the level of radical confidence at this time, however, that there was a drive to go beyond the existing party policies for diversity and provide a press that was more representative of public opinion, which would also answer concerns about the representation of Labour in the press. Two similar new schemes submitted to the media study group went beyond aiming for diversity, to use the state to attempt to eradicate bias, by establishing an Independent Press Authority (IPA). Chris Mullin's plan would use the IPA to orchestrate the representation of different viewpoints, while another proposed by Michael Meacher would make the authority impose balance. In doing so, critics could argue that both schemes illustrated some of the deep difficulties of improving Labour's representation and the profound problems of using the state to go beyond encouraging diversity.

The two schemes represented a huge incursion into press business control. Both were firmly within the public service tradition – Mullin and Meacher regarded broadcast regulation as the model for the press.[20] Both proposals envisaged there being a franchise system similar to that operated by the Independent Broadcasting Authority (IBA). Newspaper groups would then bid for membership of the system.

Mullin's system, proposed in 1981, challenged existing press ownership more directly. He wanted to provide balance by organizing the press into a range of different franchised groups, each representing a different viewpoint. He also emphasized newsroom democracy. Franchises would be tendered for, with the preference being for companies without commercial interests or for ownership groupings in which staff were represented or would be full owners. The franchises would be for profitable groups combining both lucrative and loss-making titles. This "piggy-backing" was aimed at counteracting the effects of advertising revenue on newspapers.[21] Mullin's proposal would impose rather stringent norms for newspapers under this franchise system. He insisted that a certain proportion of newspapers should be devoted to current affairs, which could well have affected the tabloids, which were occasionally the target of patronizing scorn in Labour discussions.[22]

Reflecting the wider political shifts that were under way by 1982, a less radical scheme was proposed by Meacher that year. He borrowed from the IBA the idea that the IPA should maintain balance within each press outlet by awarding franchises to individual newspapers, rather than adopting Mullin's idea of balancing through diversity. Whether it would renew these franchises depended on whether the newspapers had provided a balance of views in their news and opinion, over a period. This IPA, based on a revamped Press Council, would also have increased powers to oversee day-to-day claims of bias.[23] Thus, it would be involved with the right of reply (see below p. 67).

Both schemes were ingenious. However both had potential difficulties. First, it is difficult to see on what basis the IPA's balance of political views in the press could be imposed. Any system that involved anything other than a replication of national voting patterns would be less democratic. However, as a consequence the press would be tied to operating on party political lines, as the Marxist group Militant had argued for.[24] Also, it was perfectly possible to improve the press coverage of Labour without restructuring the newspaper market, as the situation in 1997 revealed, when Labour returned to office with the support of a substantial part of the national press. The "problem" had been solved – with Labour arguably even being over-represented – suggesting, as we saw in Chapter 1, that the "problem" is broader than simply one of providing accurate party political representation.

Second, both proposals represented a huge intrusion by the state into the freedom of the press. Mullin suggested to the media study group that the IPA had the advantage that the idea of the IBA was already firmly established. The IPA "merely" extended this idea. However, Mullin's proposals extended the IPA's tentacles into an area where it was already firmly established that newspapers could be created on any political basis – albeit with funding and the operation of advertising being decisive obstacles to this freedom. His franchise system would determine the political colour and the balance between news, current affairs and other topics in individual news-papers.[25] Titles would be forced either to reverse their perceived right-wing bias by adopting an editorial line imposed by this state-backed organiza-tion or lose their franchise. In Meacher's scheme a sizeable amount of editorial control would be ceded from the titles to the new authority – as the newspapers would have to maintain balance, overseen by the state-linked IPA. Those who are concerned by the Labour government's more recent management of the media may consider it ironic that one of the targets of this manipulation, Labour's own left-wing, had previously called for further political control of the press by a state-funded source.

Another potential objection to Meacher's plans concerns the idea that newspaper regulation would be modelled on the conception of balance applied in broadcasting (which, ironically, was controversial in Labour circles, following the Glasgow Media Group's work, as mentioned earlier). Critics could well argue that the print press should be treated differently. We saw in Chapter 1 that the British press was not constrained by ideas of balance; balance was not felt to be essential for a functioning public sphere, where political democracy could flourish.[26] The press thus had the freedom to lead discussion and play a role in agenda-setting. It is an open question whether readers find this to be part of the national newspapers' appeal. Members of the British public might well be surprised if they woke up tomorrow to find no mainstream British media sources existed, apart from those on the Internet, that could articulate a consistent opinion and show a clear viewpoint. While newspapers might well be open to a number of perspectives, critics could well argue that it is important that a space be kept for this role.

As it was, the majority of the media study group rejected both schemes. The group did not think Mullin's ideas were feasible or that the statist implications of Meacher's plans would wash with the public.[27] Instead, the group supported another scheme – the Open Press Authority – which provided some new tools to encourage diversity of newspaper ownership. But the particular concern for improved Labour coverage also articulated itself in other ways. By 1979 the question of providing a Labour movement press was being posed directly.

A Division of Labour: The Labour Movement Paper and the News International Takeover

The division described in previous chapters between those in the Labour movement wanting a broader press and those wishing for a Labour movement title emerged again after 1979. The Labour Party itself was little involved in plans to provide a Labour movement press and those interested in the matter pursued it within the unions.

Creating such a paper had initially been an important priority for Labour's decision-making bodies after the party departed from office in 1979. The Press and Publicity Committee and the NEC agreed in principle to facilitate discussions about creating a Labour title. Party officials also discussed it with the TUC press committee. Yet Labour started to shy away from the task. First, a 1979 Labour Party conference motion calling for a popular national daily was remitted to the NEC for further discussion.[28] Despite the absence of a positive vote, the media study group's original plans for press diversity focused solely on creating Labour titles, although its consultative paper was withdrawn.[29]

There were no hard and fast rules, but a division of labour seems to have prevailed. The study group discussed measures to aid diversity of press ownership, with the new left emphasis on enhancing democracy, while the TUC assessed the feasibility and prepared for the launch of a Labour movement paper. As it was, despite the efforts of supporters, most notably the Transport and General Workers' Union general secretary, Moss Evans, these plans foundered. The unions were not prepared to provide the cash needed.[30]

This division between the party and the union leadership also came into play with the takeover of *The Times* and *The Sunday Times* by News International, headed by Rupert Murdoch. The unions themselves divided over a plan jointly devised by Labour's former leader Jim Callaghan and Bill Keys, of the print union SOGAT, which featured an element of newsroom democracy. The plan aimed to turn the newspapers over to a trust, with union involvement, in opposition to the Murdoch-led takeover. As *The Sunday Times'* then editor, Harold Evans, tells it from the inside, while some of the print unions agreed to buy shares in the new trust, others refused. Evans remembers that NGA general secretary Joe Wade, "to Callaghan's displeasure, was discouraging: 'How can I put my members' money into something that is going to yield a lower return than the Trustee Savings Bank?'"[31]

In contrast, at this stage it was the Labour Party, including its leadership, which was pressing for diversity of ownership, in stark distinction to New Labour's attitude to Murdoch. Michael Foot persevered in demanding that News International's bid be referred to the Monopolies and Mergers Commission to arrest "one of the greatest concentrations of newspaper power in the history of journalism in the United Kingdom", as the then Shadow Secretary of Trade, John Smith, put it.[32] The demand was backed by the unions' more radical elements in the Campaign for Press Freedom (CPF; see below, p. 68).[33]

However, in the ensuing Commons debate Labour MPs were split on

The Times takeover, again reflecting the tension between those who wanted more press diversity and those – some of them closer to the unions – who focused solely on promoting a Labour movement press.[34] The left-wing party treasurer, Norman Atkinson, backed the unions' case for non-referral. He explicitly contrasted the case for a Labour press to challenge "the anti-Socialist monopoly" with a demand for "commercial diversity", which "means nothing at all to us". He was backed by other union-sponsored MPs.[35]

What both these MPs and the unions' leadership wanted was to advance the Labour movement. Attempts at securing press diversity were a secondary concern. It was this view – the idea that what was central was advancing Labour rather than press diversity – that would eventually win out in the party. Nevertheless, in this period, the party still committed itself to diversifying ownership of newspapers.

Diversity, the Multinationals and Internationalization: The Open Press Authority

In its pursuit of diversity of ownership, rather than accepting the statist proposals associated with the IPA, the study group agreed in 1983 with the academic James Curran on a more direct method – to strip press companies of some of their titles in order to provide for the introduction of new owners. An Open Press Authority (OPA) would oversee this operation, known as divestment.[36]

The most detailed history of the evolution of Labour Party press policy in this period, written under the name of the study group's chair Frank Allaun, conflates the OPA and IPA.[37] However, the difference between the two bodies is clear. Curran's scheme promised less state control and was again a policy transfer from the Scandinavian social market tradition. As well as defying the trend to oligopoly, Curran wanted to reduce the multinationals' hold over the British press. Demands for diversity had been given added impetus by the AES thinkers' radical analysis of the role played by multinational companies outlined in Chapter 2.

The media study group and the 1982 party conference took up Harold Wilson's point that corporate press ownership of wider business interests could threaten editorial inquiry into those broader areas (see Chapter 3).[38] And Curran used this concern, which had been first expressed in Labour documents as far back as 1922, but which, according to him, had become a reality in the period since the 1950s, to justify his new scheme for press plurality, adopted by the study group.[39]

Curran's call for divestment centred on a gap in Labour's proposals hitherto. This was in the area of competition legislation, which had been a component of some classical liberal responses to the problems of press diversity. However, Curran went beyond the classical liberal legislative response. He again based his argument on the fact that British concentration of press ownership was now among the highest in western Europe (as we saw in Chapter 1).[40] Divestment on its own would be likely to lead only to other multinationals buying the offloaded, mostly unprofitable, titles. Instead, in order to support these titles' independence, Curran also envisaged that the OPA would provide cash loans when newspapers from existing groups were sold. Thus the OPA differed from Curran's earlier proposals for financial support via an Advertising Revenue Board, from which he explicitly pulled back. In a shifting political climate less confident about large-scale intervention in the market, the Advertising Revenue Board did not have sufficient political backing.[41]

The media study group agreed to support Curran's OPA plan, with a number of key provisos. (The measures for democratic ownership are discussed below.) It also agreed to reduce the number of readers a national newspaper group could have before it was forced to sell off titles from Curran's figure of nine million – which was set to target News International and the *Daily Mirror*'s owners, Reed – and agreed to a "much lower" figure to be determined.[42] In addition, it agreed that the OPA should compensate selected titles that suffered from bifurcation, rather than concern itself with advertising revenue redistribution.[43] Yet, despite this commitment to compensation, members of the study group also felt that OPA money should be used to fund new titles rather than propping up existing failing ones.[44] Thus, overall, on this key point the study group looked two ways. As for the divisive issue of how the OPA would be funded, the group subsequently agreed that it would be paid for by the state, using an advertising tax. It also agreed that its manifesto proposals would be based on this amended OPA, an idea that, importantly, the NEC supported.[45]

Labour Policy: Labour's Programme 1982 and the 1983 Manifesto

After the Labour right regained control of the party, policy generally shifted away from confronting corporations so directly, and the press strategy followed suit. Instead, it became mired in some confusion. In formulating the media section of *Labour's Programme 1982*, the media study group retreated from three interventionist methods for achieving diversity agreed by the party and not previously renounced. It dropped the statist National Printing Corporation. It withdrew support from a revenue board and instead called for a restriction on the amount of advertising that individual publications could attract. And it also abandoned a commitment to diversifying government advertising, referred to, but little debated, after 1979.[46]

Yet, within weeks of being rejected by the study group, plans for an IPA, similar to Meacher's scheme, also became Labour Party policy at the 1982 conference.[47] The call was part of a composite motion, which constituencies proposed and seconded. The NEC supported it, with the study group chair, Frank Allaun, acting as its representative. Yet discussion of the motion, which also supported the rejected National Printing Corporation, did not explicitly refer to the IPA. So the NEC had promoted the IPA after the study group had explicitly rejected it, and the group and the NEC had backed the OPA. The rules that had been agreed on creating policy, outlined at the start of this chapter, had been flouted. This was particularly significant because the conference decisions formed *Labour's Programme 1982*, on which the 1983 election manifesto was set to be based.

Meanwhile, the media study group did not finalize its own policy until February 1983, after the series of false turns discussed earlier. This was very late in the day for inclusion in the manifesto. The proposals had not followed the intricate procedure sketched above. Policy was being formulated long after the party had produced its *Programme*.

In this confused situation neither the OPA nor IPA made it into the manifesto, leaving a major gap in the manifesto proposals and constituting another reversal from the ideas developed in the group and agreed by the conference. Nevertheless, by 1983 the party was still committed to enhancing press diversity. The same was not true for newsroom democracy.

Broader Control

Despite the resistance to implementing the findings of the Bullock Inquiry, there was an upsurge of interest in newsroom democracy in the press within the party after 1979, partly reflecting increased industrial militancy. Yet, despite internal and some external pressure from media activists, as the left's strength dissipated, so did these demands.

It was in the militant atmosphere of 1979 that the Institute for Workers' Control (IWC) held a conference on the media and democracy.[48] Some Labour Party figures addressing the conference continued to reduce the idea of democratic control to that of control by employees. James Curran and Stuart Holland envisaged a Press Co-operative Development Agency to provide launch capital for new publications under employee control, a more syndicalist position that was adopted by the party.[49] The 1979 Labour conference supported producer press co-operatives "to give all employees a voice in major policy decisions, while at the same time guaranteeing autonomy and freedom from interference in [the] day-to-day work of editorial and production workers".[50]

Perhaps ironically, it was left to the union movement at this time to consider the wider community. The TUC's 1980 pamphlet *Behind the*

Headlines considered not only newsroom democracy but also consumer representation.[51] Other Labour Party figures shared this broader concern. Two *Labour Weekly* journalists, Harold Frayman and Donald Ross, the latter of whom had represented the party at the royal commission, reiterated the Labour representatives' call for press funding to be dependent on the newspapers being trusts. But they told the IWC conference that they also felt that trusts should have wider representation of both the producers and the readers, as consumers.[52] Frayman also put this view to the media study group.

In another example of policy transfer Frayman was prepared to learn not from Sweden but from Yugoslavia, which in the 1950s and 1960s had provided hope of an alternative in the Eastern bloc.[53] The new left was particularly inspired by the Yugoslavian workers' democratic control experiments.[54] What attracted Frayman to apply the Yugoslavian model to a British system was that it gave all press workers the sort of real, but distant, involvement in newsroom decisions that the 1979 party conference had called for.[55] They would not influence day-to-day activity but could eventually be involved in sacking a consistently recalcitrant editor.

Frayman also called for broader democratic representation, going beyond newsroom democracy and towards community control. Otherwise – as we saw in Chapter 3 – newsroom democracy would not necessarily give consideration to those whom he saw as being treated badly by the press, including those he regarded as under-represented, such as the Liberal Party and ethnic minorities. Representation on newspaper editorial boards would need to be extended to the wider community, not just newspaper readers. Nevertheless, here Frayman's prescriptions were vague. His focus on the role of the community does not seem to have been picked up by other members of the media study group, other than in the limited sense of the right of reply.

Frayman provided a very radical analysis. However, it had a significant problem, which immobilized the discussion on democratic reform. Despite the detail in his analysis, Frayman argued that the party should encourage newsroom democracy but not lay down any extensive prescriptions.[56]

Curran's OPA proposals were certainly more practical. Curran advocated increased corporatist representation, without state control. He suggested that the OPA should have a governing board consisting of the major parties, press management and unions. And he envisaged reorganizing disinvested newspapers either as journalist or printworker co-operatives.[57]

However, a sign that demands for newsroom democracy were dissipating within the party, as the right regained control, was that these demands were not among the OPA measures that the media study group recommended for the manifesto. Instead, all the study group could agree by January 1983 was that the launch fund should require reconstituted publications to operate as public trusts or co-operatives "where appropriate".[58] And even this was left out of the proposals when the group finally drafted what it wanted to go into the document that would shape the manifesto in February of that year.[59]

Two study group media stalwarts, Philip Whitehead and Austin Mitchell, encouraged this turning tide in the group. Whitehead had been involved in the Free Communications Group and had acted as a bridgehead between it and the Labour Party a decade earlier.[60] Now he was reluctant to challenge existing media ownership, because he was concerned about the pressure the press businesses could bring to bear. Although more interested in the broadcast media, along with Mitchell, he explicitly counselled that radical proposals would face the wrath of media owners.[61]

Thus, although a majority of media study group members supported increasing democratic participation by journalists in the press, the most developed position on this question came from someone opposed to Labour imposing such a scheme. A minority on the study group also rejected any such moves. The result was stalemate. As with discussions on plans to encourage diversity, the elaborate nature of the decision-making process encouraged a situation where few concrete decisions were taken – an ironic problem, given that what was being discussed was the extension of democratic involvement. All the group's proposals on newsroom democracy were still being discussed by the time of the 1983 election and were agreed neither by the study group nor by the party's NEC, and did not make it into the manifesto.[62] Instead the focus of democratic input in the press was shifted to the right of reply.

The Right of Reply and the Campaign for Press and Broadcasting Freedom

The legal right of reply has not always been so clearly associated with newsroom democracy. However, the *industrial* right of reply that prevailed in the early 1980s was an attempt, particularly by the print unions, to use their collective strength to widen influence over the content of the press that they produced. Frayman estimates that their workplace control was greater than among any other group of British employees, to the extent that they effectively controlled both who was hired and what they were paid.[63] At the *Daily Mirror* Curran describes the power printers had in deciding who entered the rooms they worked in as being like "border controls".[64]

Yet the print unions had not effectively considered how to translate this power into practical measures for enhanced press democracy, increasing journalists' hostility. Instead the control was regularly abused, so there were tales of fictitious employees being paid, printers playing cards on shifts and so on. The control had been corrupted because it had not been "purified or debated", as Curran put it.[65] The printers' power only erratically translated itself into demands in the Labour Party for democratic involvement in the press. The print unions' hierarchy exhibited a maximalist approach in party debates; demanding all or nothing – "anything between fell short of Jerusalem", according to Curran. The print union representatives on the study group were concerned about workers becoming involved in making decisions when they did not have full workplace control. In consequence the union leadership passed resolutions on democratic control on paper but did little in practice to achieve these aims – aside from their role in developing the industrial right of reply.[66]

The printers operated the industrial right of reply in order to be able to respond to an article regarded as inaccurate or biased. Overwhelmingly, those seen as ill-treated were fellow trade unionists. On occasion this involved refusing to publish such an article, if threats of action failed. The industrial right of reply had a history stretching back to 1926, when one of the catalysts for the General Strike was the refusal of *Daily Mail* machine assistants to print an attack on trade unionists.

During the late 1970s and early 1980s there was a spate of instances when the printers used their power to secure a reply to newspaper coverage seen as slanted.[67] And by 1980 the TUC supported the view that the unions, rather than the government or courts, would be the arbiter of the right of reply.[68] Thus, when Labour came to discuss seeking press redress, the media study group reprinted a pamphlet on the subject, which supported the industrial right of reply in terms of newsroom democracy and community access.[69]

The pamphlet had been written by the Campaign for Press and Broadcasting Freedom (CPBF), which heavily influenced Labour's press policy during the Foot era. Originally called the Campaign for Press Freedom (CPF), the organization was set up in 1980 by print trade unionists (alongside the industrial right of reply campaign). Curran remembers that rather than involving the unions' leadership, CPF participants were from a layer "below" – different from those who represented the unions in Labour meetings.[70]

The CPF/CBPF and the Labour Party were initially linked from top to bottom. Michael Foot became a financial sponsor of the campaign in 1982.[71] Many MPs were initial sponsors, including Roy Hattersley and Michael Meacher, who as ministers had witnessed at first hand the scuppering of the Minority Report proposals. And Meacher joined the original thirteen-person CPF steering committee alongside Curran and the *Labour Weekly* journalist, Frayman.[72] More than 100 constituency Labour parties affiliated to the campaign in its first year.[73] The struggle to get a legal right of reply onto the statute book was the most prominent campaign on press control that the Labour Party was involved in under Foot's leadership.

The Legal Right of Reply

The Labour Party had previously backed policy on a right of reply in 1975 and again in 1979. At that time it regarded the press industry's self-regulating Press Council, rather than the unions, as the appropriate body to uphold the policy.[74] After 1979, however, many in the Labour Party lost faith in self-regulation.[75]

Yet a majority of the party's media study group were also uneasy about the power that the industrial right of reply gave to the unions. One of their concerns was over coverage of the Labour Party in the press. Study group members feared that newspaper businesses would not take kindly to Labour-supporting unions using industrial muscle to have input over what was printed.[76] Indeed Allaun and Meacher later told the House of Commons that letting the courts decide was a way of avoiding an industrial right of reply being exercised.[77] However, the legal method was also "universally savaged" by the press "that could spare the space to mention it", as journalist and author Tom Baistow put it, with Frank Allaun in particular being targeted.[78]

At first it was agreed that the industrial right of reply would be used as a half-way house on the road to providing a state-led legal route.[79] Then the TUC turned to a legal solution and the CPBF followed suit, uneasily at first.[80] Baistow, who was hostile to printworkers having a major input into press editorial decisions, championed the state solution.[81] The idea of a legal right of reply would cover those cases where people could not invoke libel laws either because the distortions did not involve libel or because the plaintiffs could not afford to take this route.[82] It gave individuals, companies or organizations the right to require a newspaper to print a reply to a factually inaccurate report of equal length to the original and in the same position in the paper. The study group agreed that it should consider the experience of other countries.[83] Most other countries that have adopted a right of reply have taken the statutory route.[84]

Labour debated how sizeable a role state judges would have in this process. The media study group agreed in 1981 that legal tribunals would enforce the new law.[85] Yet in October 1981 the Home Policy Committee expressed its concern about courts being used to enforce these sanctions and pressed for a specially created independent tribunal to decide.[86] The NEC finally agreed a fudge. Adjudication would either be by a court or an independent tribunal, with appeal to a High Court. A minor injection of employee democracy was also included. Both bodies could make decisions in consultation with working journalists, with a tribunal having a journalist on its committee.[87] In either case the body would be state-sanctioned, closely linked to the judicial system.

The 1982 party conference agreed to push for legislation to provide individuals and organizations with the right to reply when any of the media had been inaccurate or had grossly distorted information. This was backed up with the threat of a £40,000 fine. The right of reply was included in the 1983 manifesto.[88]

The Labour opposition front bench supported two bills in 1981 and 1982 attempting to introduce the right of reply into law.[89] But there were still concerns among Labour ranks about the role of the courts. MP Philip Whitehead, for example, preferred an ombudsman to adjudicate. As it was, the Conservative government opposed the two bills. On the second occasion the passage of the bill was blocked because many Labour MPs did not bother to turn up for the vote, indicating their apathy on the issue.[90]

Questioning the Right of Reply

Des Freedman, discussing Labour's broadcasting policy, argues that supporting a right of reply was less radical for Labour than the call to tackle bias through restructuring the media itself.[91] Despite that, it is the case that Labour's policy-making bodies were often at pains to point out that the right of reply was not a substitute for the other press ownership measures considered here.[92] Nevertheless, it is clear that the right of reply proposals were not as radical and did effectively substitute for those presented in the earlier landmark document *The People and the Media* with regard to one area – newsroom democracy. The industrial right of reply had been a foray into that particular territory. Using a state tribunal to assess complaints represented a shift to a less radical, social democratic assumption of a more benevolent impartial state than the industrial option.

But can a right of reply be seen as a democratizing measure? The answer, in part, depends on the forum deciding on it. From a democratic point of view both industrial and legal approaches are an advance on the notion that the adjudicator should be either the proprietor, the editor, a "readers' editor" appointed by the newspaper or an industry self-regulated organization. However, the industrial approach leaves a union as judge and jury. The legal approach just leaves a judge – or another court procedure with no democratic element. How a tribunal was appointed or elected would largely determine how democratic it was. The justifications used by Labour advocates of a legal solution were instructive in this regard. Frank Allaun's book considers that a union-based solution was too arbitrary.[93] This may have been true, but it indicates a more general "problem" of democracy – that of relying on people's will. In this case, it meant relying on the democratic will of the narrow, albeit significant, section of the population that actually produced the newspapers in question. To advocate using the courts was to rely on the state in one of its less democratically accountable forms. Nevertheless, it is true that an industrial right of reply again substituted the employee for the community.

A further difficulty has also been with the definition of what should constitute grounds for a right of reply. Both Labour's official position on a right of reply and the industrial variant went beyond simply targeting inaccurate reporting. Labour concluded that there would be the opportunity for legal redress when the media, including the press, had grossly distorted information – it would "mitigate the worst effects of editorial bias", to quote from *Labour's Programme 1982*.[94] Yet unless distortion was very precisely defined, it could be argued that there was a danger that any partisan journalism would be subject to a right of reply, cutting across promoting political diversity in the press and seeming to be a major intrusion by the state into newspapers' operation. Alternatively, it could be that a significant proportion of what some would see as biased journalism would not be regarded as such by the courts. In such a situation, either the right of reply would be heavily intrusive or it would be ineffective in countering bias.

A final question mark hanging over the legal right of reply is that it could be used to stifle investigative reporting. The left-wing journalist Paul Foot argued that it would impede his investigations of the powerful, who would use such laws to erase the criticisms made of them. One could indeed imagine that applying the right of reply to a publication such as *Private Eye*, for which Foot wrote, would leave it open to being filled with almost as many replies as original articles. One former prominent CPBF member and printer, Mike Power, however, countered this by arguing that Foot was complaining about "attempts to create balance in a class-driven society where none can possibly exist. That hopeless position can be applied to any effort to change or introduce new laws."[95] If taken as a defence of reformism, then the point is pertinent. However, an issue that arises in relation to the right of reply, which the debate on investigative journalism points to, is not that a legal right of reply fails in an attempt to provide balance in society, but that it is not equipped to do so. Instead, it narrowly focuses on redressing the balance in one sector – the press and media – without necessarily considering the effect of this redress on society as a whole.

What is meant by this? One argument that has been made for a legal right of reply is that it is a way for ordinary people to achieve redress in the press in a society where the rich and powerful "have PR minders to ensure their right of reply".[96] However, there is little to say that these same PR people would not further exploit this legal right to their own advantage. Press businesses could become even more reluctant to sanction expensive investigative reporting if faced with the threat that a segment of the title would be given over to replies by aggrieved businesses. One Conservative sponsor indeed saw that the opportunity for this was a positive aspect of the first right of reply bill.[97]

Thus, it can be seen that if the intention of the right of reply is to redress power imbalances, then its effect needs to be considered in relation to society as a whole. The press owners and their interconnected interests are not the only power in society. The question is not whether a right of reply provides a balance in society, but whether it serves to provide a further imbalance and weakens journalistic autonomy in the face of business pressure and flak. The debate is whether, while enhancing community control of the press, a right of reply also strengthens corporate control of it.

What Happened to the Party's Press Policy Commitments?

The policy shift in the Labour Party following the right's counter-offensive did not concentrate on press policies, which were still regarded as less important than other areas. Yet there was still a discernible change in approach from that which had been agreed by the media study group.

One pressure weighing on the right was that the existing newspapers had been allies in its revival.[98] As Dominic Wring, in his perceptive studies of Labour's political marketing, explains, in the 1970s and early 1980s Labour's campaigning innovation had stagnated, after a long period of engagement in this area, starting at the time of the introduction of universal suffrage. The period since the 1970s saw a reaction against these political communications methods, prompted by the 1970 election defeat.[99] Labour campaigners had preferred to focus on structurally altering the press. However, this was about to change. The right was now using the press to its advantage again and was reluctant to challenge it.

Roy Hattersley, who helped set up the right-wing pressure group Solidarity, was more concerned about the press than most, as we have seen. He used a regular *Punch* magazine column to voice his concerns about proprietors' influence over editorial content.[100] Yet he was loath to challenge press concentration structurally, other than in the important form of tightening anti-monopoly controls.[101] Beyond this, Hattersley claimed that party supporters had learned to resign themselves to regarding "the antics of the *Daily Mail* and *The Sun* as one of the hazards of their existence, for which they must make plans in the way that they prepare for snow and the late arrival of railway trains".[102]

Yet Hattersley's quiet resignation did not seem to reflect the mood at the 1982 party conference, where it was reported that almost every debate over the week had attacked press bias, and where delegates called for a scheme similar to Meacher's IPA.[103]

Nevertheless, with the right wing back in control of the decision-making forum of the NEC, as well as controlling the Shadow Cabinet, Labour's 1983 election manifesto toned down the agreed positions of the party. Moreover, Michael Foot, as leader, despite his previous commitment to press ownership reform, did not veto the moves.

The "longest suicide note in history", as the 1983 manifesto was famously dubbed, was rather short on press policy. The four pages in *Labour's Programme 1982* had been reduced to a few sentences with "radical-sounding" but imprecise prescriptions.[104] Most importantly, there was no mechanism for financially supporting discarded titles when the anti-monopoly law forced press companies to divest.[105] James Curran considers that the effect of breaking up press concentration, on its own, "would probably have been to close papers".[106]

Moreover, it was not clear which bodies would implement any of the manifesto proposals, since demands for an integrated communications ministry had also been discarded – despite the study group's pleas.

One reason why the left's positions could be so quickly reversed had been addressed by a Labour new left figure, Francis Cripps. He provided an analysis of the AES and the press that went unheeded. Cripps had foreseen that the AES needed to "establish its own resonance in the media". Only then would it be seen as realistic.[107] This would be more difficult to achieve for newspaper ownership policy, given whose power it challenged. Press ownership policy, incomplete as it may have been, was also almost completely internalized to the party, leaving few outside aware of its existence. Indeed, one then leading trade union press officer and CPBF activist had little knowledge of the media study group's policy.[108] If this was true of someone in the "inner circle", then it is almost certain to have also been the case for most ordinary Labour supporters. An October 1981 party political broadcast outlining press and media bias provided an isolated exception to this internalization.[109]

Tony Benn's approach was a prime example of this internalized perspective, albeit in the face of a severe press and media assault. He had opportunities to pen relatively unmediated columns in *The Guardian* and *The Times*, which he spurned at this time in favour of internal campaigning.[110] When he needed to mobilize support at key moments before the 1981 deputy leadership contest, he refused to be interviewed by the British mainstream media.[111] His attitude was perhaps understandable but probably harmful to his cause.

How should this period and Labour's 1983 manifesto be considered overall? We have seen that there were retreats before 1983 from the radical positions outlined at the 1979 conference and espoused by the media study group. The attempt to employ a public service framework to provide balance failed. Yet the strategy promoted by the study group, which might have answered some of the previous problems with press ownership policy, did not make it into the 1983 election programme.

Nevertheless, the manifesto was a sea-change from that of four years previously. It was hailed by press campaigners in the CPBF as incorporating "some of the campaign's radical proposals" and was the most far-reaching manifesto commitment to providing press diversity – thus aiding democracy – that had been made by the Labour Party.[112] If Labour had been elected and the commitments had been translated into government policy, press ownership would have been transformed. The 1983 manifesto committed the party to anti-monopoly legislation that went well beyond liberal pluralist notions. It dedicated the party to "breaking up 'major concentrations of press ownership'" by setting an unspecified ceiling on the number of titles that could be owned by one individual or press group. It also committed the government to prohibiting any cross-media ownership. Just as importantly, employing a Scandinavian-style social market orientation, it promised that a launch fund would be set up to assist new publications. It also committed a Labour government to introducing a statutory right of reply.[113]

Des Freedman compellingly argues that the media study group of the early 1980s was more timid in its public statements on Labour's broadcasting policy than the communications group discussed in Chapter 2. He suggests that, whereas the study group of the 1970s coincided with a rise in militancy, this group corresponded with a decline.[114] In seeking to emphasize the relationship with the downturn in union struggle, Freedman's analysis may well explain the study group's internal discussions and external presentation. Yet, notwithstanding the vagueness of some commitments and the circumstances of the Labour manifesto's gestation, its press policy was relatively radical. Instead, overall, it can be argued that the left's strength after 1979 was a by-product of the militancy of the 1970s. As one survey of Bennism probably overstates, when militancy faltered, so a section of trade unionists turned their attention to the Labour Party left.[115] Nevertheless, the eclipse of that militancy may well have been a key factor in explaining why the left's challenge was not sustained. The insularity of the Labour left may well have also played a part.

Another consideration, countering the overall picture of a decline in trade union campaigning, was the surge of militancy among printers, of which the launch of the CPF was a political expression. Yet this was not directly reflected in Labour policy. A key reason why the upsurge did not have a long-term effect was the vulnerability of the industrial right of reply, its major policy goal.

While the legal right of reply continued to be advocated by Labour MPs after 1983, the party moved away from some of the policies aimed at fostering press ownership diversity. Chapter 5 will explore this realignment and how it related to sweeping changes in Labour's political marketing in the press and the shifting political climate. However, it will also emphasize something which is occasionally forgotten: the fact that, given the often uneven nature of political change, there was first a shift to the left in local government, which was reflected in new press policies developed by the municipal socialists.

5
Changes and Political Communications
Labour in the 1980s

Within a year of becoming Labour leader Neil Kinnock rejoined the Campaign for Press and Broadcasting Freedom (CPBF). He robustly endorsed the organization and its aims, writing: "I strongly believe that Britain's press needs to be more open, more diverse and more account-able. We need a greater variety of press with a wider range of opinion and information."[1]

Nevertheless, the issue did not feature prominently on Labour's polit-ical agenda at this time. Denis MacShane commented in 1985 that there had been "no firm commitment from Kinnock or Hattersley, or the rest of the Shadow Cabinet to effective media reform".[2] While this may not have been entirely true for all the time Kinnock was leader, no attempt was made to promote the agreed reforms.[3]

The solutions offered became more market-oriented and, for a signifi-cant time, more nationalistic. Labour's retreat from its explicitly interventionist strategy to achieve press diversity fitted in with its broader economic policy. However, other factors were also involved. Labour's leading lights became gradually less interested in structurally changing the press market to aid party representation. At the same time they started to transform their press campaigning strategy.

Party Policy from 1983 to 1992

Organizational Changes

Neil Kinnock faced a myriad of problems on being elected leader in 1983. Labour had just suffered a humiliating defeat. The party's election campaign was disorganized. Kinnock, on being chosen with support from across the party, exploited the desire for order.

The last chapter described the upsurge of demands by activists for democratic accountability. Kinnock accepted the argument that one of the reasons for Labour's defeat was the influence of the "unrepresentative" activists on the creation of party policy, despite the fact that, as we saw, the trade union right had organizational control by 1983. He resolved to shift power away from the activists and the NEC and towards the centre.[4] As we shall see, Labour's press and media communications were central to this change.

The leadership abandoned the NEC study group system, which had conceived much of Labour's press policy. The loose arrangement with the often leftish academic advisers ended. In a prelude to the new press and media strategy the party's research secretary, Geoff Bish, argued that the party should concentrate on campaigns rather than policy. The party's problem was "not the detail of policy . . . but credibility and image".[5] The study groups were replaced with smaller and more tightly controlled joint Shadow Cabinet/NEC committees. No new policy could be developed without the Shadow Cabinet's say-so.[6] As the insightful commentator Eric Shaw demonstrates, by 1986 the leader and senior Shadow Cabinet members determined policy.[7]

Kinnock helped pay for this centralization by using the "Short money", which provided state aid to opposition parties. Unlike the Conservatives when they had been in opposition, the Labour front bench placed the money under its own control, so that the Shadow Cabinet would not be dependent on research instituted by the party.[8] The large sums involved, together with extra union funding, paid for more full-time policy advisers. Their loyalty was to the leader, rather than the party – a pattern that would continue. For the first time the leadership had developed a policy research and advice wing under its command, with the unions' support.[9]

The defeat of the 1984–5 miners' strike encouraged Kinnock and strengthened the Labour right. This was a key turning point. For the leadership the "lost year" of 1984–5, during which it had been "very difficult to open up the other ideological challenges", was over.[10] Along with the defeat of the print unions, which we will explore later, the strike's collapse undermined the left, as pressure from the unions faltered. The strike also split open a division between, on the one hand, the party's traditional left and new left, and, on the other, what became known as the "soft left".[11] The *Militant* supporters' expulsion provided a further schism. The soft left, centred on the Labour Co-ordinating Committee (LCC), decided to support Kinnock in an attempt to prise him away from the right.[12] It provided a link with other influences on the Labour Party (described below).

Some External Factors: The Soviet Union, Thatcherism and the Market

Along with Thatcherism, the inefficient Soviet economies' move towards disintegration provided an important external influence on Labour Party thinking throughout the Kinnock years. The relatively tiny, but influential, Eurocommunist wing of the British Communist Party, through its journal *Marxism Today*, helped introduce the debates prompted by the demise of the Soviet bloc into the Labour Party.

Despite possible alternatives, a critical but sympathetic reading of Frederick von Hayek's ideas influenced some left thinkers, when they both attempted to explain the Soviet economies' gross inefficiencies and applied this knowledge to Britain.[13] Economists wanted to introduce markets to regulate planning and increase consumer choice. It was believed that the best aspects of each of the two systems could be married. The inequity generated by market allocation would be tempered by planning. Efficiency would be increased without either market anarchy or planning rigidity.

Marxism Today championed this new thinking among the Labour leadership both directly and through the soft left.[14] Being closer to the Soviet bloc than much of the left, the journal's proponents were prompted by the visible collapse of the eastern states to become early left-wing market converts, albeit in a limited way. They popularized among the UK left the role of the market as the purveyor of consumer choice and had an understandable awe for Thatcherism's theoretical power and proselytizing zeal.[15] They considered that the market should replace democratic decision-making as an effective allocator and distributor. Historically, the Soviet bloc had influenced Labour Party thought towards state intervention without popular participation and control. As the sun started to set on the old regimes, arguments to marry state intervention with broader participation were rejected. Instead, the Labour leadership developed policies which linked the market with social ownership and revised party pledges to introduce employee democracy across industry, including for journalists.[16]

Labour went into the 1987 election far less committed to economic intervention than in 1983. It had rejected the AES and was more ambiguous about Keynesianism. By 1987 the Labour leadership justified interventionism primarily to bolster market vitality rather than as a tool for redistributive justice.[17]

Press Ownership Law

The Municipal Left

At the same time that Labour politics was shifting to the right nationally, a form of municipal socialism had developed locally. It grew on the back of the upsurge of demands for equality, as a democratic requirement, from the women's movement, the black community, lesbian and gay people and the disabled. From 1981 Labour councils across the country, particularly London's GLC, had pursued radical employment and economic develop-

ment policies.[18] These political positions would affect municipal socialists' press policy and were related to the "cultural industries" approach,
influenced by *Marxism Today* and the soft left. Two leading proponents,
Geoff Mulgan and Ken Worpole, who had worked at the Greater London
Enterprise Board's Cultural Industries Unit, helped the cultural industries
conception enter mainstream Labour Party thought.[19]

Two points can be made regarding these developments. First, the traditional social market position was to intervene to correct market failure. One
difference between this view and the cultural industries approach was over
what advocates of both considered to be the market's deficiencies. Cultural
industries advocates were interested not only in dealing with deficits in
press diversity; they were also concerned with the market's failure to
provide sufficient investment for the media industries to compete. In addition, followers of the cultural industries approach saw a greater role for the
market in articulating the public's views.[20] Thus, instead of answering the
problems of top-down public involvement in the press by encouraging
readers to participate in production decisions, they considered that this role
could be played by the market. Borrowing from liberal pluralist notions,
they argued that, through the market, the consumer could be king.[21]

Yet, secondly, the cultural industries approach had less influence in
shifting Labour's press ownership policy in a pro-market direction than it
did on broadcasting strategy.[22] This was because the press was entirely in
private hands and thus not influenced by the public service ethos in the
same way. So the cultural industries approach was as much an affirmation
of previous Labour Party policies on press diversity and in advocating journalist and printer co-operatives.[23]

The municipal left initially triggered a renewed interest within the
national Labour Party in restructuring the press. Labour activists and the
unions reacted to what they considered to be ruthless 1983 election
coverage by going on the offensive rather than by wooing the press as a
means of achieving more favourable representation. Reflecting the same
underlying tension between demands for diversity and Labour movement
representation that we saw earlier, they responded to press bias in two ways.
The first was to resurrect calls for a Labour newspaper, which eventually
came to nought (as mentioned in Chapter 4).[24] Second, the 1983 conference also backed policy that went far beyond that year's election manifesto
in calling for diversity in the press, by reinstating the controversial
Independent Press Authority as party policy. Delegates also wanted to
broaden involvement by journalists and others in press decision-making,
both within newspapers and among the new bodies that would control
them. Influenced by the GLC's work, the conference called for a new body,
the National Media Enterprise Agency, which would aid new newspaper
ventures. The new body's name reflected the more marketized approach
of the cultural industry perspective. Yet the conference also envisaged that

this body would be democratically owned and accountable to readers, journalists and printers. Moreover, it considered that journalist and printer co-operatives among the national newspapers would be supported, in a similar way to the GLC's proposals.[25]

However, Labour's interest in the press became much more focused on seeking positive representation in the pages of the national newspapers. The press provided brutally biased coverage of Kinnock and the Labour Party – especially its left.[26] (Kinnock also brought some problems on himself, perhaps. He laid himself open to accusations of windbaggery with his repetitive, sub-clause-ridden rhetoric, evident even in the drafts of his speeches.[27]) The miners' strike ended whatever press honeymoon Kinnock might have had.[28] By 1985 the Kinnock press office saw itself as "under siege".[29]

Press bias abounded in the lead-up to the 1987 election. The offensive on the "loony left" before the 1987 vote subjected municipal socialists and therefore the party to "an onslaught" of inaccuracies, innuendo and personal attacks.[30] Concern about the coverage Labour received would be a significant factor in the development of Labour's press ownership policy.

The News on Sunday: Representation, Diversity and Broader Democratic Involvement

Parts of the Labour Party and the unions responded to press bias with the launch of the *News on Sunday*, originally conceived by the municipal socialists as one way of countering the hostile coverage of the "loony left". Kinnock himself was enthusiastic.[31] In addition, it provided the most notable example of the strategy of the Greater London Enterprise Board (GLEB) to increase press diversity and expand democratic involvement by journalists and others who worked in the press. The newspaper was meant to rejuvenate municipal socialism. Instead, the title became "another nail in its coffin".[32]

The involvement of municipal socialists was extensive from the start. In 1983, in order to consider the options for funding, the GLEB asked James Curran and others to map out how the organization should intervene in the press sector.[33] The GLEB, along with a range of unions, also part-funded the market research, which would be crucial in deciding the title's direction.[34]

The *News on Sunday* venture was a big test for those wanting journalists and readers to have more influence over the content of the British press. The GLEB's funding came with the condition that those who produced the paper would be involved in running it though a Founders' Trust.[35] The most extensive account of the paper blames its downfall on producer democracy.[36] The legendary journalist John Pilger also states that a convoluted and muddled decision-making process drove him out.[37] So it might appear that democratic participation was the overriding problem with the paper. Or was it?

On inspection, it seems that the paper's management structure was labyrinthine and more unworkable than welcoming for key personnel to participate in. Two insiders, Peter Chippindale and Chris Horrie, describe the Founders' Trust as "[e]ssentially a self-appointed and unaccountable" grouping.[38] Another of those closely involved accepts that the workforce only elected a small minority of the trust.[39] In addition, the regional structure to provide readers' input into the paper was ineffectual and eventually collapsed.[40] Furthermore the decision to base the newspaper's operation away from London in Manchester can be seen as flawed and there was a shambolic recruiting procedure where many experienced applicants were simply not considered.[41]

Crucially, the professional journalists on the paper were not involved in decision-making.[42] Despite appearances, this newspaper's shambolic operation was not one by which to judge the effectiveness of participative democracy and accountability. It had replaced management authoritarianism with a mixture of politically dominated Utopianism, some syndicalism and a dose of admiration for the cult of the British amateur.

Rather than blaming the paper's structure, whatever its undoubted flaws, other writers have attributed its failure to the structure of the newspaper market.[43] The original GLEB report could have backed a more upmarket title, with higher advertising rates and lower circulation – a more left-wing, Sunday *Guardian*-style title, for example. Yet, perhaps surprisingly, considering the problems Curran had identified for any larger circulation title aimed at lower-income readers in an unreformed press market, his second report did advise going in that direction.[44]

The *News on Sunday* directed its attention to lower-income readers. Market research came up with the astonishing conclusion that a newspaper aimed downmarket of the *Mail on Sunday* would have sales of up to 1.5 million. And the editor, Keith Sutton, who had previously overseen the tabloid parody *Wapping Post*, made the paper much more tabloid than originally planned.[45] The initial issue sold only about a third of the more optimistic figures predicted and was judged to be of poor quality. Within days of Labour's election defeat the title went into voluntary receivership.[46]

Thus a key factor in the *News on Sunday*'s downfall was the newspaper market's bifurcation, determined by advertising revenue, combined with the inclination of some to go downmarket, bolstered by market research. Some commentators have latterly questioned whether a more upmarket title would have been viable.[47] Such a newspaper might have attracted readers with the financial clout required by advertisers. Certainly, such a title as the *News on Sunday* was conceived to be – that is, a tabloid aimed at a lower sociological class readership – was not viable, unless the circulation achieved the market research's questionable estimates. The newspaper's fortunes were a graphic illustration of the effects of bifurcation.

Other factors, especially the failure to find sufficient initial funding, contributed to the paper's rapid demise.[48] However, given the nature of the market in Britain, its pitch meant that it was very likely to fail. Government intervention had altered a comparable situation in other northern European countries, as we saw in Chapter 2. The *News on Sunday*'s downfall can be attributed to the refusal of previous Labour administrations to intervene in a similar fashion.

The *News on Sunday*'s failure added to the conviction that it was impossible to get Labour representation through either a Labour movement title or by increasing newspaper diversity. According to Peter Chippindale and Chris Horrie, more than half of the initial £6.5 million investment in the paper came from the employee pension funds of local authorities, a number of which were Labour left-controlled. The trade unions also contributed £1.6 million, and the Transport and General Workers' Union later added considerably to its original funding.[49] The paper's failure, with such relatively large sums invested, was likely to strengthen the resolve of those who had lost money never again to get involved in a similar venture. Only some on the left saw the paper's collapse as a failure of government policy.[50] For others it was merely further confirmation that the goal of a Labour movement press was fading. New methods were being developed to provide a Labour movement voice in the press. The new press and media strategy was already starting to provide an alternative.

Marketing Labour or Diversifying and Democratizing the Press?

Political Communications and the Press

Labour was now beginning to experience a clear division between what had seemed, until then, the synonymous aspirations of press diversity and party representation in newspapers. The party had for many years considered ways of trying to influence the press. Political marketing expert Dominic Wring notes that the 1950s and 1960s saw the party introduce what has been identified as a "persuasional" form of campaigning, as opposed to an educational strategy. Nascent spin doctors pursued sympathetic journalists.[51] Campaigns following Labour's 1970 election defeat had been marked by poor management and organization, and an unfocused communications strategy.[52] James Callaghan rejected being "packaged like cornflakes". Under Michael Foot the use of research pollsters was questioned.[53] However, this was to change under Kinnock. Labour's renewed interest in political communication reflected broader shifts in society, as Curran notes. As Thatcher undermined corporatism, this helped start erode the corporatist system of politics, founded on two class-based parties. With this growing instability, operating in the press and media would increasingly become a much more important factor in conducting politics.[54]

By 1983 some of those who had led demands to make structural changes to the press to promote Labour now wanted to persuade it anew. One of the Minority Report's co-authors led calls for a "new professionalism" in campaigning. David Basnett successfully proposed at the 1983 conference that a Campaign Strategy Committee be set up, as part of an organizational revamp following the election defeat.[55]

Wring identifies the involvement of the LCC in calling for a professionalization of communications.[56] It is interesting to note that in justifying this call the LCC group's organizing secretary explicitly prioritized representation over diversity. Paul Convery explicitly concluded that political communication was a more pressing concern than newspaper ownership reform. There was "little point in whingeing about press bias from the Opposition". Instead, what was required was what would become the familiar demand, that all Labour people should "speak with a united voice" and that sophisticated marketing and advertising techniques should be involved.[57] Not everything that the LCC called for was implemented. But the professionalization was an important development.

The TUC's failure to shift Conservative government press policy reform also influenced Labour in backing away from structural reform.[58] The relative success of the GLC's marketing campaign against abolition also broadened political support for professionalizing campaigning.[59]

The Labour leadership considered that trying to manipulate coverage in the established press and media would achieve its goal of a fairer press, and that changing the newspaper and media environment was not feasible. It considered that it had to deal with the newspapers before it returned to office. Indeed, the perception was that if did not successfully influence the press, then the party would never get back in.

The changing structure of journalism itself was also important. A significant and ironic shift came with News International's move to Wapping, which we will consider in a moment, and the assertion of employer power over journalists. Financial pressures have increasingly resulted in a cut in the number of journalists. Tunstall notes that national newspaper journalists' workload increased significantly from the 1960s to the 1990s.[60] The irony of this was that, as Labour's aspirations to challenge the increase in employer power started to diminish, so the new strategy of challenging bias through the media communications techniques became potentially more effective. As employers cut journalist numbers, there was a premium on getting stories with minimum effort and time. A well-managed Labour communications department could write copy for the press and have more chance of it being included in reports with fewer changes. When Labour strategists provided journalists with more accessible and effective copy, in order to counteract bias, they were pushing at a door that was already open.

A detailed account of Labour's campaigning evolution has been made elsewhere.[61] But a few points can be made. Kinnock identified part of the problem of the 1983 campaign as one of weak leadership. As such, the renewed development of a press and media focus was both important in itself and a significant part of organizational changes to strengthen leadership power and distance the party membership and the NEC from policy-making, referred to at the start of the chapter.

In 1983, under the guise of injecting professionalism but also strengthening leadership power, the Campaign Strategy Committee was instituted, followed in 1985 by the Campaigns and Communications Directorate, responsible to the leader's office and headed by Peter Mandelson.[62] Under Mandelson the secretive Shadow Communications Agency (SCA) was instituted. Mandelson oversaw presentation to the media, while former advertising executive Philip Gould busied himself with interpreting voter preferences.[63] Although the NEC, and ultimately the party, was supposed to direct the SCA, Labour's communications officers made their allegiance to the leader. They liaised largely with Kinnock's press secretary, Patricia Hewitt, and his chief of staff, Charles Clarke, along with Kinnock ally Robin Cook, who oversaw strategy from the Shadow Cabinet.[64]

The press was particularly important because of its role in agenda-setting. Sympathetic political journalists on broadsheets helped set the agenda for broadcasters. Peter Mandelson believed that the press did not have the same influence as broadcasters on political decision-making by the public. (This was a source of irritation for some print journalists, who felt they were treated as second-class citizens by Labour.[65]) However, the press was important because of "agenda-setting". Mandelson and the strategists believed that the agenda of the broadsheet newspapers in particular would, in turn, affect the political agenda of the influential broadcasters. Mirroring an influential notion in media research, they believed that influencing the agenda of the broadcasters would influence what electors saw as the salient issues, which in turn largely determined the outcome of elections. Therefore, setting the agenda meant influencing television programmes to cover the issues most positively associated with the party. Thus Mandelson, in particular, developed a series of contacts in the broadsheet press, among lobby and political correspondents, employing a particular combination of threats and flattery.[66]

With this revamped press focus the success of campaigns was measured by the manner in which the press and media treated them. An early notable example of this was the 1986 Freedom and Fairness campaign, which yielded press coverage not matched for years.[67] This was significant.

But Philip Gould and supportive commentators accorded these plaudits a particular importance. They regarded them as the judge of Labour's electability.[68] Yet the applause for such a campaign could well have come, in part, because it showed that Labour had acknowledged the press's importance and influence.[69]

The renewed press and media focus was among the factors that put a premium on leadership, conveniently dovetailing with Kinnock's determination to assert leadership autonomy. The conventions of the press do mean that newspapers tend to concentrate on the individual over the more abstract idea – to humanize the story. If Labour was to pursue the press, therefore, it would have to be promoted in a "personalized" way. This, however, could have been achieved by other methods than just promoting the leader.

Kinnock's attacks on the left, notably on *Militant*, illustrated these two tactics of seeking press and media approval and asserting strong leadership.[70] The attacks were applauded by the press and justified as gaining voter support.[71] The presidential nature of the 1987 election campaign was a product of the new press strategy. However, this strategy masked Kinnock's poor personal poll rating throughout his leadership, which Gould later admitted had acted as a drag on the party and had been deliberately withheld from party scrutiny.[72]

Maxwell, Kinnock and Journalistic Autonomy

An early indication of Labour's renewed concern with its representation in the press came with Robert Maxwell's takeover of the Mirror Group newspapers.[73] The influence of Maxwell on Labour Party policy has been a matter of controversy. Some of the biographers closest to him have regarded his effect on the party as negligible.[74] Yet there is some evidence to suggest that, in the process of getting hold of the newspaper group, Maxwell's very existence forced Kinnock to change his commitment to journalistic autonomy from proprietor control in order to gain Labour representation in the form of Maxwell's support for Labour.

Evidence suggests that Maxwell's pressure on Kinnock meant that the Labour leader was prepared consciously to revise his own position, after initially demanding that no single proprietor could own the *Daily Mirror*. Why was this important? Nothing that was written in Chapter 1 concerning the relationship between ownership and control denied the potential that editors, and even senior journalists, could maintain a level of autonomy from majority shareholder control. In the case of the *Daily Mirror*, for fifty years before the Maxwell takeover there had been no single proprietor.

Importantly, there was a level of autonomy from Reed, and the chair did not have sole control over policy decisions.[75] Instead, a five-person team including senior journalists, as well as Tony Miles (who had moved from being the *Daily Mirror*'s editor to become editorial director and later also became Mirror Group chair) and the then editor, Mike Molloy, decided political policy.[76] The editor's job was "more of a consensus position than an arbitrary dictatorship" where the paper's political stance came "more from editorial consensus than any single person's directive", as the Royal Commission on the Press was told in 1975.[77]

Journalists were thus very far from having control. Yet it was a degree of involvement that went beyond a single editor having autonomy – leading to some collective decision-making. As one of the five members of the policy team, industrial editor Geoffrey Goodman, said: "It was a more democratic situation, which led to informed discussion and debate."[78] The *Daily Mirror* columnist Paul Foot also considered that there was a measure of journalistic autonomy at this time. It was believed that not having a single proprietor would protect this.[79]

The circumstances surrounding the Labour Party's involvement in the Mirror Group newspapers' takeover are generally well known. According to Tom Bower, Maxwell's most famous biographer, the former MP seduced the Labour leadership in July 1984.[80] However, we need to trace the story back nine months. Reed International announced in October 1983, around the time Kinnock became leader, that it wished to float independently the company that owned the *Daily Mirror* and its sister papers the *Sunday Mirror*, *Daily Record* and *Sunday Mail*. Reed originally guaranteed both that it would not sell to a single owner and that the paper would stay Labour-supporting. As Bower suggests, it was crucial for Maxwell to get the Labour leader's support if Reed was to break the first part of this pledge.[81]

Within weeks of his election Kinnock had secret discussions with the title's then editor, Mike Molloy. The outcome was that the contents of a confidential letter were approved, which, it was agreed, would only appear in the *Daily Mirror* when the new chair of the Mirror Group was known. It appears not to have been published at the time. The letter underlined Kinnock's original determination to preserve both journalistic autonomy within the *Daily Mirror* and his concerns about business diversification into newspaper ownership. The document was much more hard-hitting than Kinnock's eventual public position.[82]

In this remarkable letter Kinnock wrote of his concern that the proposed sale would lead to one single owner with other business interests taking over control – just the sort of figure Maxwell was. He boldly reiterated some of the themes of this book by stating that: "Without a free and fearless press, there can be no true democracy. But a free press is no abstract idea. It means freedom, every day, from an owner's interference." In heated tones he announced: "It would be an outrage if the proposed sale left the *Mirror* open – if not today, then in future years – to a takeover by those who would curb your independence and try to make you obedient to the discipline of some big business vested interest."[83]

This was not a one-off gesture by Kinnock. The late Paul Foot said he met Kinnock and discussed the situation: "[H]e saw Maxwell as disastrous. Neil was upset and disturbed."[84] In the interim, negotiations had taken place about securing the papers as a trust with union backing, organized by Clive Thornton, whom Reed had originally appointed to oversee the sale. However, Reed scuppered these talks.[85] Kinnock's private papers indicate that at another meeting, arranged in July 1984, after Maxwell had made approaches to buy, he again committed the party to blocking any single proprietor.

Kinnock told the *Mirror*'s editor, Molloy, and its chair, Miles, that he was committed to opposing having a single owner as the best way of safeguarding the paper's independence. By now, however, he had not closed the door to accepting Maxwell as one among a number of shareholders. But Maxwell was unlikely to accept such a position, wanting, as Goodman put it, "all or nothing".[86] Miles is recorded as enthusiastically accepting Kinnock's assurances.[87]

Backbench Labour MPs also shared these fears about *Mirror* journalists losing their autonomy in the event of one person buying the paper. One newly elected MP put it thus: "[O]ne must be concerned when newspapers are to be owned by an individual who gives unenforceable guarantees of independence."[88] That MP was the future Labour leader Tony Blair, who would later entertain proprietors while ignoring calls for laws to provide journalist autonomy.

Calls for autonomy and independence for the *Mirror* dovetailed with the narrower demand that the paper remained supportive of the party. Kinnock's original letter had a subtext, which reflected the tension between courting Labour representation and stipulating guarantees on ownership. Kinnock stated that one aspect of independence that should be protected was freedom "from slavish devotion to a party line".[89] Yet "independence from big business" could well also be taken as code for traditional Labour Party concerns about the pro-Tory bias of the national press. In other words, Kinnock was insisting the *Mirror* should stay pro-Labour, as Reed had pledged.[90] His position also reflected the concerns of the senior editorial staff.[91]

Labour representation was Maxwell's trump card. He mounted a counter-operation to persuade Kinnock, using his historical commitment to the party, as a former Labour MP, enlisting the support of Michael Foot and then deputy leader Roy Hattersley.[92]

It is also now clear that Maxwell engaged in direct secret negotiations with Kinnock. Maxwell played on fears that Labour support would falter without him. On 9 June 1984 he wrote a private letter telling Kinnock that if he did not have the leader's backing, the paper's ownership could be "either wholly dispersed among City institutions or invested in [by] some predator whose political sympathies are elsewhere".[93]

Kinnock now had an unenviable choice. He could maintain Labour's support in Fleet Street, albeit on Maxwell's terms as a single owner. Or he could attempt to protect the limited autonomy of the Labour-supporting senior journalists by opposing the buy-out – as the *Mirror* journalists' representatives were doing. The latter option had no guarantee of success and could have ended up scuppering the backing of Labour's only long-term Fleet Street supporter.

The requirement that there be a Labour-supporting paper meant that, despite his deep unease, Kinnock chose the former option. Instead of intervening to stop the newspaper becoming a one-man band, he adopted a hands-off approach. He abandoned a press release implicitly critical of Maxwell and cautiously welcomed him.[94]

The shift in Kinnock's stance was clear. The existence of the millionaire businessman and the pressure of *realpolitik* had dictated the Labour leadership's policy – and had overridden Kinnock's principles on journalist autonomy. At Labour's 1989 conference the party's general secretary, Larry Whitty, implored reluctant delegates to recognize that Maxwell "controlled a newspaper whose support the Labour Party is often grateful for".[95] As Whitty suggested, and as Roy Hattersley wrote after Maxwell's death, not to have had the *Daily Mirror*'s support for Labour would have been "an intolerable psychological handicap".[96]

Contrary to the belief that Maxwell's influence on Labour was negligible, we have seen that Maxwell directly influenced the leader's press policy in the course of the takeover. The need to maintain a foothold in Fleet Street – ensuring that Labour was represented – meant that commitments were sacrificed. Moreover, the power of ownership in a market economy meant that even the Labour leader had limited choice over the manner of that representation. Returning to a point considered in Chapter 1, there was no democratic control over that representation. Despite Kinnock's reluctance to accept Maxwell's ownership, Maxwell held all the cards – and the Labour leader knew it. Paul Foot described Kinnock's dilemma well: "There is no democratic process. The only newspaper that supports Labour is sold on the marketplace and he is stuck."[97]

The 1987 Election, Wapping, Nationalism and Promoting Labour

There were other indications that the Labour leadership was starting to shift its policy on press ownership. The Labour leader dismissed the media spokesman, Norman Buchan, at the start of the 1987 election year, demonstrating the leadership's weakening commitment to the implementation of party policy. Buchan was a Kinnock ally. He had been keen on media reform and had strongly opposed press ownership concentration.[98] He had also called for a centralized arts and media ministry, citing previous party policy. However, Kinnock replaced him with Mark Fisher.[99]

As Freedman says, Buchan's dismissal appeared to be a secondary issue, yet it showed up divisions in the party over press and media policy.[100] The left's determination to co-ordinate all media policy in one ministry may be explained by an earlier debate. Proponents of press reform, notably Michael Meacher, feared that without this unitary approach – referred to earlier – any attempts at change could "fall through the cracks" between ministries. Whether the lack of such an integrated approach was a key reason why reform had not happened is not at issue. It was seen as a way of turning party policy into reality.[101]

By the time of the 1987 election press policy had changed substantially in other ways previously little discussed by other commentators.[102] Labour's underlying aim was to target the largest-selling daily tabloid – *The Sun*. However, the change also highlights that one effect of the Wapping printers' defeat was that radical policies on press diversity had retreated into populist rhetoric.

The circumstances surrounding the 1986-7 Wapping dispute are well documented. News International sacked around 5,000 printers when it moved to Wapping, prompting a bitter clash. What is less well known is the effect the dispute had on Labour's plans for diversifying the press. Labour's 1987 election manifesto saw a significant shift in press policy. *Britain Will Win With Labour* called for a bar on foreign citizens and companies from owning UK newspapers.[103]

Kinnock had showed his sympathy for the bar on foreign ownership in a rare foray into public discussion on press ownership policy at a rally for staff sacked by News International in 1986. He accused Rupert Murdoch of being an autocratic threat to democracy, who, with two other owners, presided over "one of the greatest concentrations of power in newspaper ownership anywhere in the world". He noted that, despite this concentration, "we have one of the weakest systems of controlling it".

His proposed remedy was to exclude foreigners from owning British papers. This new nationalist demand not only substituted pressure for press diversity with calls of a mildly xenophobic nature, but was also based on a factual error. Kinnock thought that it was a United States law prohibiting press ownership by foreign nationals that had forced the Australian Murdoch to take up US citizenship. He wanted the law he imagined operated there to be enacted in Britain. But the US law that forced Murdoch to become an American citizen controls broadcasting.[104]

The print unions championed the new nationalistic approach. They had been involved in bitter disputes with a former Australian and, before that, with the Asian Eddy Shah at the *Stockport Messenger*. It would not have been too surprising if these had stoked up some members' nationalist prejudices, which the unions expressed.[105] This nationalist theme came to the fore when the unions succeeded in getting the 1986 TUC conference to demand that a Labour government ensure that press "ownership and executive control [are] retained in this country".[106]

It was argued that such a law would increase newspaper accountability. Instead, it reduced the question of concentration and participation in the press to the demonizing of a single owner – Murdoch. The proprietor had stripped the printers of their jobs. The proposed step appeared an attractive riposte, a way of excluding him in a relatively painless way. Yet disguised nationalism substituted itself for democratic accountability. It was left to the NUJ at the TUC congress to oppose the attempt to "blame the foreigner" as "solving nothing". The union's Jake Ecclestone advocated the alternative of compulsory divestment. But delegates ignored his call to reject "superficially attractive solutions".[107]

When the 1986 Labour Party conference debated the new policy departure, it faced no vocal opposition. The NEC-backed motion called for a bar on ownership by non-UK companies or individuals. Speakers used delegates' anger at the Wapping printworkers' treatment to voice a nationalist sentiment again. The problem with the national press was clear, as the seconder, Danny Sergeant, of SOGAT, said: "It is not British. It is foreign."[108] This time no NUJ speaker argued that the motion cut across existing press policy, as the union was not Labour-affiliated. Yet one indication of this divergence was that the CPBF opposed the new stance.[109]

Importantly, the new "nationalist" position made it into the 1987 manifesto. The Shadow ministerial team, Mark Fisher and Robin (now Lord) Corbett, were informed that it had leadership support – and that it would "catch Murdoch now". Lord Corbett told the author that the unions strongly lobbied for the policy, with which he disagreed.[110] However, as it had leadership approval at this stage, the manifesto announced that press control, like that of broadcasting, was to be "retained by citizens of Britain".[111] Labour did not target the companies' multinational nature, but the owners' nationality. Multinationals' control of the press has reduced international diversity. Nevertheless, to argue that the remedy was a nationality bar was to conflate the question of foreign owners with that of foreign ownership.

Illustrating this, ironically, the manifesto's policy would not necessarily have been effective in excluding its most obvious target. Different members of the Murdoch family could have acquired citizenship in different countries, with effective control remaining with the same person and company. So the policy was nationalistic and potentially ineffective. It had as its inspiration the hatred of an individual – Rupert Murdoch. Over the next few years he became one of Labour's most loathed figures.[112] Yet, while concentrating on one individual, discussion concerning the structure of press ownership and measures to be taken receded.

The other measures in the 1987 manifesto reflected Labour's overall policy shift. AES-style interventionism was in retreat in press ownership policy. As Curran and Seaton point out, the manifesto reworked some of the themes regarding concentration's effect on press plurality. It is true that, in a limited sense, 1970s' radicalism still influenced *Britain Will Win With Labour*.[113] But the pledge to increase press diversity was more vague and the commitment to journalist involvement was non-existent. With the leadership dominating policy creation, the pledges made at the 1983 Labour conference did not find their way into the manifesto, despite the fact that no party body had formally jettisoned them. Apart from the important new nationalist policy, the manifesto pledged a Labour government to enacting unspecified laws to "place limits on the concentration of ownership".[114] As Allaun's book notes, it possessed even briefer commitments than the 1983 document and was "composed of generalities".[115]

At the start of Kinnock's leadership the backwash from the radicalizing wave of the previous years was felt in local government. Emulating this, the 1983 conference eclipsed the relatively strident manifesto of earlier that year. It passed policy that replicated and went beyond a Scandinavian-style social market interventionist conception. At the same time some characteristics of a more marketized social democratic response associated with the cultural industries approach were discernible. The conference ignored the leadership-dominated NEC in passing this radical resolution.

As we shall see in Chapter 6, when the leadership did come to dominate internal policy formation, press policy edged towards accommodating business and the market. As we have seen in this chapter, it was not a linear process, as indicated by the influence of Wapping. Nevertheless, the period up to 1987 had seen the leadership gradually achieving dominance over the NEC in forming policy, while the left divided, a development reflected, for the most part, in the press ownership policy in the 1987 manifesto. However, the fact that even in 1987 there could still be detected some references to intervention showed that the radical upsurge from 1979 onwards had not yet been completely quelled.

Rather than drafting policy to control newspaper companies, which Kinnock's inner circle rejected as an outmoded method for improving newspaper coverage, the leadership would further develop a new strategy to woo the press. It became more interested in other methods for garnering Labour support in the press, associated with political marketing. This strategy was considered successful and would eventually further undermine the case for structural change, which was seen as counterproductive for those trying to woo newspaper businesses.

6
Policy Reviewed
Neil Kinnock and John Smith

The later years of Neil Kinnock's period as Labour leader and John Smith's short time in the post were more of an uneven journey than a gradual evolution as far as the party's policy on press ownership was concerned. The period from 1987 to 1992 saw proprietorial policy slip down the agenda as the Labour leadership pulled back from intervening in the economy, while strategists regarded marketing Labour in the newspapers as a much more important task than addressing the question of ownership.

Yet in 1993 the policy vehicle that sought structural change tried to make it up the hill one last time. The Labour shadow minister responsible for policy on press ownership, Ann Clwyd, announced that the "unregulated growth of Mr Murdoch's empire" was "an affront to a democratic society".[1] And her counterpart with responsibility for trade and industry, Robin Cook, concurred that the "empire" needed to be curbed by law.[2] However, within a month of making that statement Clwyd had lost her job and the new incumbent, Mo Mowlam, opted for deregulation – riding on the back of what she saw as the inevitable demands of globalization. Again this development should be seen within the context of Labour's overall policy shift, alongside Labour's new marketing strategy.

Party Policy from the Policy Review to the Death of John Smith

The 1987 election failure provided an opportunity for Labour to re-evaluate its policy and its approach to decision-making. It instituted the Policy Review, which ran from 1987 to 1991, the effect of which was to put the leadership and the marketing strategists directly in control of policy-making. The Policy Review included development of a series of new position documents. The leadership retreated from plans to control the unfettered market and eventually rejected Keynesian economic management, at least on a national basis.

The soft left Shadow Trade Minister, Bryan Gould, had successfully championed Keynesian interventionism within the party.[3] He was influential in maintaining the view that the government needed to control the financiers and the City of London in order to aid manufacturing industry. Yet by the late 1980s Kinnock and his shadow chancellor, John Smith, were convinced that financial capital, which had been further strengthened when the government freed up exchange controls in 1979, was too powerful to challenge head-on.

International and domestic factors influenced Labour's perspective on economic management. The "French lesson" that Labour learned from President Mitterrand's reflationary failure after 1981 was that the international economy and financiers had greater power than ever before in determining the economic development of individual countries.[4] When the Berlin Wall fell in 1989, it paved the way for the West's zone of influence to be expanded (limiting the possibilities of reforming the market system in the minds of many, and not just social democratic Soviet fellow-travellers). Moreover, ten years of rule by Margaret Thatcher had changed the political landscape. In this context the Labour leadership proceeded to accept some of the new economic medicine. It argued that the threat of capital flight had overwhelmingly weakened nation-states in a qualitatively new way, making Keynesian intervention impossible at a national level.

With left alternatives dismissed, in place of Keynesianism at first came "supply-side socialism". Government intervention across the whole economy would now more approximately replicate Britain's existing minimalist press ownership laws. Neil Kinnock outlined in a Policy Review document a policy whereby the state would not directly intervene to reorganize markets but would restrict "monopoly practices in the interests of competition".[5] Business would predominately be left to "get on with business", while most Conservative restraints on the unions would remain.[6] These monumental shifts would help shape the approach taken to press ownership.

The shift was facilitated by changes in the decision-making process, which were of profound importance. The Policy Review saw the soft left and the right in the party come together to reorientate the party's policy, with union support, against the rest of the left. But this process "emasculated" the party, including the soft left and the unions, as the leader's office and the marketing strategists came to dominate policy-making through the review structures.[7] Meanwhile, the leadership-dominated NEC successfully persuaded the 1989 conference to accept the proposal that Policy Review documents could not be amended by Labour conferences – they could only be accepted or rejected.[8] The 1990 conference approved, in principle, the creation of a National Policy Forum, which also provided for greater party centralization, as the forum, rather than the party membership, would decide which motions were debated at the party conference.[9]

Despite all these changes, which were meant to aid electability, and the fact that Labour went into the 1992 election with its lead buoyed by opposition to the Community Charge – something party strategists were reluctant to focus on – Labour failed once again. After standing down as party leader in 1992, as we saw at the start of this book, Kinnock bitterly blamed his defeat on what he saw as the national newspapers' bias against his party. The question was posed as to whether Labour could ever gain office again, facing such press hostility.[10]

On the back of this fourth consecutive defeat, John Smith was elected Labour leader. Whereas his predecessor had lost with the press and media strategists at the helm, Smith's reign was marked by a struggle between two factions. The language describing the contenders has been so successfully touted by one of the factions that it is difficult not to adopt it. The ascendant new right,[11] who styled themselves "New Labour", fought with others in the party, for whom they invented the term "Old Labour" – thus grossly simplifying the complex recent history considered here. In turn, the right were described by anti-left commentators in the press as "modernizers", thus accepting the right's terminology at face value.[12] "Old Labour" blamed the 1992 defeat on the marketing strategists. The "modernizers", meanwhile focused on the largely irrelevant issue of the union block vote in explaining the loss, thus successfully deflecting attention away from the marketing strategists' failure.[13] And psephological evidence produced by the strategists, who also attempted to blame the result on memories of the municipal socialist "loony left", was also flawed.[14]

In turn, New Labour suggested that to win office Labour needed to change. It needed to accommodate itself to allegedly shifting social attitudes, targeting aspirational Thatcher supporters and further embracing the market in order to demonstrate "economic competence".[15] The diagnosis of the modernizers was based on research that was selectively leaked to sympathetic journalists, to provide a skewed analysis. The research bore the imprint of the marketing consultant Philip Gould and relied on selective quotes from qualitative analysis, which deliberately ignored the role of Kinnock himself.[16] It was not borne out by quantitative polling research.

The New Labour prescription also faced the problem that, despite all the claims of a changing electorate, another discernible attitude shift was that voters were turning to Labour. Evidence suggests that after the failure of their ERM strategy in September 1992 "the Conservatives never recovered their reputation or unity".[17] The public questioned Tory economic management, making the traditional social democrats' call for just "one more heave" relatively convincing. Nevertheless, it is questionable whether the "traditionalists" had a complete strategy for government, as it was not clear which tradition they wished to return to.[18]

In this situation, it is perhaps not surprising that Smith himself wavered between the two camps. In the early phase of his leadership, at least, he avoided siding with either faction when he could honourably do so, a policy that led the new right to accuse him of "sleepwalking".[19] Nonetheless, the new right did influence Smith's organizational control over party policy-making. Although he valued the trade unions' role, Smith weakened their influence.[20]

Smith's oscillation between the two camps was mirrored by Labour's economic policy. It is easy to forget that before the autumn of 1993 Labour flirted with solutions to bring about Keynesianism on a European scale. The shadow chancellor, Gordon Brown, later adopted a more neo-liberal strategy, influenced by a notion of economic globalization.[21] Analogously, the party's position on newspaper ownership also went through a more radical moment, as we shall see, before moving closer to one guided by the concept of globalization.

The most important aspect of this acceptance of globalization has been its impact on regulation. Some commentators have emphasized that, because of capital flight – the ease with which multinational corporations can shift their investments between different locations around the globe – international business can now hold nation-states to ransom. Multinationals can dictate to governments the extent to which they are subject to regulation, knowing that if government action is not to their liking they can invest elsewhere. A similar argument now guides Labour's press and media cross-ownership policies.

Labour also came to imply that this process was part of an objective and inevitable "tidal wave" of change, in which globalization was the agent. It obscured the fact that the process was a product of choice by conscious agents, be they governments, international financiers or multinationals. Moreover, the Labour leadership carefully employed language to mask this fact and to absolve itself from responsibility for its own actions.[22]

Press Diversity and Cross-ownership Policy Reviewed

Following the 1987 election defeat, in line with other policies on industrial intervention, even the Labour manifesto's minimal commitment to press diversity started to wane. In the late 1980s the Labour front bench still expressed concern that the lack of press ownership diversity provided "an increasing threat to genuine democracy", as the shadow Home Secretary, Roy Hattersley, put it.[23] But as nation-state Keynesianism made an exit from the Policy Review, so the commitment to intervening to provide press diversity also started to dissolve.

The Policy Review was now dominated by a new emphasis on political communications. In explaining Labour's 1987 defeat, the Shadow Communications Agency (SCA) came into its own.[24] The SCA was decisive in mapping out the new agenda of Labour's Policy Review. The marketing strategists continued to provide biased evidence of the "loony left" municipal socialists' responsibility for defeat.[25] Nevertheless, the input of the SCA also became part of a process whereby the party was circumvented by the leadership. The press and media began to be used to present information directly to potential supporters, and seemingly sophisticated techniques were used to gauge public opinion.[26] The bypassing of the party membership meant that power was concentrated in the hands of the leadership, at the expense of the activists and the NEC. The old approach of attempting structural change of the press was not even part of the press strategists' lexicon. Yet, along with the leader's office, it was the strategists who took control of the Policy Review.

The leadership under Kinnock became far more concerned to appeal to what strategists considered to be the wants and needs of the electorate; in other words, there was a shift from a media-led strategic approach to one based on political marketing. Thus, prior to 1987, Labour's political communications had reverted to what Dominic Wring describes as a "persuasional" schema (rather than the "educational" school of thought, to which Michael Foot had adhered). After the 1987 election, while the Policy Review accepted the dominance of the market in the economic sphere, it also embraced the dominance of the market in politics.[27] Central to the political marketing strategy, where the public was reached directly, was the press. As Labour marketing strategists became key, so did their allies in the newspapers.

In return for privileged access, sympathetic journalists provided a conduit for the leadership to influence the political agenda of the membership and the wider public. Before the Policy Review the Labour leadership had attempted to influence the membership by focusing on left newspapers such as *Tribune* and in-house publications such as *Labour Weekly*. The closure of the latter under Kinnock "was symptomatic of the leadership's concentration on the anti-Conservative *Guardian* and the *Mirror* group" of national newspapers. During this time both sets of titles and Alastair Campbell at the *Mirror* and Patrick Wintour at *The Guardian* were particularly supportive. By targeting these papers the Labour leadership could reach a far larger percentage of the party than through the Labour-supporting publications such as *Tribune* and *Labour Briefing,* which in any case were more critical of the leadership in their coverage.[28]

This struggle to use the press to aid agenda-setting described in Chapter 5 was a battle with what the SCA fully accepted as "the hostile press (with which we are stuck)".[29] Yet what was striking was how resigned the marketing strategists were to "Conservative control of the media" and how scant were the structural alternatives they proposed. We saw that Kinnock blamed the "Conservative-supporting press" for the 1992 defeat. Yet Philip Gould, while also identifying this bias, advocated challenging the way individual journalists worked but not the structure within which they operated.[30] Previous policy on structurally changing the press to challenge newspaper bias was written out of history as these new methods were adopted. Even implementing the right of reply was not seen as significant. So Gould's meticulous chronicling of the implementation of Kinnock's media strategy facing a "fearsomely hostile" press did not even hint that the SCA contemplated restructuring the newspaper market when considering this imbalance.[31]

The policy of employing the strategists' methods to guide policy-making was based on the assumption that the strategists would accurately gauge the views of the public, which were assumed to be a million miles away from those of activists. However, political communications specialists have outlined the bias in the methods the marketing strategists employed to assess the electorate's opinions, particularly in qualitative focus group research. For example, Mandelson and Gould painted a picture of an electorate that had rejected collectivist values for individualist ones – something not borne out by the British Social Attitudes Survey. Gould admits he suppressed evidence when it challenged his pre-set agenda. Even Kinnock himself later admitted that the SCA consciously gave presentations which "assisted in the efforts to sustain the review in the desired direction".[32] There was no way to scrutinize the marketing strategists' interpretations, as they made sure their work was kept secret.[33] Yet focus group experts have argued that it is only with such access that this research can be legitimated. They have also questioned the representativeness of such small groups.[34]

Moreover, the most extensive analysis of the relationship between the beliefs of party members and voters indicates that activists, Labour voters and the electorate as a whole shared many opinions. For instance, both voters in general and Labour members supported industrial democracy at this time – a cause, of course, central to activist demands for press participatory democracy.[35] There were significant areas of divergence, but any idea that the electorate shared the Conservative tabloids' prescription of a low-tax and non-interventionist economic policy, for example, is not supported by the evidence.[36]

The Policy Review and Press Ownership Diversity

Although the way the Policy Review operated meant the cards were stacked against them, campaigners still attempted to influence the press and media section of the review. This was overseen by the Democracy for the Individual and the Community Committee, chaired by Roy Hattersley, who jointly managed media policy as Shadow Home Secretary. He had written *Democratic Socialist Aims and Values*, an intellectually ambitious attempt to be the Policy Review's "ideological foundation". His document's relatively radical aim of diversifying the press to "represent and reflect every strand of political opinion and cultural characteristic", with "diversity of ownership", was offset by his reluctance to challenge market control.[37]

By 1988 the Policy Review, supported by the interventionist Shadow Trade Minister, Bryan Gould, had agreed to introduce laws to strip the press oligopolies of some of the titles they owned, similar to the 1983 manifesto policy. Such was the importance still placed on placating campaigners in the Campaign for Press and Broadcasting Freedom that Gould unveiled the new policy to a meeting of the organization, pre-empting the 1988 Labour Party conference by a few days. Both organizations' delegates would learn that, as with the 1983 manifesto commitments, there would be no help for new owners in running the discarded titles – leading to the possibility that these newspapers would go under. The 1988 conference also called on the review to re-consider both an advertising levy and that there was concentration of newspaper ownership by individuals "who neither reside in the United Kingdom nor have United Kingdom citizenship".[38]

New left elements on the review tried to flesh out this more interventionist approach. Ken Livingstone, later to become Mayor of London, spearheaded a shift in Labour conference policy on press diversity. When the NEC met at the start of the 1989 conference, he successfully proposed a motion that had come from the Democracy for the Individual and the Community Committee. This called on a Labour government to establish and fund a Media Enterprise Board, providing funds and advice to aid start-ups. Its terminology also indicated a more market-oriented cultural industries approach, which reflected both the GLC and soft left influences.[39] Although Livingstone's initiative became party policy at the 1989 conference, it did not figure in later Labour thinking.[40]

Instead, as the Kinnock leadership turned to supply-side socialism and away from any direct intervention – which was associated with soft left figures such as Bryan Gould and Robin Cook – so the party's commitment to press intervention was ignored. With the input of the leader's office and the strategists, the later review document *Opportunity Britain* and the final report, *Meet the Challenge, Make the Change*, did not reflect the party's position. Both documents only bound Labour to a review of concentration by the Monopoly and Mergers Commission. There was a vague reference to strengthening that body to deal with ownership changes. Media union representatives rejected the review documents' new position.[41] One pleaded to the 1989 conference: "We do not have the time to refer to the Monopolies and Mergers Commission."[42]

Democratic Control

The Policy Review not only affected ownership policy. Calls for democratic participation in and control of the press were also extinguished. It is true that another attempt to provide an intellectual backdrop to the Policy Review, authored by David Blunkett and Bernard Crick from the soft left, at first provided a more radical stance. Their document called for more democratic employee and user participation in the press.[43] However, little more was heard from the mainstream soft left. More typical was Hattersley's *Democratic Socialist Aims and Values*, a version of which was finally agreed by the Labour Party, where calls for "equality of access" were also undermined by its author's refusal to consider the need for private ownership to be democratized.[44]

A failed attempt to challenge Hattersley's reticence regarding press democratization came from another quarter. Labour Party members involved in the new left GLC experience had maintained their commitment to broader participation in the press. In contrast, by now the NEC's union representatives were strongly backing the leadership in quelling this radical line of thought. In Chapter 5, we saw that the media unions, while happy to support theoretical aspirations, were reluctant to embrace democratic participation in newspapers when faced with it in practice. By the late 1980s, however, they were so intent on supporting the leadership that they now rejected resolutions on democratizing ownership, at least behind closed doors. Yet at the same time the media unions still complained publicly that the party hierarchy ignored their input on broadcast diversity and democracy.[45]

At a meeting of the NEC before the 1989 conference, Ken Livingstone proposed that the Labour Party should again support co-operatives in the press. But the failure of the *News on Sunday* militated against this bid. SOGAT official and former media study group member Ted O'Brien spoke in opposition, citing the *News on Sunday* débâcle and other negative experiences.[46] Livingstone's was the last attempt to introduce press co-operative policy at the NEC.

The pledge to introduce legislation on a right of reply was also eventually dropped under Kinnock, despite the efforts of several Labour MPs: Austin Mitchell picked up the baton in 1984, Ann Clwyd in 1987 and Tony Worthington in 1989.[47] The commitment to a right of reply did not make its way into the 1992 manifesto, although no party forum had explicitly rejected it.

Thus, the Labour leadership's interest in press ownership reform of any sort dwindled in the 1980s, despite pronounced newspaper hostility to Labour. While the marketing strategists looked to other remedies to deal with this, Robin (now Lord) Corbett says that Hattersley, who had overall responsibility for the policy as shadow Home Secretary, "never showed much real interest" in detailed work on press and media ownership despite his previous concerns.[48] The problem of both dealing with bias and encouraging press plurality that had bedevilled policy development had now come to a head. This was reflected in the saga of how Labour treated the newspaper owners News International and its parent company News Corporation.

News International/News Corporation and the Revamped Strategy

The saga of Labour's changing attitude to News International in the late 1980s and early 1990s provides a contrast with the attitude adopted later by Tony Blair and was a by-product of the Wapping dispute (referred to in Chapter 5). Rather than using the dispute as a launch pad to challenge the power of News International and other press companies, Labour concentrated its action on a boycott of the Murdoch titles and their journalists.

Labour's attitude to News International was counterproductive in dealing with the problem of press bias and would have been even more so if the boycott had been applied rigorously. It may have appeared that the motion agreed by Labour's National Executive Committee to decide on the boycott was ambiguously worded, merely calling for a boycott of the News International newspapers.[49] However, it was taken to mean that Labour barred reporters from interviewing or receiving information from party members.

By doing so, the Labour Party excluded papers from which publicity was needed, whatever their anti-Labour bias. The boycott also laid Kinnock open to accusations that, by withholding information, the party was inhibiting press freedom and undermining the democratic process.[50] Because Kinnock refused to answer questions from News International reporters, Westminster journalists in turn barred Kinnock from lobby meetings.[51] Kinnock's response was to hold a weekly conference in his Commons offices to which News International journalists were not invited. A by-product of this arrangement was that Kinnock controlled contacts with individual political journalists more directly.[52] It encouraged the idea that particular journalists could be cultivated, a notion that the marketing strategy later developed.

Problems with the boycott came to a head during the 1986 Fulham by-election. The Labour candidate, Nick Raynsford, made clear that he was going to ignore it and answer questions from all journalists. Eventually the leader's office – intimately involved with the shifts in political communications – conceded that all journalists should be admitted to press conferences, "however much we dislike it". However, Kinnock's office advised him that, to placate the unions, News International journalists would not be given "exclusive" interviews.[53] This compromised boycott was publicly observed for the remainder of the dispute.

The boycott may well have been an effective consciousness-raising exercise; it certainly demonstrated a willingness to show solidarity with the sacked printers and probably dented News International's profits. Yet it did not follow that Labour significantly raised the profile of its policy on diversity or democratic ownership of newspapers, or reopened debate on it.

Kinnock was personally reluctant to court the News International tabloids, along with the other titles hostile to Labour, for the rest of the time he was leader. One of Labour's preferred journalists at the time, Alastair Campbell, later described Kinnock as having a different view of the press from his own – if equally fatalistic. Like Kinnock by now, Campbell did not want to challenge press structures but wished to build more positive relations with them than Kinnock felt able to do. "It was one of the things I used to argue with Neil about – and I completely understand why he found it difficult because they were complete bastards to him – but I held the view that, however bad the press is, it can be worse, and it can be better, and you have to work at it all the time."[54] Later Campbell followed this nostrum when he headed Labour's communications team.

Unlike Kinnock, some key figures in the leader's office and among the marketing strategists shared Campbell's view and did not sever all contacts with News International, viewing the partial ban as counterproductive. Among them, according to the then *Sunday Times* editor, Andrew Neil, were Peter Mandelson and his ally Tony Blair.[55] In fact, a little later Blair cemented this early relationship with News International by making *The Times* his sounding board. His articles formed a regular column more or less every fortnight for a period in the late 1980s.[56] In January 1992 one senior member of Kinnock's office – his chief of staff, Charles Clarke – even went behind the leader's back to contact "Fortress Wapping" to try to improve relations. Clarke recalls: "It's the only thing I ever did without telling Neil beforehand."[57] Nevertheless, it is important to note, for all the new aspects of the press and media strategy, that Labour still regarded News International and News Corporation as a breed apart.

The antipathy to News Corporation was a factor in Labour's policy on press cross-media ownership. Cross-media conglomeration was a very significant development in the 1980s on both sides of the Atlantic.[58] This process saw News Corporation dominating the satellite sector and leading the national newspaper market. Because of these developments, the Labour Party now concentrated more on broadcasting policy than on issues of press ownership.[59]

Related to Labour's interest in cross-ownership were the party's nationalist response to the Wapping dispute, the individual targeting of Murdoch and the promotion of Labour in the press. For some in the Labour Party, Murdoch was a totem figure regarding newspaper diversity, representing all the problems of press and cross-media concentration. Yet, for many the main concern was simply his view of Labour – he was an "old-style" right-wing interventionist proprietor, in league with the Conservative Party to advance each other's interests. Notwithstanding the attempts to neutralize News International outlined here, during Kinnock's time as leader, he regarded the "bastards" at Wapping as an enemy, over whom he had little influence. If he could therefore limit News International's grip over the British press, he would at the same time be able to confront newspaper bias.

The personal vilification of Murdoch described in Chapter 5 and here was thus a pivotal point in Labour's policy evolution. The Labour leadership was moving away from focusing on press concentration policy, through the individual targeting of Murdoch, with an eye to promoting Labour, towards later diluting diversification policies and using other methods to market the party.

Labour concerns were heightened by the launch of Sky Television in 1989 and its subsequent takeover of a rival satellite station to form BSkyB in 1990, with Conservative government approval. Sky Television had been launched amid a welter of positive publicity from the "shameless cheerleaders" at *The Sun* and other News International titles – heightening fears about cross-promotion.[60] The Conservative government had in fact stated its opposition to cross-ownership. And it had formalized an IBA policy to reduce press interests in broadcasting in the 1990 Broadcasting Act. The government's position was that no newspaper owner could possess more than 20 per cent of a terrestrial television station. Yet this was ignored when it came to non-British satellite channels, freeing News International to pursue its joint satellite and newspaper interests.[61]

In 1988 Bryan Gould, still speaking from the Labour front bench, called for stricter control on cross-media ownership, and the following year the Labour Party publicly committed itself to this. The rhetoric denouncing Murdoch was strident.[62] At first, the Shadow Cabinet argued that newspaper owners could not also own broadcasting stations – satellite or terrestrial.[63] When the Conservatives sanctioned the takeover to create a monopoly with BSkyB, Labour's broadcasting spokesperson, Mark Fisher, described it as a "craven decision taken by a government in hock with Mr Murdoch", an accusation that was also to be levelled against the Labour leadership only a few years later.[64]

Yet, importantly, a rift was opening between this rhetoric, from those who fronted the policy and were keen on some limited intervention, and the leadership and strategists in control of the Policy Review, who did not want to alienate media business interests. In official review documents Labour's commitment to stifling cross-ownership became much vaguer. It amounted to no more than a pledge to refer the issue again to a strengthened Monopoly and Mergers Commission.[65]

By the early 1990s, however, pressure was mounting to shift policy away from this minimal commitment to press diversity and towards an accommodation with News Corporation. The arguments again reflected the tension between the concerns, on the one hand, to promote the Labour

Party and, on the other, to encourage press diversity – foreshadowing, also, later disputes in the party.

One close Kinnock ally, Austin Mitchell, had already advocated a similar diagnosis to the marketing strategists to explain Labour's electoral woes.[66] In 1989 he had caused a furore by accepting an offer to become a BSkyB presenter. In 1990 he called on Kinnock and Labour to follow its Australian and New Zealand sister parties' example and work with Murdoch rather than against him. Mitchell argued that those parties regarded promoting their own fortunes as more important than challenging a media conglomerate. They had "seen the virtues of working with someone who owns powerful communication media so that they can put over their case". In other words, in the tension between press diversity and the marketing and promotion of Labour in print, the Australian and New Zealand Labor parties regarded their short-term advance as more important than advancing media diversity. Mitchell saw that for the British Labour Party the name of the game was no longer to attempt to restructure press ownership to get a "fairer" hearing. Labour needed to accommodate the owners and, at least, ameliorate policy on press diversity and accountability. This was especially the case, Mitchell pointed out, as Labour's policy on crossownership was by now dominated by the consideration of "one medium [television], one channel [BSkyB], one television system [satellite] and one person [Murdoch]". As Mitchell said, this stood in stark contradiction to the Policy Review's generally pro-business spirit. He argued that, while the events at Wapping were "monstrous", if the Labour Party did not have policies to undo the wrongs, then "hitting out is irrelevant and . . . damaging to the Labour Party's case".[67] At this stage the Labour leadership denied that there was a vendetta against Murdoch. But it was becoming clear that "one person" was indeed still being targeted.

Press Ownership Policy and the 1992 Election

By 1992 the role of the strategists and their auxiliaries in the press was key to the changes in the party's organization, as we have seen. The strategists also had extensive power over policy development, including on controlling press ownership – an area which they held in low regard.

The power of the SCA was such that, together with Patricia Hewitt from the leader's office, it was involved in rewriting and drafting parts of the Policy Review's reports, under Kinnock's control.[68] The strategists, together with the leaders' office, collectively ran the 1992 campaign.[69] (Peter Mandelson had by now left his post in order to become an MP, to be replaced first by John Underwood and then David Hill.[70]) Those controlling the actual campaigning also decided which policies were prioritized.[71] Although Shadow Cabinet member Jack Cunningham, as campaign co-ordinator, was a member of a secret group which oversaw the SCA, according to Philip Gould, other than the leader, "senior politicians were never fully involved".[72] Indeed the minister with overall responsibility for the media, deputy leader Roy Hattersley, says that he had no involvement even in planning his own election programme.[73] Entirely unaccountable outsiders were also influential, such as the media entrepreneur Clive Hollick, who would later become a press businessman aligned with Labour.[74] Examples of problems associated with the SCA's influence included the débâcle over a broadcast dubbed "the war of Jennifer's ear" and the self-congratulatory election-eve Sheffield Rally.[75]

There was now again a divide within Labour. One former shadow minister describes the two different parts of the party as "operating in isolation" from one another after 1987, with each developing policy independently.[76] Some, mainly on the left, were still trying to persuade the party to implement thoroughgoing policies to promote diversity – and a few to democratize the press. However, the fatalism that had previously characterized those mainly on the right about countering anti-Labour press bias was also shared in a particular way by the media strategists who had become such a key influence, together with the inner core of the Labour leadership. Wholesale structural change was simply not an option; containment of News International's ownership was as far as anyone went.

It is in this context that Labour's policy on press ownership can be best appreciated. One indication of the combined power of the strategists and the leader's office was that a then shadow minister, Robin Corbett, says he was treated like a "mere backbencher" by them and the inner leadership in planning the manifesto. Yet he was aware of the discussions of the political communication strategists and the leadership, where the concern was not to challenge media businesses directly. For some time Labour activists had complained that they had not been involved in drawing up the party's manifesto. Now even shadow ministers were being excluded from an input in their own area of policy. And the leader's office was forging more links with Wapping journalists while developing a political marketing strategy. By the time the 1992 manifesto emerged, the best-known aspect of the press ownership policy, and the one that affected News Corporation – cross-ownership legislation – was "kicked into the long grass", according to Corbett. "The party strategists were saying 'No, that is far too hard-edged'."[77]

So, despite all the previous pledges on press reform, and Tory claims that Labour would revert to its previous radical position, Labour's 1992 election commitments on press ownership were minimal.[78] The manifesto limited itself to restating the Policy Review's commitment to refer the question of cross-ownership to an "urgent inquiry" by the Monopolies and Mergers Commission.[79] In other words, a social democratic interventionist policy had been rejected in favour of the possibility of a limited liberal pluralist notion of anti-monopoly curbs. As Austin Mitchell, of all people, put it, merely referring ownership to the commission "is the classic formula for any party that cannot decide what to do".[80]

It was clear which company was the target of this cross-ownership policy – News Corporation – but this only made it easier to reject the policy as one born of spite. Concerns centred on Murdoch because of his dominance in the British national newspaper market, his globalizing ambition, his political links and his anti-union record. Yet he was also a media hate figure for Labour to unite around because of his then hostility to the party, his nationality and his acumen.[81] With satellite television, as with other areas, "Rupert Murdoch got in first and scooped the market . . . Capitalism is all about taking a risk. Rupert Murdoch got in and did it – successfully."[82]

The Labour leadership concentrated more on this individual, with the hope of tackling the problems of party representation, and focused less on robust policies to regulate the market in which Murdoch operated. The result was that a new, even more market-oriented clique of Labour politicians found it easier to reject such policies. Indeed, Tony Blair later publicly embraced Mitchell's logic of not offending Murdoch (while Mitchell himself, perhaps ironically, started to go in the other direction). Policy became focused on containing the existing press conglomerates rather than on actively promoting further diversity or participation. However, even calls for an inquiry, with no guarantees of any legislation, prompted concerns that BSkyB's cross-ownership was going to be targeted, which would have forced Murdoch to choose between News Corporation's five national newspapers and its satellite broadcaster. The effect even of mere talk of the Labour Party legislating should not be underestimated. Fears of any such legislation sent shares plummeting in those press companies that were BSkyB shareholders – News International (as part of News Corporation), Pearson and Reed International.[83] As Murdoch's sympathetic biographer put it for News International, "no company stood to lose as much from a Labour victory", despite Labour's minimal commitments.[84]

Press Policy under John Smith

Press and Media Strategy under Smith

In the early part of John Smith's time as Labour leader the party's policy on both press ownership and Labour marketing in the press differed from the later Kinnock period. Smith shunned the more overt press manipulation techniques and, in the early period, his front bench vigorously promoted the cause of press plurality and accountability.

The sea-change in Labour's media relations and the techniques employed saw Smith leave many of Kinnock's key players "out in the cold" and one of them, Mandelson, left "kicking his heels". Smith also closed down the Shadow Communications Agency.[85] He restored some NEC accountability over Labour's marketing and, unlike Kinnock, he gave senior colleagues access to the party's private opinion research.[86]

Why was this? One reason was simply the 1992 election defeat. Smith also had a personal animosity towards Mandelson's coterie.[87] But the main reason for the change of approach was that the new leader was resistant to the media strategists' methods and their weighty influence. In the period before Smith's sudden death Labour did quietly begin using some of the Clinton campaign's electoral techniques.[88] Yet Smith publicly rejected what he called "the black art of public relations".[89] He had an "innate detestation of trickiness with the press".[90]

Thus, on this issue, Smith mostly sided with the Old Labour traditionalists.[91] (Importantly nevertheless, the target of Labour's policies continued to be those of Policy Review – i.e. what had been dubbed "Middle England".[92]) The battle between the modernizers and the traditionalists was intimately linked with perceptions of the media strategists' role. If there was the need for a completely new political approach to win over the press and broaden the party's support, then Labour needed the media strategists. If it could win without the Conservative newspapers' backing, then "such people were surplus to requirements".[93]

Press and Cross-Media Ownership under Smith

At first, the Labour front-bench team also rejected the message of those MPs wanting a rapprochement with press businesses. In November 1992 Smith appointed the soft left stalwart Ann Clwyd as Shadow Heritage Secretary, responsible for press policy. He was aware of Clwyd's involvement in press and media campaigns and that the former journalist championed the right of reply, as we saw. In fact, under her, Labour press policy limited itself to the same targets as the later Kinnock years. Yet, as was suggested, Clwyd employed a radical public zeal, notably with regard to News International and News Corporation, which associated her approach more with the remnants of the Labour new left. Although by this stage others in the party had little input in policy development, an indication of the direction taken was that Clwyd brought in the CPBF's Mike Jempson as an adviser. She may have clashed with Jempson on policy, but she was close to the CPBF and relied on it as a "think tank", according to one prominent activist.[94]

Clwyd followed the party's conference policy and rejected calls to weaken rules on cross-media ownership. If anything, she intended to strengthen them to challenge oligopoly – a market failure that needed government action to correct. In February 1993 Clwyd publicly told the government to take action against News Corporation's "totally unacceptable concentration of media ownership".[95] Later that year, in renewing calls for the Monopolies and Mergers Commission to hold an inquiry into ownership, she called for a targeting of News Corporation's "insidious monopoly . . . of opinion".[96]

In the early part of Smith's leadership, then, in stark contrast to the situation that later arose under Blair, Labour regarded economic globalization of the press and media as a development that could and should be challenged. So Clwyd slammed Murdoch as "the globetrotter" who "must and will be stopped" after he had publicly boasted that technologically determined globalization would let him overwhelm national media regulations.[97]

Thoroughly Modern Mowlam

However, those associated with the modernizers fought back. They were aware of Smith's aversion to their conception of how to gain Labour representation in the press. They promoted more liberalization in the area of media ownership. Clwyd's attacks on News Corporation had prompted a strong riposte in one of the group's newspapers, *The Sunday Times*. Its political editor, Michael Jones, had arrogantly counselled Smith not to follow Kinnock's "mistake" "in involving his party in a commercial tussle well outside its orbit". Tellingly, he contrasted Clwyd's view with the "struggle for modernity".[98]

Little noticed by other writers, Peter Mandelson, languishing in obscurity on the back benches, put out early feelers towards this new policy direction. In a Commons debate he initiated in July 1983, he demanded a review of broadcasting ownership. Contrary to party policy, he entertained the notion that this could consider further deregulation.[99]

Clwyd subsequently lost her job as shadow minister, ironically, because left MPs did not support her in the elections to the shadow Cabinet. Her position on press policy was not a factor, however.[100] In a move that replicated other shifts towards a more pro-business agenda, she was replaced by a "modernizer" – although it is not clear that Smith understood the direction in which Clwyd's replacement would take party policy. In October 1993 he installed Mo Mowlam in the shadow Heritage post. Although Mowlam, like Clwyd, was from the soft left tradition, she now closely aligned herself with the new right.[101]

The following pattern started emerging more than six months before Blair assumed the leadership in 1994. The Labour front bench vied with the Conservatives as the two parties sought to outdo each other in arguing for liberalization, as part of an emerging accommodation to a particular vision of globalization and a Tory paradigm. Within this framework Mowlam, as a former key player in the business-friendly "prawn cocktail offensive", in particular attempted to ingratiate the party with a series of media conglomerates, of which News Corporation was just the most prominent. As her deputy shadow minister, Robin Corbett, has put it: "Along comes Mo and Mo wants to tear it all up and start again . . . We have to stop being old fashioned, and childish . . . Minimum regulation and that is all we are about."[102] Labour still mentioned the importance of maintaining a diverse press to facilitate democratic debate. But this was, by now, increasingly rhetoric.

On her appointment, Mowlam's determination to start anew made the policy shift more abrupt.[103] The poor communication between successive Labour spokespeople was another factor in the change. According to another insider, they did not pass on information on policy initiatives – an indication, perhaps, of the relatively low importance attached to press and media policy.[104]

Mowlam first called openly for deregulation in November 1993, after facing concerted representations from press companies, which were arguing that globalization had left national regulations outmoded.[105] Rather than opposing a government review to consider deregulation, she took up the modernizers' cudgels in the battle to shift Labour's policy so as to accept this new "reality". At this stage, under Smith, Mowlam was mindful that the change of party policy had not fully occurred. Yet instead of seeing globalization as a process that should and could be challenged, her words reflected New Labour's language, described fascinatingly by the linguistics specialist Norman Fairclough.[106] In this language the market became an independent agent, rather than a human creation that could be regulated by government – a process that others have termed as reification. Mowlam thus told one newspaper that "politicians are not keeping up to speed with changes in the market place. My personal view is that we should have a change of policy."[107]

Mowlam's new line soon extended to calling for less restraint on cross-media ownership. Once the Conservative government's deregulation review was in place in January 1994, the discussion switched to newspaper proprietors owning broadcasting companies. Newspaper businesses, through the British Media Industry Group (BMIG), had been campaigning for the Conservatives' 1990 Broadcasting Act 20 per cent cross-ownership rule to be altered.[108] Labour had previously opposed the act as leading to "dangerous concentration" by allowing any cross-ownership.[109] Now, along with successfully lobbying the Conservative government, the BMIG also used the review to lobby Labour.[110] It used the language of an all-conquering globalization and a multimedia revolution to argue that it needed greater access to TV ownership to expand, in order to survive. The companies saw it as unfair that Murdoch could indulge in satellite TV cross-ownership while they could not do likewise with terrestrial television.[111]

Yet, along with the danger to diversity, cross-ownership potentially threatened public service broadcasting and led to cross-promotion. Commercial television's takeover by proprietors who were used to influencing the political direction of reporting and by editorial staff schooled in this tradition would, at least, provide a potential challenge to ITV's practice of public service balance.

A key ally of Labour's marketing strategists, Clive Hollick, also called for the cross-ownership rules to be liberalized.[112] And under the combined pressure of the Conservatives' influence on the political climate, the new understanding of globalization and the newspaper businesses' demands that this dictated a fresh course, Mowlam followed suit.[113] At first, she said she feared that a deal would be struck between the Conservatives and press businesses to end the 20 per cent rule. And within days, as if to pre-empt this, she made those fears a reality for Labour. Without reference to any agreed Labour conference policy, she decided that the 20 per cent rule was "irrational" and had to be changed. At first, she said that she did not know what the new figure would be, and she disputed claims that media groups needed to be bigger to compete internationally.[114] However, her scepticism about expansion soon faded.

The party leadership took its business-friendly neo-liberal deregulatory approach a step further forward at the 21st Century Media Conference, presided over by Mowlam in July 1994, just prior to Blair becoming leader. Media campaigners had originally proposed this event. Yet, rather than organizing a party gathering to which outside speakers would be invited, which would reflect Labour's traditional alliances in media reform, Mowlam organized a conference for media business to tell the Labour leadership what it should do. A participant from one of Labour's traditional allies considered that the conference represented "the very clear statement that New Labour was going onto a corporate media agenda".[115] A more blunt assessment of its role comes from Mowlam's deputy, Robin Corbett. He said: "We had a great bloody conference . . . which some media moguls paid for . . . And that was it really. It [the media policy] just went out of the door after that."[116]

When Mowlam was questioned over this before her untimely death, she denied that she had wanted to loosen the ownership rules.[117] However, the facts speak for themselves. Mowlam had taken on board the liberalizing message from the newspaper owners.[118] Before and at the conference she argued that "some loosening of cross-media restrictions" was "inevitable".[119] Again, as in other areas at the time, Mowlam invoked globalization as a justification for deregulation. She regarded liberalization as part of as an unstoppable "media revolution". And again in line with wider thinking, she also thought that globalization could be managed in order to bring benefits.[120]

Mowlam added: "I was doing nothing to add to Murdoch's strength. It was the furthest thing from my mind."[121] Yet again the reality was different. As we have seen, the relaxation of controls on cross-ownership would benefit News Corporation and BMIG, because the existing regulations barred them from having a stake in terrestrial TV, which analysts increasingly saw them as craving.[122] It was certainly the case, by this stage, that the policy commitment developed by Clwyd to challenge News Corporation's existing ownership had evaporated.[123] Labour's former bogeyman, along with other media businesses, was starting to be accommodated. One conference witness reported that a News Corporation representative even thanked the organizers for the opportunity to influence party policy.[124] By this time high-spending media conglomerate lobbyists seemingly had Labour's ear. As Mike Jempson views it: "She [Mowlam] may well not have realised it, but . . . the significant thing, I suppose, was that it [Labour] was saying: 'We're listening to you'."[125]

Nonetheless, nothing was decided formally at this stage. The Labour movement strongly opposed this new line, but the leadership ignored the wider party and flouted its decisions. The TUC and socialists outside the Labour Party rejected the new trajectory.[126] A section of Labour MPs, including Chris Mullin, Ann Clwyd and Denis MacShane, demonstrated these concerns when they brought the Media (Diversity) Private Member's Bill to the Commons in January 1995. It aimed to enforce press diversity by barring any national newspaper proprietor from owning more than one daily or Sunday title, again restricting ownership rather than providing for new titles. It also called for the 20 per cent rule to apply also to satellite TV ownership, which would have led to News Corporation having to sell part of its empire.[127]

What other accounts have downplayed was that the 1994 Labour Party conference also opposed the new neo-liberal line. The first conference with Tony Blair as leader overwhelmingly backed a motion calling for the party to oppose any moves to deregulate the media industry further. Indeed a succession of speakers called on Labour to commit itself to diversifying the oligopolistic press: "proper newspaper regulation . . . to break up the monopolies", as one delegate put it. Mowlam dutifully pledged to the conference to act against further deregulation[128] – and then the Labour front bench promptly ignored her commitment. The extent to which deregulation would be encouraged, rather than opposed, while considering newspaper business interests and invoking the issue of economic globalization, will be key to the next chapter.

7

Living with the Enemy
Press Policy under Tony Blair

As we saw in Chapter 6, in 1993 the Labour shadow ministers briefly responsible for press ownership policy, Ann Clwyd and Robin Cook, considered that "Murdoch's empire" should be curbed by law.[1] Nine years later, the two Labour ministers responsible for government policy in this area jointly announced a self-avowed deregulatory package that gave the press magnate the opportunity to expand into a hitherto unexploited area – terrestrial television.[2] How did this change come about?

Central to the volte-face in Labour policy was the control Tony Blair had over the party and its members, dating back to well before Labour assumed office. Although there was an appearance of collective participation, Blair withheld power from members and, particularly, activists. Policy was now formally developed by a new body, the National Policy Forum (NPF), which had been instituted by John Smith. The role of the party's conference was "effectively undermined" and the NEC's role "significantly reduced", as one academic relatively well disposed to New Labour put it.[3] The NEC became in fact a largely administrative forum, but the input of the left-of-centre Grassroots Alliance provided a source of debate.[4] Constituencies and unions had relatively little representation on the NPF.[5] No resolutions from the constituencies or unions could now be taken directly to the party conference, other than very narrowly defined "contemporary motions".[6] Constituencies primarily operated as non-voting listening-posts, passing any proposal on to the largely unaccountable forum, where there was "no way of tracking what happened to the idea", as Labour's general secretary eventually admitted. Motions from these forums would not be amendable at the party's conference. With little opportunity to influence policy, after an initial surge following Blair's election as Labour leader, party membership halved to the lowest level since the 1930s.[7]

Instead, Labour's strategy was often developed by "policy entrepreneurs" in prominent think tanks.[8] We saw in Chapter 5 that the Labour leadership eventually attempted to fill the intellectual void formed when the study groups closed down by creating the Policy Review. Later Blair "privatized" policy creation, as Margaret Thatcher had done before him, using think tanks such as Demos, which included many of the stalwarts of *Marxism Today*.

Industrial Policy under Blair

As Labour leader, Blair adopted more noticeably pro-market policies than Neil Kinnock.[9] His leadership team expunged the last vestiges of Keynesianism, demand management and planning from party economic policy.[10] The market accommodation was articulated in the watershed new Clause IV.[11] Previous Labour leaders had combined a pro-market bias with a nagging insistence on regulation. Instead, Blair's administration promised from the start that, as it was "business, not government, that creates lasting prosperity", any "unnecessary outdated regulation" would be junked.[12] New Labour married this anti-regulatory assault to a supply-side economic approach. Just after entering government it demonstrated this in its battles alongside right-of-centre parties in the EU against demand-led macroeconomic policies.[13]

Behind the shift from mixed-market pragmatism – notwithstanding New Labour's slogan of "what counts is what works" – was a particular reaction to radical right neo-liberalism.[14] Philip Gould advised Blair, after the latter became party leader, that he faced "Conservative hegemony" and that New Labour needed to be rebuilt "completely from the ground up".[15] The shift was not as fundamental as this. Yet Richard Heffernan convincingly argues that, simply put, Thatcher had developed a new paradigm and the Labour leadership progressively came to accept it. New Labour viewed that the party had "lost" the 1980s and thus decided to follow the Conservatives, who were said to have "won" that decade.[16] There was "an acceptance of the economic legacy of Thatcherism", as the neo-liberal *Economist* crowingly put it.[17]

The view that globalization was inevitable, as discussed in the last chapter, fitted neatly with some Thatcherite diktats that the Labour leadership had progressively accepted as its election defeats mounted up. The new right's particular analysis of globalization acted as an impersonal justification for the course Labour had taken and a way of deflecting blame from the Labour leadership for accepting that neo-liberal path. Globalization was used to justify shifts in such areas as business regulation, taxation and market liberalization.[18] New Labour effectively constructed "neo-liberalism itself as a given and irreversible fact of life".[19] As Peter Mandelson latterly put it, "globalization punishes hard any country that tries to run its economy by ignoring the realities of the market or prudent public finances. In this strictly narrow sense . . . we are all 'Thatcherite' now."[20]

This is not to say that there were not policy differences between New Labour and the Conservative Party.[21] (Nor did the shift happen as incrementally as this summary narrative suggests.) What New Labour grandly termed the "Third Way" – between undiluted neo-liberalism and Keynesian corporatism – also involved an emphasis on supply-side measures, for instance with "New Deal" employment initiatives. A communitarian influence, imported from Bill Clinton's advisers, on crime and welfare policies provided the call that rights should be matched by responsibilities.[22]

Other features of New Labour's consideration of globalization also marked it out from pure Thatcherite neo-liberalism. The new right leadership, at least at first, saw that minimal government intervention could manage globalization to bring benefits, for example, by improving education in a globalized economy.[23] Also, some of the widely held hopes of non-Conservatives on domestic policy, dashed in Labour's first term, were realized to a small degree in the government's second term, as spending increased significantly from 2001.

But overwhelmingly, in economic and industrial policy, there was a sense of a political "ground broken and reset", first and primarily by Thatcher and then by John Major, towards which Labour gravitated, in the face of the Conservatives' repeated electoral success.[24] Going beyond a Downesian model, which sees that electors influence parties, and on from Patrick Dunleavy's description that parties influence electors, Richard Heffernan recognizes that parties can influence one another.[25] One legacy of this was that, despite Labour's welfare spending, research showed that "overall income inequality was greater at the start of the twenty-first century than any time in the last fifty years" – and wealth was more unequally distributed than income.[26]

However, implicitly New Labour had left some small room for movement, even within the globalization "strait-jacket". The "hyperglobalist" thesis sees self-sufficiency and sovereign power as having withered away.[27] New Labour has tended to alternate between this view and that of the transformationalists – those who make no claims regarding the future direction of globalization. Indeed, part of the slippage of New Labour's approach to globalization was explicitly to state that globalization had happened, was inevitable and was following a set direction, while at the same time implicitly recognizing that the process was indeterminate and still taking place.[28] Thus, New Labour appeared to accept implicitly that government could have some influence on the direction of the process.

Press Policy under Blair: Globalization Shaped by Representation

How have Labour's policy developments generally shaped its press policy? New Labour accepted a neo-liberal globalization agenda, the logic of which would bring its views more into line with press business demands for freedom from regulation. It justified this as promoting international competitiveness. However, there were still choices as to how closely to co-operate with the newspaper companies. The particularity of New Labour's press alignment may be coincidence but looks suspiciously like collaboration, resulting from its concern to prevent a repetition of Neil Kinnock's mauling by the press. New Labour still considered the press as a potential enemy. In fact, one senior government spin doctor revealed that those at the centre of New Labour regarded it as its main foe, above and beyond the Conservatives.[29] Whatever the accuracy of that assessment, rather than legislate to create a positive press, Press Secretary Alastair Campbell led an offensive strategy to neutralize or create allies of those elements of the press that had attacked Kinnock, while Labour strengthened the hand of the press conglomerates, as we shall see.

Labour's bid to market itself in the press also benefited from the leadership's general economic strategy. Support for Blair did not hold the dangers of the past for the hierarchies of traditionally Conservative newspapers. In addition, New Labour's politics could appeal to the different layers of the press workforce. One disillusioned modernizer, Bryan Gould, describes those, found markedly in the national media, who wanted a party that could "salve their consciences . . . without threatening the comfortable privilege which they enjoyed and expected".[30]

The broadsheets' reporting of Blair was similar to their initial treatment of Kinnock. The difference was that Blair's press honeymoon was far lengthier. Another key difference was that Blair was more naturally in tune with the instincts of the press and media agenda. Unlike Kinnock, who had to adapt, to some extent unsuccessfully, Blair was at ease with the sound-bite culture.

However, a most significant change from the pre-Smith days was the targeting of the tabloid press. Alastair Campbell, whose background was on the tabloids and who had worked on the latterly defunct News International title *Today*, provided a vital link and became the central figure in the new media strategy. From the time he became Blair's press secretary Campbell superseded Peter Mandelson as the central figure in Labour's media strategy.[31]

Now *The Sun* was in Labour's sights. In Kinnock's time Mandelson had considered the broadsheets as the primary target, in order to set the agenda for the all-important broadcasters. Campbell accurately saw that the tabloids also helped set the agenda for broadcast journalists.[32] In addition, as we have seen, Kinnock had believed that "it was *The Sun* wot won it". Academic research by Martin Linton, a journalist who had been involved in the communications study group and was to become a Blair-sympathizing MP, gave important support for this view. The tabloids had influenced sufficient voters.[33] Whether or not Linton's was an accurate assessment, it confirmed the judgment of Blair and Campbell. Their view was that the Labour Party needed the support of the tabloid newspapers, and particularly *The Sun*, if it was to be elected – even if Cherie Blair allegedly would not allow the paper in the house.[34] Subsequently, *The Sun* and the other News International titles were given preferential treatment, such as in its briefings by Labour, for instance on the 2001 election date in *The Sun*, on Robin Cook's marriage breakdown in the *News of the World* and with the particularly extensive briefing by special advisers in *The Times*, while reporters from other newspapers were attacked.[35] Former BBC political correspondent and media commentator Nicholas Jones and Labour political marketing expert Dominic Wring have outlined Campbell's "robust news management techniques" after Labour gained office.[36]

Marketing Labour: Meeting Mr Murdoch

If this was Labour's new press strategy, it helps explain why the formerly Conservative-supporting newspapers, particularly those belonging to News International, softened their support for the Tories and edged closer to Labour. The former *Marxism Today* editor Martin Jacques attributes this development to class dealignment.[37] His argument, however, which is similar to that used by New Labour to explain the party's previous electoral defeats, would have more validity if the press organizations had not been, at the same time, engaging in crude "class war" tactics by derecognizing the main journalist union.[38]

A more convincing explanation is that, as we saw, New Labour consciously wooed those newspapers as part of a bid to achieve a fairer press, and this was reciprocated. The idea of structurally changing the newspaper market was part of a past to which New Labour did not wish to return.

Murdoch's motives for supporting Blair, however, can only be inferred.[39] Murdoch appears have made both a political and a business decision. A deeply committed right-wing advocate, Murdoch has shown himself to be tactically adroit – he "covered political bases", as he told one interviewer, to advance his business interests.[40] He had let some of his papers support a British Labour government in the 1970s and also the Australian Labor Party – before withdrawing support for both.[41] In Britain in the 1990s Murdoch first became hostile to the Conservative leadership – and then came to find Blair attractive. He told close confidants that Major was "useless and finished".[42] *The Sun*, which the then *Sunday Times* editor Andrew Neil described as "Murdoch's mouthpiece", made clear its opposition to Major's government, wailing: "What fools we were to believe this lot."[43]

The feeling was mutual. Major had felt the newspapers' wrath after the ERM débâcle in 1992, and he loathed press intrusion – having "built up no immunity", according to his biographer.[44] What is more, according to one confidant, he had specific reasons for this hostility, to do with his personal life.[45] Major was said to have vowed: "If I had a majority of a hundred and fifty, I would crush Rupert Murdoch."[46]

This may have been an idle threat, but Major made sure that those close to Murdoch were aware that he was considering legislation.[47] His Conservative predecessor, Stanley Baldwin, with the help of his speech-writer and cousin-in-law Rudyard Kipling, had famously railed in the 1930s against those who had "power without responsibility".[48] Now Major contemplated a law similar to that which the Labour Party had considered previously – a nationality clause for the ownership of titles.[49] He was said to have revealed: "It would have been much worse if the others had had their way in the Cabinet. They want to close some of his newspapers immediately." Indeed, Conservative ministers were privately castigating foreign newspaper owners – using "Bennite" language, according to one journalist.[50] Major and Murdoch's mutual antagonism was exemplified and amplified by the proposals for newspaper owners and cross-ownership contained in the government's Broadcasting Bill.

Box 7.1: The Market, Murdoch, Focus Groups and Democracy

New Labour's fêting of the tabloids has been described by one press commentator as an aspect of "a ruling ideology of élite populism".[51] More specifically, Blair appealed to Murdoch's business élite, market populist outlook, which styled itself as opposite to a "liberal Establishment élite".[52] Imported from US business thinking by writers who would become Blair's advisers, this conception, when theorized, saw the entrepreneur as representing the people's will, expressed through demand and supply. Borrowing from Hayek, it was pitted against "élitist" social democratic-style regulation and demands for economic democracy.[53]

However, the market populist view – the idea of one dollar, one vote – was plutocracy, not democracy. People voted for neither Rupert Murdoch nor Bill Gates. Also, the view that dumping regulation motored prosperity was exposed by the 2001 stock market falls in the USA, which highlighted the demand for intervention.[54]

Nevertheless, market-place techniques, when applied to politics, were also seen to provide "democratization". The view was not only that, rather than trying to democratize business, government should be pro-business, but also that democracy should learn from the market by updating political communications strategies, as discussed in Chapter 6.The use of such strategies was part of "the demise in the faith of the efficacy of representative democracy", a notion made famous by Mandelson and applied equally to the use of focus groups, polling and other PR-based techniques, as "part of a necessary dialogue between politicians and people".[55] As is well known, both the qualitative and quantitative polling techniques identified in Chapter 6 were operated by the Blair leadership.

The techniques were part of a strategy that led to further party centralization. While disagreeing about much, Peter Mair and Anthony Barnett concur that New Labour attempted to provide a "partyless democracy". There was an attempt to eliminate intra-party dissent.The party as a level of mediation between government and citizen was dispensed with. The strategy was undemocratic in the sense that the potential for intra-party choice and debate was done away with.[56]

Instead, market research methods were used, in part, to target New Labour's disproportionately indulged constituency: the floating voters – those "aspirational" voters in marginals of the south-east, west midlands and north-west. Those ignored included blue-collar workers, the public sector workforce, trade union members and the poor.[57]

Voters were seen as individual marketized consumers. Moreover, the focus group technique had been employed since earlier on in the twentieth century by PR agencies and advertisers to unmask unconscious desires, which could then be satiated. People were encouraged not to talk rationally in the groups organized by political strategists, but to discuss their feelings.[58]

New Labour saw the use of focus groups as a triumph for a new form of democracy and the end of élitist politics. However, what was being offered was not a democratic process. In encouraging these "unelected and unaccountable groups of individuals"[59] to express their "maze of contradictory desires",[60] they were not giving people the chance to provide their own rationally and consciously developed alternatives and to select between them. Instead, the focus group staff interpreted the deliberately undeveloped desires. Equally, as Bob Franklin makes clear, through its news management techniques Labour was shaping the information on which these focus groups were forming their ideas.[61] This mode of consultation, rather than decision-making, had echoes in what was now happening in the local Labour Party policy forums.

Globalization Shaped by Representation: The Broadcasting Bill and Labour

In 1995, following corporate lobbying from the British Media Industry Group, the Conservative government announced that it would liberalize cross-ownership rules to bring them more into line with general policy on competition. Yet this was to be achieved in a way that would exclude News Corporation and the Mirror Group. The Conservative government's 1995 White Paper opened the way for newspaper groups with under 20 per cent of national newspaper circulation to wholly own as many television channels as they wanted – up to 15 per cent of the entire television market. The government justified this move on the grounds of the inevitable rush of technologically determined globalization and convergence.[62] The Labour front bench turned its back on the party's conference policy and followed suit with Chris Smith, who had taken over from Mowlam as Shadow Heritage Secretary, in supporting the White Paper.

The proposal left Murdoch in a "furious rage", however, since News Corporation, as well as the Mirror Group, was left out in the cold – unable to expand into terrestrial TV because of the size of its newspaper holdings.[63] An insider tells that Murdoch was also influenced by the fact that the Major government was investigating News Corporation's monopolization of digital set-top boxes. Despite lobbying from Murdoch personally and others, Major refused to budge.[64]

Blair saw a gap in the "political market" and exploited it. He and his coterie had had meetings with Murdoch on his trips to London, as insiders have revealed.[65] The best-known illustration of this rapprochement was Blair's attendance at the News Corporation Leadership Conference on Hayman Island in July 1995. In this, the parallels between how New Labour and the Australian Labor Party treated Murdoch, as has been explored by Julianne Schultz, were striking.[66] Blair was said to have become close to the Australian Labor leader, Paul Keating.[67] Significantly, Blair chose this island conference to make one of his most important speeches embracing globalization. One of the consequences of going with the grain of globalization, he told the corporation's top executives, was that press and media legislation would aim to facilitate an "open and competitive media market".[68]

If going with the grain of globalization was important and wooing Murdoch was seen to be significant, then there was an overwhelming pressure to downplay press ownership policy considerations such as diversity. New Labour MP Martin Linton admits a "price has been paid" to gain press business support, in that Labour will not "take any action about the press itself".[69] Campbell's former deputy in the No. 10 press office, Lance Price, suggests that the government viewed Murdoch as an ally, whose policies were not generally to be challenged.[70]

Murdoch and New Labour developed an "understanding", as Andrew Neil described it[71] – one of non-aggression "to take account of what the other's reaction would be", as Linton puts it.[72] Former News Corporation employee Campbell was a conduit, providing a link with the organization's top brass.[73] Later examples of the "understanding" in government, according to Campbell's former No. 2, were that News International's people understood that, on the euro, New Labour wouldn't "make any changes without asking them". Blair was also very anxious to keep Murdoch on board when BSkyB bid to buy Manchester United Football Club. Other sources have suggested that Tory-inspired cuts to single parent benefits in 1997 were backed by Campbell, who allegedly feared their rejection would attract *The Sun*'s wrath.[74]

In contrast to Major, the Labour hierarchy briefed that it would not seek to break up News Corporation's holdings. Blair was quoted in 1995 as saying: "It is not a question of Murdoch being too powerful."[75] And later that year Labour's deputy leader John Prescott slapped down Shadow Competitiveness and Regulation Minister Richard Caborn when he called for BSkyB's pay-TV monopoly to be investigated.[76]

When the Conservative government published the 1995 Broadcasting Bill, the Labour leadership progressed from playing catch-up, by agreeing to loosen the cross-ownership rules, to engaging in leapfrog, by arguing for the complete scrapping of the laws.[77] In taking this stance, the Labour leadership was defining press and media policy in terms of its general competition strategy, as the Conservatives had done.[78] Yet, unlike Labour, the Conservatives explicitly justified having a separate 20 per cent rule in order to protect diversity.[79]

New Labour's justification cited globalization and international competitiveness. The new Shadow Heritage Minister, Jack Cunningham, argued that cross-ownership regulation impeded such companies as News International – now regarded as British – from being able to compete in the globalized market, where other media companies were getting larger. The nationalist objection to News International under Kinnock had been turned on its head. Nor did size – and implicitly market dominance – matter as much. As Labour's press and broadcasting spokesman, Lewis Moonie, who had attempted to amend the Conservative legislation in committee, put it: "There is nothing intrinsically wrong with big companies. There are lots of nasty small ones."[80]

But what is also interesting, compared with later, was that the shadow minister involved, Jack Cunningham, went beyond globalization in explaining the move and also invoked the question of Labour's press support. Cunningham did not refer to News Corporation, which Labour now supported in its bid to buy into terrestrial TV. Instead, he justified ditching cross-ownership legislation by pointing to the Mirror Group. Cunningham complained that "the government's friends are being looked after in the legislation, and the single newspaper that supports Labour is being excluded".[81] If it were just concerns about the Mirror Group that motivated the policy shift, then it would remain true that diversity across the media was being sacrificed in the attempt to market Labour. However, the Mirror Group was already "on board" with Labour. What was novel was Labour's "understanding" with News Corporation, which welcomed Cunningham's initiative.[82]

Another indication that the Labour front bench was going further than simply catching up with the Conservatives in accepting neo-liberal deregulation was that two right-wing Tories resigned from the government to support the Labour position. Despite this pressure to remove the controls, the Major government stood its ground and the amendment was lost.[83]

Socialists inside and outside the Labour Party challenged New Labour's neo-liberal volte-face. One of those outside the party, Paul Foot, saw that it gave increased power to the media owners, which could be used against Labour.[84] More importantly, a number of Labour backbenchers broke ranks to support amendments opposing New Labour's deregulatory thrust.[85] An amendment proposed by Chris Mullin and Austin Mitchell, in a shift from the latter's previous standpoint, aimed to bar all newspapers with more than 10 per cent of the market from being able to buy into television. This, the "rebels" noted, would exclude all companies owning tabloid titles from TV ownership.[86] Mitchell pointed to fears that importing newspaper values into broadcasting could threaten TV balance and lead to cross promotion.[87] While Mullin obliquely reflected that Murdoch's hand was behind Labour's latest move, the other parties' members explicitly talked of "pay-back" after the Hayman Island trip.[88] More than 70 members of the House supported the Labour backbenchers' motion. But both the amendments of Mullin and Mitchell and those of the Labour front bench were defeated.[89]

The Effect of the "Understanding"?

The "understanding" between Blair and Murdoch did appear to bear fruit in terms of press coverage for New Labour. Alastair Campbell provided privileged access to News Corporation's papers.[90] At the same time, Labour's coverage in *The Sun* shifted perceptibly, while *The Times* also became less hostile. Blair's by-line appeared on numerous articles, some written by his staff, in the newspapers of News Corporation and other groups – to such an extent that Blair was even named freelance of the year in 1999.[91] The day after Blair had written an article in *The Sun* characterizing himself as the defender of Britain's national identity, and with Major having called the 1997 election, came the announcement that "*The Sun* backs Blair". The wording was telling. As the paper's editor said later: "[W]e had reservations about the rest of the party." The paper was backing a Labour victory within its own neo-liberal terms.[92] A number of senior *Sun* journalists were shocked and initially hostile, providing an indication that the decision was one made by senior management.[93] The surprise was not confined to newsrooms. One prominent Labour supporter, rock musician Paul Weller, who had been part of the party's 1980s' youth initiative Red Wedge, spoke for many bewildered, but not necessarily hostile, party members and trade unionists when he said: "It was like in Orwell's *1984* – one minute everyone's told to hate some country and the next day they're the allies again and it's the other lot you're supposed to hate."[94]

By the time of the 1997 election Labour had the support of as many tabloids as broadsheets.[95] For the first time in living memory more than 8 million voters were reading a Labour-supporting title. This well outshone the explicitly Conservative-supporting titles' 4.5 million voters.[96] There was also a huge disparity among the Sunday papers.[97] And even Conservative-supporting papers' management showed less hostility to Labour than in the past.[98]

Whether Labour needed to shift its position on newspaper cross-ownership to achieve *The Sun*'s backing is open to question. According to the diaries of one confidant, Lord Wyatt, Murdoch's close adviser Irwin Stelzer identified two reasons for Murdoch's *rapprochement* with Labour – his anger with the Major government and his fear of being on the losing side.[99] It was in News Corporation's business interests to be with the winners.[100] *The Sun*'s editor thought that not to do so would be "a complete nightmare".[101] Note that he was not even implicitly claiming credit for the Labour victory. He was more concerned that Labour might well have won without him and his paper.

Labour in Office: Press Ownership and Cross-ownership Policies While Maintaining Newspaper Support

Three interrelated factors helped guide Labour Party press ownership policy on entering government. First, the new government had accepted a particular conception of globalization. Second, Labour was concerned to merge press policy with competition policy, in line with EU policy. Third, while concerned to maintain newspaper support, its thinking on these issues was shaped by lobbying from press and media organizations intent on continued expansion. At times the Labour government explicitly acknowledged this guidance. It moved closer to the large press and media companies' stance of regulation and away from that of Labour's former allies – the party-aligned and trade union campaigners for media plurality. Diversity continued to have a low priority. All of these pressures were on display in the debate concerning predatory pricing.

War! The Competition Bill

A long-running battle between newspapers had been launched in 1993 over the sum of 15p – the amount News International had cut from the price of *The Times*.[102] Under John Smith, Labour front-benchers had consistently called for an investigation into this, as competitors accused the company of "predatory pricing": selling the paper below cost price. Yet the Office of Fair Trading (OFT) examined the issue three times and found no basis on which to act.[103]

In office Labour introduced the Competition Bill in 1997.[104] Labour MPs were among those demanding that the bill be amended in the light of the OFT investigations. They felt the government was not acting on concerns it had had when in opposition about the need to protect press diversity's special requirements. Yet the Labour front bench dismissed these demands.

On this and a number of non-media issues opposition to the government united left MPs with several members of the House of Lords. Lord Borrie was a party member, a Labour adviser on competition policy and a former Director-General of Fair Trading. Lord Tom McNally was the former head of the political office at No. 10 under James Callaghan and now a Lib Dem peer. Together they introduced amendments to the bill, aimed at strengthening provisions to curb predatory pricing.[105] Yet New Labour argued that the amendments were unworkable and unnecessary. It was "wrong in principle" to treat the press differently from any other commodity.[106]

Labour MPs backed similar amendments tabled in July 1998, which were defeated. The Europeanist and New Labour loyalist Giles Radice was one of those who expressed concerns at the time about the influence on British politics of News Corporation, whose chair, Murdoch, it was subsequently revealed, had had dinner at No. 10 the month before.[107] Yet one of the few Labour backbenchers vocally to back the government, media activist Austin Mitchell, again argued that obtaining a fairer press for Labour was more important than an "explosion of impotent anger against Rupert Murdoch".[108] The government defeated the amendments more narrowly in the Lords, with some notable Labour figures still defying it.[109]

At first glance subsequent events appeared to bear out New Labour's stand regarding the amendments. Peter Humphreys' sophisticated review of New Labour's media policies notes that a later, fourth inquiry by the OFT in 1999 found *The Times* guilty of deliberately cutting prices to affect competition – predatory pricing.[110] The Labour government's claim that the rules were tight enough to snare News International abuse seemed therefore to be justified. However, the reprimand for this was a minimal "slap on the wrist" – in contrast to the action taken over a far smaller-scale local title accused of a similar practice.[111] OFT director John Bridgeman decided merely to put News International "on notice", arguing that the predatory pricing scheme had stopped.[112]

In retrospect we can see that the basis of the amendments from Mullin and the Lords was wrong in a formal sense. Despite his expertise in the area, Lord Borrie was inaccurate in his assessment that the government's bill would be ineffectual against *The Times*. And Mullin followed Borrie's line. However, in attempting to amend the bill, they kept up the pressure on the OFT to confront News International, and so an important dynamic was uncovered.[113] The government refused to directly target News International, which was indeed later found to be engaged in predatory pricing. This indicated New Labour's concern to bring press law in line with general competition law, as well as its timidity in challenging, in the name of diversity, its new potential ally in marketing Labour – a view expressed by Labour MPs.[114] The minimal reprimand handed out by the OFT to News International for predatory pricing may also have been an indication of this tentativeness.

Cross-ownership Policies and Press Diversity

Alongside the move to converge with general competition law, as considered in this chapter and the preceding one, New Labour's perception of economic globalization was another factor influencing press ownership policy, as illustrated by the pre-election media and arts document *Create the Future* and the 1997 election manifesto. The manifesto contained little specifically on the press, and only one paragraph on the media as a whole. Yet it insisted that globalization dictated deregulation – reflecting "the realities of a far more open and competitive economy, and enormous technological advance".[115]

The Department of Culture, Media and Sport (DCMS) was created in 1997 and, as if to prove this industrial profit-driven approach and the link with general competition law, started working closely with the Department of Trade and Industry (DTI). Thus, in 1998 the DTI and DCMS together launched the Green Paper *Regulating Communications*. At this stage Labour rejected complete convergence with general competition law and cross-media deregulation.[116] Yet it pushed the argument that a reduction in press diversity was an inevitable consequence of globalization. It used the determinist language that we have noted before, attaching as little importance to subjective choice as the most crude Marxist economism does.[117] New Labour said that there were no options about how the economy would develop – there was a wave of globalization, and the government's role was to make sure the British economy surfed it.

This perspective was consistent with other non-media government policies. But press and media companies were also pressurizing the government to go yet further in distancing itself from Labour Party policy on diversity. The government's response to the consultation on its Green Paper on ownership was *The Way Ahead*, which made no mention of the need for cross-ownership rules at all. Instead, the DTI and DCMS emphasized that general competition law would be enough to stop abuses.[118] The Labour government paper made clear that a factor in forming this conclusion was that respondents – a large majority of which were individual press and media companies, industry bodies or regulators – had "accepted" this shift. Yet again the government expressed this move as an objective process of market forces – neither it nor media businesses were agents in this process. Contrary to the experience of increased concentration in the media industry, there was a need to expunge "unnecessary regulation".[119]

Deregulation went a step further with the December 2000 White Paper *A New Future for Communications*, which proposed a new industry regulator, the Office of Communications, known as OFCOM. The White Paper's promotion of markets, competition policy and regulatory reform replicated the Labour government's general approach to industrial policy mentioned at the start of this chapter.[120] New Labour had a tentative and vague position on cross-ownership at this time. However, the White Paper opened up the possibility of further liberalization and "a lighter touch" for newspaper mergers.[121]

Labour's 2001 manifesto mentioned nothing about media ownership itself. However, its business manifesto vowed that it would bring in communication reforms that would remove "the archaic regulations that are slowing the pace of innovation and change".[122] Possibly coincidentally, the election saw the press businesses, and particularly News International, provide Labour with new levels of support. Labour's then director of communications, Lance Price, has revealed that Blair secretly met Murdoch prior to the election and was assured of his backing once again.[123] In the 2001 election, *The Times* followed *The Sun* and supported the party for the first time. Following on from the argument its tabloid sister paper had used four years previously, *The Times* suggested that New Labour had entrenched some core Thatcherite tenets.[124] Although *The Sun* had wobbled in its support during Labour's first term, at times calling Blair "the most dangerous man in Britain" and the Cabinet the most arrogant in history, it still backed the Labour leadership when it came to the crunch.[125] And the *Express* newspapers also temporarily came on board (see Box 7.2). By then, seven of the ten national daily newspapers and six of the Sundays supported Labour. In terms of circulation, 72 per cent of the voters by then read a pro-Labour title, while an astonishingly meagre 7.8 per cent read a Conservative-supporting paper.[126]

Box 7.2: The Curious Cases of Lord Hollick and Richard Desmond

Media focus on New Labour and the *Express* newspapers has concerned the pornographer Richard Desmond, who first supported and then abandoned Labour. Media historians have characterized Desmond as the key architect of the traditionally Conservative titles' short-lived realignment with New Labour.[127] However, the *Express* titles' previous proprietor, Lord Hollick, was perhaps more pivotal, providing a potential challenge to the traditional problem of bipolarization and Labour representation (see Chapter 1).

Hollick was a Labour insider. The founder and trustee of the Labour think tank the Institute of Public Policy Research, he was a central figure in Labour's 1992 election campaign. In February 1996 Hollick's company, MAI, merged with United News and Media, which owned the *Express* newspapers' owners, headed by the Tory peer Lord Stevens. Later that year, after a period with the two politically antagonistic managers in charge, Stevens took a back-seat role.[128]

Following Labour's 1997 election victory, Hollick became a government special adviser on regulation and competition.[129] The *Daily Express*'s editor, Richard Addis, shifted the paper's stance to back Labour, calling the government a new "conservative" administration.[130] Yet Hollick soon replaced him with Rosie Boycott. Insiders suggest that Hollick wanted to entrench the paper's support for New Labour and use it to increase his political influence.[131]

Formerly, Labour had denounced the ability of press management to influence political debate. Now, with their own management insider, they became involved in changing a newspaper's direction to influence the political discourse. Alastair Campbell advised on the appointment of the *Daily Express*'s political editor. Also, New Labour adviser Derek Draper wrote a column that he said was vetted by Peter Mandelson. And the *Express* titles sponsored Labour information packs.[132]

There was perceived to be a business logic to this move, although this was questioned.[133] The mandate given to Boycott was for the papers to go "upmarket, to make them appeal to a younger, progressive audience", and by implication a New Labour readership.[134] Past Labour readers were too poor and old for advertisers. The niche market of New Labour's core supporters, by contrast, could be seen to attract advertising, as they were part of the social strata that Bryan Gould had described (see p. 113). The *Express* titles were explicitly aimed at readers who were both aspirational and campaigning – wanting "social justice which provides opportunity".[135]

However, by 2000 the *Daily Express*'s line had abruptly changed again – displaying the media barons' power, albeit in a curious way. As the paper's deputy editor explained later, Hollick's ambitions to become a major media player had been scuppered by a Competition Commission broadcasting decision, and Hollick lost interest in the titles.[136] The government competition adviser believed that New Labour had not rewarded him for his efforts.[137] This gave Boycott free rein to attack a government that she was to the left of.[138] It also made Hollick open to offers for the titles, which were sold to Richard Desmond in November 2000.

A potential dilemma for New Labour was that Desmond owned a range of pornographic magazines – which angered a sizeable section of the party. Senior Labour MPs wanted the takeover to be referred to the Competition Commission on the same public interest grounds that had stopped pornographer David Sullivan gaining control of the *Bristol Evening Post* a decade earlier.[139] Trade and industry secretary Stephen Byers refused, and shortly afterwards Desmond's company donated £100,000 to Labour Party coffers.[140] Under his ownership the *Express* titles supported New Labour, before turning against it once again.

The Communications Bill: 'The Most Significant Legislation on the Media in Nearly 50 Years'[141]

Following Labour's re-election another chain of events took place, reflecting News International's potential influence. In October 2001 the government used a newspaper industry function to launch a consultation paper on media ownership, which presented the option, among others, that cross-media limits be repealed.[142] Respondents included News International and the Campaign for Press and Broadcasting Freedom (CPBF).[143] And the following month, Rupert Murdoch publicly threatened to withdraw his support for the Blair government after a potential set-back to BSkyB.[144]

After Murdoch reminded Labour that his support was conditional, when the draft Communications Bill finally arrived in May 2002, important new provisions were included, which had not been previously discussed by the government in its long consultation over media reform – and thus had been addressed only briefly by the campaign organizations that had submitted responses. Yet these provisions had been prominently championed by News Corporation.[145] In the end, although the draft bill did cover a much broader range of issues than national press ownership and cross-ownership,[146] in these areas it was strongly deregulatory, again going well beyond Conservative policy.[147]

On cross-ownership, the draft bill moved towards policy that the Blair leadership had pioneered from the mid-1990s – that restrictions should be completely removed, except for those imposed by general competition law.[148] The 20 per cent rule was to be scrapped for ownership of the terrestrial TV channel Five (sometimes known as Channel Five).[149] This would open the possibility of a complete takeover by any of the large newspaper groups, most notably, the largest: News Corporation. Despite government protestations, this became widely known as the Murdoch clause. The 20 per cent rule would still apply to ITV.[150] When asked, the justification put forward for this discrepancy by the minister co-piloting the legislation, the Secretary of State for Culture, Media and Sport, Tessa Jowell, was that Five had fewer public service obligations and was not a universal service, and that ownership was not an issue. She rejected claims that News Corporation was being given preferential treatment – the government was "proprietor-neutral". However, Jowell was wilfully missing the point. By treating all businesses equally, the government was also potentially aiding News Corporation, as well as the owners of *The Mirror* and the *Daily Mail*, as Jowell herself admitted.[151]

The self-avowed deregulatory proposals would increase newspaper cross-ownership in national and local radio as well. Importantly, the Labour government explicitly justified this as aiding press and media businesses. Again the proposals went beyond the former Conservative government's position.[152] The previous government's 1995 legislation had allowed only those newspaper groups with less than 20 per cent of the press market to acquire a percentage of the radio market. The new proposals said that those groups with more than 20 per cent of the national newspaper market could now own radio stations. (The original stipulation in the draft proposals was that there needed to be at least two other commercial broadcasters, as well as the BBC, reaching more than 50 per cent of the adult population in the radio station's area.[153] After further media business lobbying this was reduced to two commercial stations in total.[154])

Labour's 2002 Communications Bill also provided for the possibility that the new overseer of this legislation, OFCOM, would review the legislation every three years.[155] The process was thus laid open to the spectre of constant lobbying. But more importantly it represented a significant democratic shortfall, as the government acknowledged. Despite this, it saw fit to ensure that Parliament would not have the final say over such important legislative reviews.

Initial opposition to the bill among Labour ranks did not concentrate on the question of cross-ownership, even though this had been a theme of the critique introduced by leading opponents outside the House, such as Professor Steven Barnett. He feared that it would be undesirable to give as much power to Murdoch even if he was a version of "Mother Teresa and the son of God rolled into one".[156] Former Sky presenter Austin Mitchell, who had sung News Corporation's praises in the past, even when the Labour leadership was hostile, was among MPs and Lords who had problems with the bill, some of whom initially saw "the Murdoch question" as a "red herring".[157] The NUJ, which again was among leading opponents of the legislation, initially shared this assessment.[158] Labour movement critics attached more importance to provisions in the bill to increase international ownership of broadcasting and on broadcasting content regulation. This was to change.

New Labour's attempt to railroad the legislation on newspaper business ownership of Five hit a potential obstacle. Among the 148 recommendations made by a joint committee of MPs and peers, headed by Lord Puttnam, was the suggestion that the government defer plans to allow press groups, including News Corporation, further access to Five.[159] The committee, half of whom were Labour MPs and peers, divided on this question. Only one Labour MP, Brian White, sided with a Conservative member to back the government's plans for Five. Those Labour MPs with professional experience backed the committee majority. Paul Farrelly had been a senior national newspaper journalist and John Grogan had worked as a Labour Party press officer.[160] The latter appears to have become radicalized by this experience and started organizing amendments to the draft bill. As a result, by the end of 2002 opposition to the bill, at least among the unions, shifted significantly, as we shall see in a moment.

Despite this, the Department of Culture, Media and Sport (DCMS) rejected most of the committee's major recommendations, even before they were published. According to newspaper reports, the government announced that the provisions were "not tentative proposals, they were decisions" – making a mockery of the legislation's description as a "draft bill".[161]

Opposition in the Labour Movement

For a long period, New Labour's strategy on press representation was regarded as successful. Its media liberalization trajectory faced relatively little effective resistance internally. As we have indicated, MPs and peers voiced some opposition, which delayed, but did not derail, legislation. As Curran and Seaton note, part of the reason for the weakness of opposition was the decline of the media unions, which we outlined previously.[162] And, as we have seen, no groups aside from the leadership had much organizational influence on Labour Party policy.

Thus the media unions had to rely on the TUC's relative collective strength. Yet, although the TUC was now generally frozen out of policymaking, the little pressure which it could have placed on the leadership on press diversity was repeatedly not exercised – a point which has been underplayed. The TUC general council made only a limited attempt to honour its commitment to campaign for diversity.

Union attempts to change press ownership policies and set up a Labour movement title had "run their course", according to the former head of the TUC's Press and Information Department.[163] One reason was that the TUC was paralleling the party by concentrating on getting better representation for itself, rather than following the media unions' demands to concentrate on attempting to increase diversity. The TUC's strategy was to engage with the existing press rather than challenge it. As Aeron Davis's work makes clear, the unions generally had shifted from a position of supporting alternative newspapers as a key demand, to professionalizing their PR operations – "a policy of accommodation rather than structural reform", as one union representative and media academic put it.[164] As mentioned, one reason for this collapse of enthusiasm for creating press diversity may have been the demise of the *News on Sunday*. Sizeable parts of the trade union leadership felt they had wasted large sums of money and wanted nothing to do with any similar project – "most people thought it was like a dear friend that had died: 'Don't talk about it'".[165] The demoralization, as one senior media official said, strengthened the union leaders' conviction that they were not "interested at all in running their own media" and so concentrated on improving their coverage in the mainstream press.[166] So, although the media unions demanded that the TUC challenge Labour, with motions overwhelmingly agreed to conduct a large-scale campaign against Labour's cross-media ownership proposals at the 1996 and 1998 conferences, action never materialized.[167] This was despite general secretary John Monks's vow concerning News Corporation – "to take on this juggernaut which is running through so many parts of British life".[168] Media activists saw attempts to resurrect the resolutions "stonewalled".[169] According to Mike Smith, head of the TUC Secretariat, the TUC saw itself as playing a limited role as it had other priorities and few resources.[170]

However, small pockets of resistance to this view appeared in some media unions, notably in the NUJ and the broadcasting union BECTU. As we have seen, the NUJ was at the forefront of opposition to the draft Communications Act. It attempted to mobilize dissent among other unions.[171] The tenor of its disagreement subtly changed during the act's passage. Although broadcasting content and defence of public service broadcasting were still priorities, its opposition to the changes on ownership regulation strengthened.[172]

With this pressure, the TUC again overwhelmingly passed a motion at its 2002 congress, proposed by Equity and seconded by the NUJ, that spoke of fear concerning further media concentration. It opposed relaxing ownership rules – at least until reciprocal legislation was adopted in other countries.[173] But again, action was limited.

Despite the act's importance, no motion was taken on it at the 2002

Labour Party conference, for reasons that were procedural as much as directly political. It was unlikely that the conference could have taken a contemporary motion on the bill because of how such resolutions were narrowly defined. And Labour's National Policy Forum had not timetabled a discussion on the media to be taken at the conference, which is the other route such a motion could have taken.[174] Such was the relatively low priority given by party activists to media reform by this stage, it is not clear that it would have been selected as one of the four contemporary resolutions allowed in any case. Nevertheless, this absence of debate on the bill also indicated traditional activists' demoralization over new Labour Party procedures and, in particular, the difficulty in getting motions taken that were not deemed contemporary. Instead, as we shall see in the next and concluding chapter, the most effective influence from non-business civil society on the Communications Act came not from the Labour movement but from NGO campaigners.

8

Epilogue and Concluding Remarks

How Did We Get Here?

Epilogue: The 2003 Communications Act and its Aftermath

This government, and previous ones, should have learnt from the experience of News International over the last 30 years that, if you do not please them, you can be out of office at the next election. Too much power in the hands of a few can influence the outcome of elections and indeed government policy, regardless of democracy. Allowing further concentration of the press would only be putting further power into the hands of those who already have a disproportionate influence on the electorate of this country.[1] (*Daily Telegraph* owners, the Barclay brothers, 2004)

The billionaire newspaper owners the Barclay brothers highlight here the tension that Labour faced in the period covered in this book, even if the assessment of News International's influence on elections is again debatable. While the party leadership was trying to stay on good terms with those who already had press power, some within the party saw it as a democratic imperative to maintain a plurality of the press that many noted was traditionally hostile rather than friendly.

When what became the 2003 Communications Act was presented as a bill in November 2002, there was no direct modification of the draft rules on newspaper business ownership of Five and on foreign ownership. And as we saw, the government allowed more extensive newspaper business ownership of radio.[2] This left the Labour peer David Puttnam complaining that policy-makers assumed, in what he referred to as the battle of "shareholder values in contrast to democratic values", that there was "God-given supremacy of the market-place". The former film producer ruefully argued that: "You cannot expect the government to tackle Murdoch when it needs the support of his newspapers."[3]

As if to prove the point, Labour had shifted its position on national newspaper policy since its first term. Peter Humphreys suggested in 2000 that at that time the government's press policy hardly differed from that of the Conservatives.[4] However, reports that assumed there was little in the Communications Bill exclusively related to the press were not true – either for the bill or the act.[5]

Once again Labour went beyond Conservative catch-up, explicitly justifying this move in terms of the need to appease press owners. In the act the special merger regime – the minimal monopoly provisions that came in with the 1973 Fair Trading Act – was scrapped, as News Corporation, for one, had prominently demanded.[6] No longer would a minister automatically have to intervene to give prior approval for any merger in which the newspapers involved had a total paid-for daily circulation of 500,000 or more. It is true that the 1973 act had been ineffective. Yet, rather than arguing that the rules should be more rigidly adhered to, or that issues of international concentration should be considered, the fact that few mergers had been rejected under the law was used to justify taking the act off the statute book. Indeed, the government explicitly rationalized the move on the basis that the "rules, and the uncertainty and costs they create, are disliked both by newspaper proprietors and by regulators".[7] The act imposed "unnecessary burdens both on business and on the authorities".[8] The government appeared less concerned in this assessment with the position of readers, citizens and ordinary journalists than with the "proprietors" and regulators.

In place of the Fair Trading Act, there was a fine example of New Labour's penchant for harmonizing press law with rules on competition, while deliberately addressing the concerns of media enterprises.[9] The takeover law would be subsumed under a new system for non-media mergers that was introduced in the Government's 2002 Enterprise Act. In other words, newspaper mergers would be treated in the same way as any other, based on a competition test. Just like any other company, from one producing oil tankers to one selling toilet rolls, if the new company has more than 25 per cent of the market or increased its share beyond that level, or alternatively if the UK turnover of the company being taken over was more than £70m, then it would be assessed by the competition authorities. If one of the companies already had 25 per cent of a market and the takeover did not increase this, the competition test would not apply.[10]

Again, the watering down of press ownership legislation was seen as technologically determined and rationalized in terms of the need to increase international investment. It was suggested that "developments in technology and the desire to promote a more competitive communications industry that will attract greater investment have encouraged the deregulation of the industry".[11] The fact that multinational companies had been active in demanding these changes was not emphasized.

However, challenging this, Lord Puttnam led a cross-party alliance of

Lords, including some associated with New Labour, such as Melvyn Bragg, who were concerned about the removal of the cross-media ownership rules applying to Five. In June 2003 the peers by a large majority secured an amendment insisting that OFCOM's "principal duty" was to look after citizens' interests.[12] The amendment was backed by the lobbying of Public Voice, a coalition formed during the gestation of the act, representing the voluntary sector and citizen media groups.

When it looked as though the Lords' persistent support for Puttnam's concerns about cross-ownership of Five and foreign ownership could delay the act's passage through Parliament, the Labour government eventually persuaded Puttnam to compromise. At the third reading of the bill in July 2003 the government introduced a "public interest" clause for media takeovers to head off the Lords' revolt. This was supported by Puttnam and agreed by Parliament.

The public interest clause had been included in the original Enterprise Act. It was to be enacted if there was concern that issues of national security might be involved when two companies merged.[13] So the DTI explained that the public interest clause would provide some protection and continuity of assessment, "while lifting much of the regulatory burden on the industry".[14]

With the new clause, the only difference for newspapers above and beyond the standard set for all company mergers was that in "special merger situations" a public interest consideration could also apply and the Minister of Trade and Industry could intervene. Along with other mergers that increased ownership to 25 per cent and beyond, this would apply when one of the companies involved in the merger already had more than a quarter of the UK newspaper or broadcasting market. The minister might also intervene if it was more indeterminately considered there was a risk to the "accurate presentation of news", "free expression of opinion" and "sufficient plurality of views in newspapers in each market", albeit "to the extent that it is reasonable and practicable". There would, nevertheless, be no automatic compulsion on ministers, now committed to a "lighter touch", to call for an inquiry.[15]

Any takeover of a newspaper by News International would already have fallen under the jurisdiction of the Enterprise Act because it would have increased its newspapers' share of the market above its existing figure of more than 25 per cent. But because the new legislation also affected cross-ownership of newspapers and broadcasting, the DTI could now intervene over a cross-ownership merger. But it need not necessarily refuse a company, such as News Corporation, which had more than 25 per cent of newspapers, from taking over the terrestrial broadcaster Five. More about this later, when we look at the discussions on this issue that took place.

Of course, in a situation involving the national press, the Secretary of State would be under intense pressure from a range of sources, not least citizen group campaigners, to conduct a comprehensive inquiry. However, it is still important to note that the decision would be hers or his.[16] Thus, a public interest test and a case-by-case approach, while a significant achievement by campaigners, would still face profound difficulties regarding the power of ministers to decide on newspaper ownership based on political or corporate partisanship. It would replicate the problems of previous newspaper and cross-ownership limits. The new regime would be still particularly susceptible to narrowly politically motivated government decision-making. It has evolved, as we know, under the auspices of a Labour administration that has shown itself to be much more open to corporate lobbying.

If it was considered that the clause applied, a merger would be referred to the OFT and then to OFCOM, which, after public consultation, would produce a report on public considerations for the Secretary of State, with recommendations. In providing advice, OFCOM would seek to obtain information from the company on its operation, for example on the relationship between owners and editors and the "likely level of involvement of proprietors in editorial decisions". The company would also have to provide the "opinions of all newspapers, and details of personal editorial contributions to newspapers", staffing levels and how the company would ensure accuracy in news presentation. The company's history as an employer would also be considered. However, it would be up to the minister alone to decide on an appropriate course of action, such as the appointment of an editorial board. And indeed, the guidance produced by the DTI in May 2004 recognized the subjective element here.[17]

The public interest clause did provide some continuity with the old system. The DTI pointed out in its guidance that previous public interest regulations were the basis on which the pornographer David Sullivan had been barred from owning the *Bristol Evening Post* (see Chapter 7).[18] Nevertheless, after the alarm was publicly raised over "state control" of the press, the press companies voiced their concerns when the proposed provisions came up for consultation with both OFCOM and the DTI.[19]

OFCOM's website lists ten responses to its consultation held in 2004. A possible indication of how narrowly this process was promoted among citizens' groups and the wider community, including those who had called for the public interest test in the first place, was that all the responses were from lobbyists, newspaper groups or industry organizations. Included were two from News International, as well as Trinity Mirror, the regional owners' group, The Newspaper Society and the Daily Mail General Trust's regional newspaper group, Northcliffe Newspapers. Another similar consultation by the DTI did, nonetheless, include contributions from unions and the CPBF.[20]

News International complained that OFCOM had been formed from authorities with no previous experience of newspaper regulation. It considered that bringing the DTI's previous advisory role into OFCOM set a "dangerous precedent". It wanted assurances to allay "the newspaper industry's concerns about regulatory creep". It was concerned at the "enormous detail and volume of information" that OFCOM was to require in the event of a merger.[21] Trinity Mirror also described the information required as "excessive".[22]

Following these protests, OFCOM saw a system akin to newspaper self-regulation as the answer. It looked as though OFCOM might have to give its first advice on a national newspaper takeover when the *Telegraph* papers were offered for sale in 2004. Rather than considering broadening popular democratic involvement, it announced in May that year that a panel of former newspaper editors and company executives, along with some academics, would advise the trade minister over this and possible future mergers. OFCOM argued that this answered industry concerns that it did not have enough in-house expertise.[23]

Nevertheless, it would still be up to the minister alone to decide whether there was a public interest consideration involving any press or cross-ownership merger. This offered an opportunity for the Labour government to reduce plurality of press ownership to aid its political preferment. These political considerations were in the minds of some of those involved in the takeover of the *Telegraph* newspapers. Thus the political editor of the *Daily Telegraph*, George Jones, was quoted as describing the Barclay brothers as a "more acceptable owner to the government than possibly Richard Desmond or Associated Newspapers", owners of the *Daily Mail*. Despite the Labour government spending years trying to woo the title, the *Daily Mail* had become more hostile, and the antipathy was mutual. And indeed before purchasing the *Telegraph* newspapers in June 2004 the notoriously private Barclay brothers themselves publicly reminded the government that they were not hostile existing newspaper owners, as we saw at the start of this chapter.[24]

At the start of 2005 another twist to the saga of the 2003 Communications Act was revealed. It was uncovered that News Corporation's representatives had met with government officials six times during the bill's passage through parliament to engage in behind-the-scenes lobbying. Just prior to the insertion of the public interest clause, a high-level delegation met with the Culture Secretary, Tessa Jowell, to be reassured that "there was no intention" that a duty to maintain plurality in the act "could be used to block a merger". Jowell had been told by government officials that it was understood that OFCOM would "not be able to block mergers by virtue of this duty, nor [would] it be able to make a 'U-turn' on the Channel Five ownership policy. In other words, it will not be allowed to reinstate the ownership rules preventing Channel Five licences to be held by newspaper proprietors."[25]

Indeed, the documents reveal that the government and News

Corporation agreed that the act amounted to a "significant deregulation" of the rules on newspaper ownership. Jowell wrote to the executive chair of News International, Les Hinton, to express her pleasure that they were agreed on this point. Before offering another meeting to discuss any concerns, she reassured him that: "We don't think that the involvement of both OFT and OFCOM in merger decisions should be too onerous."[26]

After the secret talks had been revealed, Lord Puttnam was quoted as wondering whether he "was naive and being manipulated" to withdraw his objection to a national newspaper company owning Five, before agreeing to the public interest compromise. He said he had been convinced "to back off because I was persuaded that there had been no discussions whatsoever with any national newspaper group". [27]

Yet the public interest clause that he had agreed with the government had not yet been tested by 2005. As for OFCOM, its position was explained by its chair, David Currie. In May 2005 he addressed the Newspaper Society, telling the regional press owners' organization that OFCOM operated with a "bias against intervention" and that he was "somewhat closer to those who want regulation out of the way".[28]

Overall, the impact that media business lobbyists had in the passage of Labour's Communication Act is clear. The Labour and trade union movement, however, had little visible input. Des Freedman's research into the views of a range of policy-making participants showed that, despite the seemingly broad range of people involved in developing policy, decisions were actually taken by a tight group consisting of government members, advisers and civil servants. It was driven by a handful of figures in Downing Street, particularly Ed Richards in the No. 10 Policy Directorate. There was a far more welcoming environment for lobbyists who wanted to effect change by emphasizing their affinity with the ideological position of the policy-makers. To be taken seriously, pressure groups needed to be seen to make a practical contribution to the debate and thus accept the ideological parameters within which the debate was conducted – that is, to accept neo-liberal and business assumptions.[29] As we saw, even on the public interest test, when civil society campaigners managed to have an impact, it was carefully circumscribed by the government within a framework that was deregulatory and influenced by industry lobbying.

Also, voluntary sector campaigners with less formal connection to the Labour movement had greater influence on the act than those in the Labour Party and the trade unions. In other words here, as in other arenas, links to the Labour movement could well be an actual hindrance to winning the ear of this Labour government. In the meantime, the state of internal Labour Party democracy, as measured by membership levels and involvement, was at a historic low. And while these momentous decisions – with long-term implications for the future of wider democracy – were taking place, there was a paucity of debate within the party, with no scrutiny of the policy.

Overall, New Labour had gone even further than previous Conservative regimes dared in relaxing ownership rules. The Communications Act represented the failure of the hopes of generations of media activists inside and outside the Labour Party who had put their faith in a Labour government to deliver communications diversity.

Concluding Remarks

Rupert Murdoch is one of those in the industry who, along with many commentators, have highlighted the fact that national newspapers find themselves increasingly under serious challenge from new media. However, the rise of the new media does not diminish the historical importance of the press and, therefore, press policy – in Labour politics and in government. It is striking that James Curran, who was a Labour Party member for many years, treats the struggle for a diverse and democratic press and media within the party sympathetically but rather pessimistically.[30] Yet Des Freedman, who declares himself to be a socialist outside the Labour Party and cites a series of left authors openly dismissive of Labour left currents, is pleasantly surprised by the breadth of internal radical discussion on broadcasting.[31] While the glass is more than half empty for Curran, it is its content that has also interested Freedman.

This book has taken the latter emphasis when it comes to press policy. For myriad reasons, it is clear that the glass is at a very low level. The history of the Labour Party in this period operates like an eye reading a line in a newspaper – it goes from left to right. More recent calls for a press advertising tax, for instance, seem to be a product of a different age.[32] In the context of the last thirty years, and from a normative policy-making perspective, Curran is acutely aware of his own sense of failure as he plays down, in an unnecessarily self-effacing way, his own pioneering work. One factor in this – the crushing of the optimism felt when Labour came into power in 1997 – has contributed to a sense of the whole policy-making enterprise being unreasonably diminished however.

To minimize the importance of debates on improving the press in the development of Labour Party thought can give the wrong impression. It can mistakenly leave the reader fitting this historical sweep into the same partial perspective as *New Media, New Policies*, which reduces Labour Party discussion on the media before New Labour to Labour's 1974 policy document *The People and the Media* and two pages in the 1991 *Arts and the Media* pamphlet.[33]

Leo Panitch's and Colin Leys's significant work on the Labour Party attempts to recover its history from the revisionism that saw New Labour triumphing over an undifferentiated "Old Labour" of Dennis Healey and Tony Benn or, in our more defined arena, Gerald Kaufman and James

Curran.[34] In an extremely modest sense this book has tried to contribute to this body of contemporary historical work – noting the profound problems with the new left solutions but also the quiescence of the Old Labour right and New Labour's neo-liberal reality.

Promoting Labour and the Evolution of Press Diversity Policy

The relationship between newspaper ownership diversity and the Labour Party's concern to promote itself in the press has been a constant theme of this book. (The press and media models discussed in Chapter 1 are useful for facilitating analysis of this.) The first major discussion in the party on the media in 1972 was a response to perceived press hostility, particularly directed towards the trade unions. And even while the communications study group was deliberating, the public debate at the time, for example in *Labour Weekly*, justified the need for change in order to create a specifically Labour press, rather than a more diverse one.

To advance diversity, *The People and the Media* policy document reflected the tension between a Scandinavian-style interventionist model and a public service conception of the press. The methods of intervention it envisaged reflected a social market interventionist model, as advocated by some from the new left tradition, such as, notably, the academic Curran, who were most interested in directly diversifying the newspaper market. Yet Tony Benn, for example, insisted that the document should describe itself as being in the public service tradition. And most trade unionists on the group were primarily concerned with the issue of securing more positive press coverage of the Labour movement – an idea that fitted in better with a public service conception, which wanted to balance the press.

The tension between the social democratic and new left traditions and between concerns to promote Labour, on the one hand, and increase press ownership diversity, on the other, should not be overstated. Those involved were not necessarily even aware of it at this stage. Yet the tension was real and continued with the Royal Commission on the Press, initiated by the 1974 Labour government. In order to guarantee greater press diversity, the Labour Party had made a series of proposals including the setting up of an Advertising Revenue Board, which though far more interventionist, had its origins in the Scandinavian social market model. Nevertheless, the emphasis of party officials reporting to the royal commission and the Labour government itself was more on creating a Labour press than on developing a diverse one. The original concern of the Labour government had been also to improve press coverage. The 1974 commission had been set up by Harold Wilson in part as a response to the end of his long press honeymoon. The Labour administration's reluctance to support interventionist policies meant it eventually rejected all the proposals from its party and those contained in the Minority Report. In contrast, the Labour Party officials supported intervention, but they also emphasized to the royal commission that their aim of changing the structure of the market was in order to provide "fairer" newspaper coverage. However, the problem with that aim was that the effect of the schemes would have been solely to increase diversity. They might have enhanced Labour movement representation, but they wouldn't have had a predictable political outcome.[35] The schemes would not have guaranteed anything like political parity in terms of press coverage.

For that to happen, there needed to be some sort of control of the newspapers, which could have either come through state control from above – as in the public service model – or it could have come from below through participation in the newspapers' control. Alternatively, there could have been a combination of both. Work was attempted on developing the first approach after Labour left office in 1979. The proposals developed by Michael Meacher and Chris Mullin for an Independent Press Authority (IPA) were in the public service tradition and eventually became party policy, although they did not make it into the manifesto. Meacher and Mullin went beyond "broad-brush" attempts to achieve diversity to trying to obtain balance and thus representation of Labour and the left. In having done so, they are among the few currently serving politicians to have thought seriously about challenging the idea of the media being controlled by just a few companies. But their efforts indicated the huge problems of attempting to achieve balance in the press and reflected difficulties inherent in the public service model's positive view of employing the state's coercive force.

Perhaps a less problematic solution, concentrating on press ownership diversity, came with the Open Press Authority concept, which reflected the Scandinavian social market model but had already been discarded by the time of the 1983 election. The 1983 manifesto commitment was nevertheless a sea-change from that of four years earlier. Its anti-monopoly law went beyond the liberal pluralist model, while its commitment to a launch fund was a policy transfer from Scandinavian-style social democracy.

After Labour's defeat in 1983, and given the part that newspapers were perceived to have played in it, the emphasis in this last radical phase was again on correcting bias and achieving balance as much as on diversity. The Labour conference again put its faith in the flawed public service model IPA. Yet, the collapse of the *News on Sunday* dealt a huge blow to attempts to provide a Labour movement voice in the press with some influence from the movement itself. One consequence was that some unions became less enthusiastic about promoting Labour through structural change of the newspaper market.

As intervention to restructure the market became politically unacceptable, many of those who were concerned about how Labour was reported in the press sought other attractive solutions to the problem of anti-Labour bias. Aeron Davis has considered how the unions concentrated on political communications to deal with problem.[36] More importantly, the Labour leadership had made a similar assessment. One by-product of the new media strategy was a renewed pressure to seek press business approval – to avoid upsetting the apple cart by bringing forward proposals for structural change. Backbenchers had already advised Neil Kinnock that Labour's case would be advanced if it accommodated News Corporation's demands over cross-media ownership. In the retreat from interventionist policies on press ownership, we are entering the difficult territory considered by writers such as Steven Lukes, where the agenda now avoided consideration of various press ownership options – something not apparent even to some of those involved.[37] But, as the higher echelons of the party abandoned interventionism in other areas, at least after 1987, they placed less emphasis on structural change of the newspaper market and much more on political marketing.

The demand for active intervention in the press market was not just some left fetish. As this book has indicated, measures that merely restricted existing ownership could well lead to papers being shuffled around between existing companies. Worse still, jettisoned newspapers could go to the wall. Such proposals would need to be accompanied by some sort of launch body for new publications, which itself would need to be guaranteed independence from the state and democratic legitimacy, going beyond appointed representatives. Nevertheless, it is a sign of how far Labour has departed from previous discussions on diversity that within party circles such measures now seem Utopian, outlandish, impossible and even dangerous.

Labour thinkers had grappled with the problem, for democratic expression, of newspapers operating in a dual market; this heavily disadvantages lower-income readers, who are less attractive to advertisers. However, there is no way of redistributing advertising revenue that does not have potential problems that will need to be dealt with over time. The answers that Curran advocated in the 1980s – to impose a levy on all advertising to finance new publications, or more recently to fund such a press from the National Lottery – seem appealing.[38]

However, these forms of redistribution would not directly deal with bifurcation. Titles financed by such a levy would still face the problem of seeking advertising revenue, while a levy placed on papers charging high advertising rates would excite the wrath of companies producing those advertising-subsidized newspapers aimed at higher-income readers. Subsidies would need to be given to lower-income reader newspapers with a strong current affairs content, as Curran suggested.[39] Such a scheme is not acceptable under New Labour's Third Way. Nevertheless, there remains a democratic flaw in a market system that skews press provision against lower-waged readers.

One might have thought that New Labour's Third Way communitarian influence would logically demand that with the rights of press business come responsibilities. Philosopher Onora O'Neil, whose Reith lecture on a similar topic provoked some comment, has argued forcefully that, put simply, a theory of obligations impacts on communications.[40] She argues that accepting the notion of obligations leads to a state commitment to "developing and sustaining institutions" that foster diversity of communication and protect voices faced with the danger of marginalization.[41] This is a concern with which Labour formerly identified itself, notwithstanding its difficulties and contradictions with representation. Yet the New Labour government's interests seem to lie elsewhere.

Third Way advocates have argued that one reason for the decline of traditional social democracy is that its interest in equality was in conflict with policies to create cultural pluralism.[42] Yet there is an irony here. As we have seen, left variants of social democracy, especially the Labour new left, were concerned about cultural diversity and its representation in the press and media. For all the problems regarding its solutions, this part of the left was actively involved in trying to create strategies to provide for plural representation through diverse ownership and increased participation. In contrast, New Labour's "actual existing Third Way" has stripped away some of the few remaining regulations concerning press ownership and cross-ownership. It has allowed for increased domination by fewer multinational corporate players, greater international concentration, less cultural plurality and less diversity of ownership.

Wider Involvement in the Press

So much for the idea that diverse press ownership is needed for democracy. Yet it could be argued that even some powerful advocates of this view have underplayed the role of democratic participation in aiding political democracy. It is true, as has been argued, that no society can guarantee that all communicators can express all possible content in all contexts. Yet, as Onora O'Neil indicates, one justification for state media regulation is that, in its absence, it is unaccountable businesses that will regulate access instead.[43]

For a time, Labour supported legislation to involve those working in the press industry in deciding what was produced. The ways this would work are associated most closely with the new left/neo-Marxist and social market models. As we saw earlier, the broader question of employees' democratic involvement in industry had excited some western European social democratic parties in the 1970s as part of the new left upsurge, and British Labour Party policy had to some extent followed suit. However, in the early 1970s the journalists' union representatives did not share this concern for worker control. The NUJ leadership's position took a view that shared elements of a classical liberal pluralist model. However, this conception was under pressure, notably from the new left Free Communications Group (FCG), which by then was influencing the Labour Party as well as some in the NUJ. One journalist and FCG supporter, Neal Ascherson, used the 1972 communications study group to call for direct forms of newsroom democracy, which echoed the neo-Marxist views of Raymond Williams. Although most of the group supported workers' participation in the press, there was a dissenting social democratic voice. Hence the general statements of intent on participation in *The People and the Media* did not lead to clear policy. While the proposals called for participation, they did not specify how it would be accomplished.

As for broader involvement in press decision-making, going beyond staff democracy, Tom O'Malley considers that the new left, associated with *The People and the Media*, did try to demand more public accountability.[44] However, we saw that here too the communications study group was divided and, although there was a concern to fund newspapers that met a community need, priority was given to industrial democracy.

By the time of the 1974–7 Royal Commission on the Press the Labour Party both publicly and in its policy positions supported staff participation in press decision-making, reflecting the neo-Marxist model. Yet the royal commission Minority Report, which the Labour Party promoted, went further, towards a broader participatory social market or democratic media model. It cautiously considered reader involvement. The Labour government's involvement in the closed shop legislation highlighted potential tensions within new left notions, when it was shown that greater staff involvement could clash with public participation and access.

However, what stymied demands for journalist participation was the Labour government. It shelved both the demands for journalist autonomy made by the royal commission and its Minority Report, which went further than the commission in this respect.

The left's radical challenge to Keynesianism and the democratic upsurge in the party again put press worker control on the agenda at the party conference in 1979. Yet calls did not extend to the broader community and, in any case, this left momentum was relatively short-lived. An attempt to put flesh on this proposal in the party's media study group, which went beyond Raymond Williams's model towards again considering broader community involvement, was scuppered. It faced reluctant media unions, with their maximalist approach, in demanding full workplace control, leading to minimal conclusions. Some MPs were also reluctant to back the proposals because they feared newspaper businesses, whose support they wanted, would resist them.

In the course of the 1980s Labour shifted away from the municipal socialists' approach, reflected in the 1983 conference motion, whose participatory emphasis included reader involvement and fused neo-

Marxist and social market models with a more marketized sensibility. Ken Livingstone's attempt to revive this approach was spurned, with a print union representative spearheading this rejection. The unions instead called for the industrial right of reply, which partly reflected the neo-Marxist model. Eventually party policy concentrated on a legal right of reply. Labour made a last attempt to provide this with the support of the front bench during John Smith's brief period as Labour leader.

The legal right of reply did not necessarily require any restructuring of the press market. One analyst of Labour media policy saw this as an advantage. It would aid public acceptance of the measure.[45] However, Freedman sees it as a retreat.[46] This work has argued that the legislation to guarantee the legal right of reply had a potential difficulty, but not necessarily quite in the way Freedman envisaged. The right of reply went beyond the self-regulation of the Press Council regime, with its "independence from any external accountability beyond the market",[47] but the question mark was over the role of the state. Some of the options Labour policy-makers considered substituted self-regulation for decision-making overseen by state appointees or judges connected to the state, but others looked to broader public or staff participation. Influenced by citizen groups such as the CPBF, these options attempted to seek public accountability rather than direct nationalized state control. They attempted to be representative. But most Labour Party variants followed the social democratic public service tradition in their attachment to the state and were a policy transfer from social democratic governments and those to their right.

The Labour hierarchy eventually abandoned the right of reply. Instead, in government, campaigners clashed with Labour when it attempted to marketize participation in the 2003 Communications Act. In the preamble to the draft version of the bill – the more public face of the bill – the government repeatedly used the term "citizens", indicating an understanding of the particular role of the press and media in democratic debate that we have previously considered. Yet in the bill itself the minimal provisions for democratic representation, a merely advisory panel, was termed the "Consumer Panel" – reflecting the language of customers and consumers – words that appeared more than a hundred times in the bill, while the word "citizen" was used only once.[48] Also, the panel's remit was not intended to include newspapers. As we saw, however, after successful lobbying by campaigners, the Lords amended the proposed legislation to make citizens' interests OFCOM's prime concern, which was reflected in the language of the parts of the Act. This tussle over commercialization reflected a more general trend in New Labour thinking. As one commentator put it: "The increasing marketization of the political system and its evocation of the 'citizen-consumer' have subsequently placed greater emphasis on the value of economic activity as a form of public participation."[49] In other words, the ability of citizens to have a voice had become dependent on their economic power in the press and media market – a forum where, as we have seen, their power is severely limited by factors outside their control.

Policy Changes and Global Shifts

Apart from Labour's renewed emphasis on political communications there were other reasons for these shifts away from more radical models of diversity and democratic control, reflecting the party's general drift to the right with the demise of Keynesianism and the rejection of employee democratic control. Labour was also affected by the general loss of confidence in public intervention following the collapse of the Soviet Union, by union demoralization and by the impact of Thatcherism. New Labour's determination to converge press policy with general competition policy was also in line with EU policy, as has been indicated elsewhere.[50]

However, another key reason for this shift was that the Labour leadership accepted that it needed to go with the grain of globalization, another key influence on the Communications Act. The government's summary of the proposals that would eventually make it into the Communications Act had again talked of globalization as an unstoppable objective process. It implied that globalization was not something that governments actively created or, at the very least, shaped. This objective process, which, seemingly, had no conscious agents, determined legislation. Thus, it was suggested that: "Today's world combines a fast changing consumer environment with an increasingly international and competitive market place ... Unnecessary regulations need to be removed wherever possible."[51]

This ignored the fact that the act's provisions would indeed make the British broadcasting sector more open to takeover by international media conglomerates – potentially allowing Five, for example, to be taken over by a group with a huge newspaper interest. Thus, the legislation would make the British media market potentially far more globalized than before. The government's determinist language also justified an evolving role for the regulator OFCOM, which, as "competition in the media sector increased", would have a brief to deregulate further.[52]

One question is whether globalization of the press and media is a qualitatively new phenomenon. It is true that there has been concentration, conglomeration and internationalization of the British media. It is also the case that technology is eroding traditional market boundaries. The world economy has evolved, one aspect being the liberalization of capital movements. Internationalization and convergence have accelerated. Yet economic internationalization afflicted centre-left left governments before the term "globalization" was ever coined. It grossly constricted the Blum government in France in the 1930s, for example.[53] Subsequently, centre-left governments consciously acted to regulate financial markets, thus challenging this economic liberalization, before Margaret Thatcher and other governments following her example began equally deliberately to deregulate these markets. It was government action, not some automatic process of globalization, as is often implied, that facilitated capital flight. Meanwhile, the Labour left considered the implications of economic internationalization, and the Labour right rejected previous party policy to rein in the City's control over the economy before the right even started discussing globalization.

Similarly, well before globalization was talked of, there was a significant post-war internationalization of British press ownership, as Colin Seymour-Ure points out.[54] And it was precisely concern about the international economy's effect on the press that prompted left media activists to call for government intervention. As in other areas, the idea of globalization, with no agents, was used to justify decisions being made and events already taking place in press and media policy. The commitment to intervention to achieve press diversity was crumbling under Neil Kinnock well before the globalization defence was tacked on as a justification.

If globalization has constricted the room to regulate, as the Labour leadership implied, then it would be regulation in small, open economies such as those of the Scandinavian states that would have been most at threat. As we saw in Chapter 2, those same small, open Scandinavian states have continued to lead the way in social democratic Keynesian-style interventionism to achieve a more diverse press. Such a situation suggests persistent evidence of the importance of national institutions, which goes against some of the wilder globalization claims. It is undeniable that the "Scandinavian/Nordic model" is in retreat. However, the willingness to stand against the tide of globalization has still been greater there than in other European economic powerhouses.[55]

This book has gone beyond arguing that New Labour's press policy has simply been determined by its acceptance of going with the grain of globalization. It has argued as well that, along with the influence of the EU in harmonizing with general competition law, policy was also shaped to appeal to other agents, particularly business interests. New Labour accepted the neo-liberal interpretation of globalization and alternated between, on the one hand, arguing that this was an inevitable process and, on the other, suggesting it could be shaped. Thus we have seen that the New Labour government itself specifically indicated that it had geared some provisions of the Communications Act to deal with the concerns of "the newspaper proprietors", as well as regulators.[56] Aligning itself closely with the interests of certain companies here could have been mere coincidence but has looked suspiciously like collaboration, related to the concern that Labour should be promoted in the press.

Meet the Challenge, Make the Change?

When considering the relationship of readers to newspapers, it is a common belief that the market operates as a democratic tool. The market is seen as the simplest way that readers can "vote" with their pennies and pounds in order to buy a paper that, along with a bundle of other interests, including entertainment and information, best represents either their political positions or their desire to have those positions challenged. Yet some Labour thinkers have seen the market as flawed because of the huge financial barriers to those seeking to enter it and because of the way the advertising market has historically functioned. In this sense, they saw the press as operating in an imperfect market, which requires intervention to create diversity.

There are other senses, however, in which the market approach to analysis of the press and its relationship to democracy are flawed. Money may be a simple instrument to indicate intentions, but it is a blunt one. Readers cannot specify which parts of the bundle or what aspects of the political line of a newspaper they approve of by handing over their coins to a newsagent.

Even more importantly, Labour thinkers considered that the readers are not the only "voters" who can use their money to influence the already flawed market. Newspaper group shareholders and stockholding companies have overwhelmingly more money and power with which they can buy more "votes" and thus potentially affect content. Chapter 1 suggested that the questions of democracy and diversity were interwoven, but to repeat, some saw that diversity of the press was not enough to ensure equality in decision-making. Input by citizens was also seen to be required. To argue merely for Labour representation in the press was to ignore the nature of the organization that was providing the representation and, indeed, what payback media businesses would want in return. It was to call for representative democracy without any way of democratically influencing that representation, as provided by the market. Clearly, this is a contentious question, which encompasses debates such as those regarding whether there is any role for a party press in the twenty-first century, which this book has not considered. However, given the centralization of the party described herein, any call for democratic representation of the Labour Party would need to be allied with a long-term intra-party democratizing project, not least because of the relationship between the party and a Labour government.

Stanley Harrison was being rather simplistic when he wrote in 1974 that a "handful of ultra-wealthy men" commanded the press. Nevertheless, it is true of newspaper businesses and shareholders that "[t]hey submit themselves to no election, acknowledge no control or responsibility, and stand completely outside British democracy".[57] This threat to democracy still exists. As the preceding chapters have demonstrated, New Labour's policies have, if anything, reinforced this threat.

The New Labour MP and media thinker Martin Linton has expressed his fear that press support for Labour may be temporary.[58] With regard to the News Corporation press, the way that *The Sun* turned against Labour in the 1970s reflects this possibility, as does the history of the Australian Labor Party's relationship with News Corporation. Moreover, coverage in the *Telegraph*, *Mail* and *Express* titles in Britain has become more explicitly hostile since 2000. Also, the other side of the coin, Labour's "spin" strategy, partly intended to improve press coverage, has become distinctly frayed at the edges. Although doubts have been cast on the evidence that the spin strategy has undermined politicians' credibility,[59] after a honeymoon period the public fairly rapidly started to indicate their disaffection to pollsters. So by 2000 a poll revealed that a significant majority saw Blair as more concerned with image than issues.[60] Pollsters were seeing spin as "counterproductive".[61] Hostility to spin was also blamed for a dramatic turnaround in how honest and trustworthy the Labour government was seen as being. In 1998 a clear majority saw Labour as honest. Four years later the figure had halved, while nearly two-thirds regarded the government as lacking in trustworthiness.[62] Also the newspapers increased coverage of the spin phenomenon, leading to accusations from the government that the national press was obsessed with the process of government rather than its policies.[63] Although the Labour leadership had also been successful in maintaining the support of the papers it had gained in the 2001 election, bar the Express group, the press's fixation with the spin process was an indication that the majority of newspaper businesses may not always be so supportive of a Labour government.

And this fixation was evident in the period up to and including the 2005 general election, when the Labour government's communication strategy reflected concerns about shoring up its core support. Following the fateful day of 20 March 2003, when Britain invaded Iraq, different considerations have come into play from those that had dominated the previous elections. To improve its press coverage as its natural supporters became more disillusioned, along with trying to cultivate the regional newspapers, Labour also targeted those newspapers that had never been part of the Conservative press. The readers of these papers, such as *The Guardian* and *The Mirror*, were the core Labour voters formerly taken for granted but whose support the party now needed.[64]

Overall, the problem for Labour has not necessarily been solved. Labour could again be faced with an overwhelmingly hostile press. Linton's prediction as to what might happen in this situation may oversimplify the relationship between ownership and control, but it has a ring of truth: "When it does happen, you will still be left with this irreducible problem that you have a press which is owned by four or five people . . .

and they want to push their right-wing agendas in their publications, so far as their readers will put up with them."[65] Crystal ball gazing is a risky business. Yet, in the circumstance Linton describes there may be a pressure in the party to revisit the discarded policies on press ownership. The question would then be whether the liberalization of press and cross-ownership policy had made it much more difficult to put the genie back into the bottle.

It would be easy to conclude from discussion of the problems of spin, and attempts at government interference in reporting, that the last thing that would be required is increased state-sponsored intervention in the press. It could easily be concluded that, if there was intervention, it would be bound to lead to a more quiescent press. Certainly, there would need to be strict independence from direct government interference in any body overseeing intervention. Part of its job might be to monitor and make transparent the role of spin, aggressive news management or, indeed, collusion between the government and the press. Nevertheless, as we saw, the case of Norway shows that tightly specified intervention need not lead to negative political interference in the press. One of the Norwegian government's most historically insistent critics, the leftist daily *Klassekampen*, has existed only because of the subsidy system.[66] This sort of limited government intervention works there. Critics of the present press might ask: why not in Britain?

In summing up media policy, Colin Seymour-Ure argues that no one has successfully put the case "that the need to hold an increasingly integrated media industry accountable to the public through the government was greater than the need to hold the government accountable through the media".[67] However, what this book has shown is that, in the period under consideration, no one successfully developed policy for a Labour government to enact in which forms of press accountability went beyond a social democratic conception to one where this accountability relied less on the state. In failing to do so, legislation got stuck with considering the state and the market as mutually exclusive. Before these issues had been excluded from debate and citizens were reduced to consumers, Labour at least considered these crucial problems for the democratic functioning of society.

Calls for democratization of the mainstream press subsequently diminished. This work has discussed some of the problems, or at least areas of contention, in the models for democratic participation and diverse ownership put forward by those involved in debates in the Labour Party. The problems of these flawed models need to be addressed when deliberating over this important area for the advance of democracy.

Nevertheless, if tested and amended, they might well have proved more broadly democratic than a system where a few conglomerates and a handful of millionaires dominate – to adapt New Labour's famous dictum, where the reading of the many is controlled by the few. There are examples where, in the slow process of policy implementation, problems have been ironed out. The Scandinavian press schemes provide evidence of this in terms of press diversity legislation.[68] There are further examples in other areas in British policy-making.[69]

With policies for broadening democratic input, for instance, it is only through implementation that the power of those such as journalists or pressure groups can be assessed and adjusted. The difficulties of improving the press set out above explain why there were disagreements in the Labour Party over implementing a democratic model that went beyond liberal pluralism. However, the problems and disagreements were not a justification on their own for the failure even to seek to implement such a model.

Notes

Preface

1 Quoted in Schultz, *Fourth Estate*, back cover.
2 Newspaper Publishers' Association, Evidence to the Royal Commission on the Press, 30 November 1976, pp. 14–15.
3 Quoted in David McKie, "'Fact is Free but Comment is Sacred'", in Crewe and Gosschalk, *Political Communications 1992*, pp. 121.
4 Hall, *Change, Choice and Conflict*.
5 James Curran interview, 9 May 2001. James Curran stood for the Cambridge parliamentary seat in 1974. He went on to become an academic advisor to the Royal Commission on the Press, discussed in Chapter 3. Since 1989, he has been Professor of Communications at Goldsmiths College, University of London. He is an author and editor of numerous books on the press. As a journalist, he was founding editor of *New Socialist* from 1981 to 1984 and was a *Times* columnist from 1982 to 1983.
6 Freedman, *Television 2000* and *Television 2001*.

1   Introduction: *Labour's Problems with the Press*

1 Franklin, *Packaging Politics* (1994), pp. 216–17; Harrop, "Voters" in Seaton and Pimlott, *British Politics*, p. 46.
2 Miller, *Media and Voters*, esp. p. 165; Franklin, *Packaging Politics* (1994), pp. 219–20.
3 Negrine, *Politics*, pp. 178; MacArthur, "The National Press" in Crewe and Harrop, *Political Communications 1987*, p. 97.
4 For example, Humphreys, *Western Europe*, and Sanchez-Tabernero and Denton, *Concentration*.
5 For instance, Negrine, *Politics*, and Curran and Seaton, *Power Without Responsibility*.
6 For example, Curran, "Press Reformism", and, to a lesser extent, *Allaun, Spreading the News*.
7 See Minkin, *Labour Party Conference*, p. 318.
8 *Ibid.*, p. xiv.
9 Habermas, *Structural Transformation*, esp. pp. 57–72.
10 Gurevitch and Blumler, "Political Communication Systems and Democratic Values", in Lichtenberg, *Democracy*, pp. 269–89, 270; Street, *Mass Media*, p. 253.
11 See Street, *Mass Media*, p. 258.
12 Arblaster, *Democracy*, pp. 94–6.
13 Meier and Trappel, "Media Concentration", pp. 42–3; Doyle, *Media Ownership*, pp. 11–12, 170–1; Lively, *Democracy*, p. 35.

14 Gurevitch and Blumler, "Democratic Values", in Lichtenberg, *Democracy*, pp. 269–89, 270.
15 See Street, *Mass Media*, pp. 258–9.
16 Doyle, *Media Ownership*, pp. 177. See also Meier and Trappel, "Media Concentration".
17 Entman, *Democracy Without Citizens*.
18 Compaine and Gomery, *Who Owns the Media?*; Compaine, "The Myths of Encroaching Global Media Ownership", 8 November 2001; Benjamin Compaine, "A World Without Absolutes", 9 May 2002, <www.opendemocracy.net>.
19 McCombs, "Concentration, Monopoly and Content", pp. 129–37.
20 Bagdikian, *Media Monopoly*, p. 129.
21 Meier and Trappel, "Media Concentration", pp. 44–5.
22 Doyle, *Media Ownership*, pp. 13, 17, 25.
23 For instance Bagdikian, *New Media Monopoly*; Herman and McChesney, *Global Media*; McChesney, *Corporate Media*; McChesney, *Rich Media*.
24 Meier and Trappel, "Media Concentration", p. 46.
25 See, for instance, Bagdikian, *New Media Monopoly*.
26 Doyle, *Media Ownership*, pp. 13, 18–22.
27 Humphreys, *Western Europe*.
28 Doyle, *Media Ownership*, pp. 13, 18–22, 25, 27–8.
29 Seymour-Ure, "National Press", p. 266.
30 Crosland, *Future of Socialism*, esp. pp. 14–18; Thompson, *Political Economy*, pp. 150–1.
31 Burnham, *Managerial Revolution*, Chapters 6, 7 and 8.
32 Mattick, *Marx and Keynes*, pp. 302–5.
33 Scott, *Corporations, Classes and Capitalism*, Chapter 5 and p. 175.
34 Quoted in Richards, *The Bloody Circus*, p. 3.
35 For the latter, see Chapter 7. For Lord Matthews' own view of his role, see Baistow, *Fourth-Rate Estate*, p. 5.
36 Evidence to the Royal Commission on the Press, submitted by Mirror Group Newspapers Ltd., April 1975, (1) 31.
37 Tunstall, *Newspaper Power*, p. 85 and Chapter 5.
38 *Ibid.*, p. 125.
39 Neil, *Disclosure*, esp. pp. 215–17.
40 See Hastings, *Editor*, esp. pp. 81, 250.
41 Tunstall, *Newspaper Power*, p. 114.
42 Ayerst, *Guardian*.
43 The book does not include the exclusively Scottish titles, the limited-circulation *Morning Star*, the *Daily Sport* and the sports dailies, which have not been regarded as part of the national press (Williams, *Murder a Day*, p. 215).
44 Tulloch, "Managing the Press", pp. 64–5.
45 Doyle, *Understanding*, p. 126. "*Today* and *Sunday Today* were launched with an initial outlay of £22.5 million [rising to £46.5 million]; the *Independent* with an establishment fund of £21 million; the *News on Sunday* with around £6 million; the *Sunday Correspondent* with £18 million; and the *London Daily News* with an outlay of well over £30 million in its first year" (Curran and Seaton, *Power Without Responsibility*, pp. 99–100).

46 Sparks, "Concentration", pp. 179–206; McNair, *News and Journalism*, pp. 161–2, 216–17.

47 Doyle, *Understanding*, pp. 8–9.

48 For Europe see De Bens and Østbye, "The European Newspaper Market" in McQuail and Siune, *Media Policy*, pp. 7–22, 8. For the United States, see Bagdikian, *New Media Monopoly*; Herman and McChesney, *Global Media*; McChesney, *Corporate Media*.

49 Meier and Trappel, "Media Concentration", p. 50. The dominance of the national newspaper market is unusual in Europe (Doyle, *Understanding*, p. 125; Sparks, "The Press", p. 44).

50 See Table 1, Source: Audit Bureau of Circulation, National Newspapers – Audit Period December 2005, <www.abc.org.uk>.

51 Royal Commission on the Press, *Final Report*, pp. 73, 185.

52 Doyle, *Understanding*, pp. 14, 27, 123; Doyle, *Media Ownership*, pp. 38, 59, Collins and Murroni, *New Policies*, p. 8.

53 Doyle, *Understanding*, pp. 9, 126. For reasons why the 'hidden hand' of the market has not effective here see Sparks, "Concentration".

54 Doyle, *Understanding*, pp. 30–33; Doyle, *Media Ownership*, p. 13; Meier and Trappel, "Media Concentration", pp. 41–2.

55 Doyle, *Understanding*, pp. 14–15, 28–9; Doyle, *Media Ownership*, pp. 38–40.

56 Bagdikian, *Media Monopoly*, pp. xii–xiii, 243–4.

57 So specialist business newspaper owner Pearson can provide synergies by exploiting economies of scale and scope across different media products, such as the *Financial Times* newspaper and FT business magazines etc.

58 Bagdikian, *New Media Monopoly*, p. 115.

59 Doyle, *Media Ownership*, pp. 68–72. See also Hesmondhalgh, *Cultural Industries*, p. 141.

60 Doyle, *Understanding*, p. 12; Sparks, "The Press", pp. 51–2.

61 Sparks, "Concentration", p. 192.

62 Sparks, "The Press", p. 53. See also Tunstall, *Newspaper Power*, pp. 12–14.

63 Sparks, "Concentration", pp. 192–7.

64 Doyle, *Understanding*, p. 121.

65 Sparks, "Concentration", pp. 195–7.

66 See Sparks, "The Press", pp. 53–4. A possibly contrary example is that of the *Mirror* in the period leading up to and during the Iraq war. However, the attempt to buck the market trend saw readership levels fall, albeit with rivals facing similar problems (Peter Cole, "Have the 20p tabloids shot themselves in the foot?", *The Guardian* (19 May 2002); Ciar Byrne, "Mirror Sales Hit All-time Low", *The Guardian* (6 September 2002)).

67 Bagdikian, *New Media Monopoly*.

68 Tunstall, *Newspaper Power*, pp. 8–9, 14–17.

69 Sparks, "Concentration", pp. 190–1.

70 It may be true that the *Herald*'s fall in readership was significant, as Negrine suggests. Nevertheless, as Negrine himself writes, it also had the 'wrong' sort of readership (Negrine, *Politics*, pp. 69–70). See also James Curran, "Advertising and the Press", in Curran, *The British Press*, pp. 250–53; Allaun, *Spreading the News*, pp. 20–8.

71 MacBride, *Many Voices One World*, pp. 174, 267. It has also been argued that

the demand for democratic communication was key to the "New World Communication and Information Order", which UNESCO advocated (Hagen, "Democratic Communication", in Wasko and Mosco, *Democratic Communications*, p. 22).

72 Gillmor, *We the Media*.

73 Lively, *Democracy*, p. 35.

74 Hagen, "Democratic Communication", in Wasko and Mosco, *Democratic Communications*, pp. 23, 25–6.

75 MacBride, *Many Voices One World*, pp. 172–4.

76 Hagen, "Democratic Communication", in Wasko and Mosco, *Democratic Communications*, p. 21.

77 Gillmor, *We the Media*.

78 Alastair Campbell, The Internet as Seen by the Technophobe, <discuss.aol.co.uk>.

79 See Curran, *Policy for the Press*.

80 Curran, "Democracy Revisited", pp. 83–98; Curran, "Public Sphere", p. 29.

81 See, for instance, Curran, "Rethinking", pp. 93–4.

82 Bagdikian, *New Media Monopoly*, Curran, "Rethinking", pp. 123–4, also cited in Street, *Mass Media*, p. 262.

83 Curran and Seaton, *Power Without Responsibility*, pp. 72–5, 86–8. See also Neil, *Disclosure*, pp. 27–34.

84 McChesney, *Corporate Media*, pp. 45–6.

85 Street, *Mass Media*, p. 262.

86 McChesney, *Corporate Media*, p. 45; Frank, *One Market Under God*, pp. 86–7, 97, 93, 366–9.

87 See, for instance, Harrison, *Poor Men's Guardians*, Chapter 10, esp. 218, 232.

88 Curran, *Policy for the Press*, p. 1.

89 Curran, "Different Approaches to Media Reform", in Curran, *Bending*, p. 99.

90 Scannell, "Public Service Broadcasting", pp. 25–6; *Tracey, Decline and Fall*, p. 26.

91 Tracey, *Decline and Fall*, pp. 30–1.

92 Scannell, "Public Service Broadcasting", pp. 14–18.

93 Michael Meacher, Reform of the Press, RD 2222, March 1982; Media Study Group, Minutes of the 6th Meeting, 19 January 1981.

94 Keane, *Media and Democracy*, pp. 94–114, 116; Curran, "Public Sphere", p. 48. See also Williams, *Communications*.

95 Keane, *Media and Democracy*, pp. 119–24; Curran, "Public Sphere", p. 48.

96 Williams, *Communications*, p. 170.

97 Baistow, *Fourth-Rate Estate*; Curran and Seaton, *Power Without Responsibility*, pp. 346–7.

98 For a broader argument concerning economism and industrial democracy see Bobbio, *Which Socialism?*, esp. p. 84.

99 Hagen, "Democratic Communication", in Wasko and Mosco, *Democratic Communications*, pp. 18, 25.

100 Pateman, *Participation and Democratic Theory*, p. 29; Hagen, "Democratic Communication", in Wasko and Mosco, *Democratic Communications*, p. 22.

101 Curran, *Policy for the Press, Media and Power*, pp. 13–14; Curran, "Different Approaches", p. 91.

102　Curran, *Media and Power*, pp. 240–47.
103　Curran, "Rethinking", pp. 120–54; Curran, *Media and Power*, pp. 240–7; Street, *Mass Media*, pp. 268–70.
104　Street, *Mass Media*, p. 270.

2　The People and the Press: Party Debates up to 1974

1　Quoted in Thomas, *Newspaper Crisis*, pp. 67–8.
2　Labour Party, *People and the Media*, pp. 24–5.
3　Tunstall, *Newspaper Power*, pp. 380–1; Stephenson, "Tickle the Public", p. 22; Robertson, *People Against the Press*, p. 121; Curran, "Different Approaches", pp. 288, 289; Levy, *Press Council*, pp. 15–16, 405; Curran, *Policy for the Press*, p. 4. See also Humphreys, *Western Europe*, pp. 94–5.
4　Levy, *Press Council*, p. 410; Robertson, *People Against the Press*, p. 121; Tunstall, *Newspaper Power*, pp. 380–1.
5　Tunstall, *Newspaper Power*, pp. 380–1.
6　Tunstall, *Media in Britain*, p. 265.
7　Koss, *Political Press*, p. 667.
8　Wickham-Jones, *Economic*, pp. 34–8.
9　Panitch and Leys, *Parliamentary Socialism*, pp. 1, 5, 19–21.
10　For various assessments of the early British new left see Kenny, *First New Left*; Widgery, "The Double Exposure"; McCann, *Theory and History*; Anderson, *Arguments Within English Marxism*.
11　Panitch and Leys, *Parliamentary Socialism*, pp. 2–4; Wickham-Jones, *Economic*, pp. 42–3; Wickham-Jones, "The New Left", in Plant, *Soul*, p. 25. See also Kenny, *First New Left*, pp. 42, 133–4.
12　Wickham-Jones, *Economic*, pp. 5, 55–9, 61–4, 66–8, 79–80, 126; Thompson, *Political Economy*, pp. 8–9, 219–222, 226, 231, 233; Callaghan, *Retreat*, pp. 58–9. For the argument that operating a national enterprise board was not the same as conventional nationalization see Holland, "Ownership, Planning and Markets", in Plant, *Soul*, pp. 163–86.
13　Thompson, *Political Economy*, pp. 203, 209; Panitch and Leys, *Parliamentary Socialism*, p. 73.
14　Hatfield, *House*, p. 54; Wickham-Jones, *Economic*, pp. 68–9; Thompson, *Political Economy*, p. 207.
15　Wickham-Jones, *Economic*, pp. 69–70, 185–7.
16　Panitch and Leys, *Parliamentary Socialism*, pp. 21–6, 56–9; Thompson, *Political Economy*, pp. 209–12.
17　Panitch and Leys, *Parliamentary Socialism*, pp. 26–38, 66.
18　Wickham-Jones, *Economic*, pp. 118–22.
19　Home Policy Sub-committee Advertising Report, December 1971, Labour Party Research Document RD 201, pp. 52–3, 62–4, 67.
20　Home Policy Committee Note on Communications Meeting, RD370, June 1972; NEC, Minutes of the Home Policy Committees on Communications, 1973–4; O'Malley and Soley, *Press*, p. 72.
21　Curran interview.
22　*Ibid.*
23　Interview with Martin Linton MP, Wednesday 18 July 2001. Linton was a journalist on the *Daily Mail* and *Financial Times*, before joining *Labour Weekly* in 1971. He moved to the *Daily Star* and then *The Guardian*. He became a Labour MP in 1997. He has written on Swedish socialism and in 1995 published *Was It The Sun Wot Won It?*

24 Curran interview.

25 Trades Union Congress, *104th Annual Trades Union Congress*, p. 533.

26 Anon, "Briginshaw Bashes Trade Union Bashers", *Labour Weekly* (11 August 1972).

27 TUC Economic Committee, The Newspaper Industry, 13 December 1972, p. 1.

28 Home Policy Committee Note on Communications Meeting, RD370, June 1972, p. 2. See also Geoffrey Goodman, Quality and Diversity in the Press, RD 651, February 1973, p. 3.

29 Martin Linton, Policies for the Press, RD 536, January 1973, p. 2.

30 Hugh Jenkins, A Framework for a Communications Policy, RD 597, February 1973, p. 1. Hugh Jenkins became Arts Minister in 1974. He was MP for Putney from 1964–79, before becoming a peer (Baron Hugh Jenkins archives, London School of Economics).

31 Curran interview.

32 Anon, "Case for a Labour Press: Where the Dream is a Reality", *Labour Weekly* (30 June 1972). See also Martin Linton, "The Case for a Labour Press"; Bjorn Hansen, "Where Labour Has a Good Press", *Labour Weekly* (9 June 1972).

33 Linton, "The Case for a Labour Press".

34 Home Policy Committee: Communications, RD 324, April 1972, pp. 2–3, 5.

35 Home Policy Committee Note on Communications Meeting, RD 370, June 1972.

36 Minutes of the Second Home Policy Committee on Communications, 10 January 1973, p. 2.

37 Trades Union Congress Economic Committee, The Newspaper Industry, 13 December, 1972, pp. 16–17; Goodman, Quality, p. 3. Geoffrey Goodman had worked on a range of national newspapers before becoming the *Daily Mirror*'s Industrial Editor in 1969. He served on the 1977 Royal Commission on the Press, where he was the co-author of the Minority Report, which advocated a similar solution. He had previously been a member of the Labour Party Committee on Industrial Democracy (*Who's Who (1979)*, p. 967; Morgan, *Callaghan*, p. 627).

38 Linton, Policies, p. 2; Eric Moonman, Saving the Press, RD 532, January 1973, p. 1; Goodman, Quality, p. 3.

39 Linton, Policies, pp. 2–4.

40 Sixth Meeting on Communications, Communications: Draft Report, n.d., pp. 25–6.

41 George Viner, NUJ Policy on Concentration of Ownership, RD 647, February 1973, p. 8.

42 Minutes of the Second Home Policy Committee on Communications, 10 January 1973, p. 2; W. R. Richardson, Proposals on the Press, RD 632, February 1973, p. 3; George Viner, Comments on RD 324, RD 529, January 1973, p. 2; Viner, NUJ Policy, p. 3; Trades Union Congress Economic Committee, The Newspaper Industry, 13 December 1972, p. 18.

43 Eric Moonman, "Future of the Press – Does Anyone Care?", *Labour Weekly* (9 June 1972); Moonman, Saving, pp. 3–4.; Linton, Policies, p. 2.

44 Rose, *Lesson-drawing*.

45 Richardson, Proposals, pp. 3, 9; Moonman, Saving, p. 4.

46 This did not necessarily mean democratic participation (Moonman, Saving, pp. 4–5; Richardson, Proposals, p. 9).
47 James Curran, The Newspaper Press: Salvage or Save?, RD 662, March 1973, pp. 30–2.
48 Moonman, Saving, p. 2; Moonman, "Future".
49 Minutes of the Second Home Policy Committee on Communications, 10 January 1973, p. 3. See also Viner, NUJ Policy, pp. 8–9; Richardson, Proposals, p. 3.
50 Richardson, Proposals, p. 8.
51 Curran, Salvage or Save?, p. 24.
52 See, for instance, Humphreys, *Western Europe*, pp. 102–5.
53 In Scandinavian countries there is a long history of a party press; the local press has been much more significant and most of the press schemes' spending has been on safeguarding existing diversity, rather than on encouraging new publications (Murschetz, *State Support*, pp. 116, 135–6, 195–6; Murschetz, "Europe", p. 301).
54 Curran, "Press Reformism", p. 46.
55 Murschetz, "Europe", p. 294.
56 Murschetz, *State Support*, p. 124.
57 Swedish Press Subsidies Council, <www.presstodsnamnden.se>.
58 Sanchez-Tabernero and Denton, *Concentration*, p. 238.
59 Murschetz, *State Support*, p. 189.
60 Murschetz, "Europe", p. 303 and Gustafsson, "Press Subsidies", in Smith, *Newspapers and Democracy*, p. 121.
61 Skogerbø, "Norway", pp. 106–7; Østbye, "Norway", p. 173.
62 Skogerbø, "Norway", p. 105; Murschetz, *State Support*, pp. 133–4, 193.
63 Høst, "Norwegian Newspaper System", p. 296; Norwegian Ministry of Cultural Affairs, *Media in Norway*.
64 Østbye, "Norway", p. 174; Høst, "Norwegian Newspaper System", p. 295; Skogerbø, "Norway", pp. 109–10.
65 See, for instance, Norwegian Ministry of Cultural Affairs, *Media in Norway*.
66 Curran, "Press Reformism", p. 46.
67 Communications Study Group, Minutes of 4th Home Policy Committee on Communications, 8 March 1973, p. 1.
68 Hugh Jenkins, Communications and Advertising, RD 530, January 1973, pp. 1–3; Communications Study Group, Minutes of the Second Home Policy Committee on Communications, 10 January 1973, pp. 1–3.
69 See Curran, "Different Approaches", pp. 112–13.
70 Curran, "Different Approaches", p. 112.
71 Curran, Salvage or Save?, pp. 2, 35–7.
72 *Ibid.*, pp. 3, 35–40, 41.
73 Communications Study Group, 4th Meeting, p. 3.
74 Smith, *British Press*, p. 290; Wintour, *Pressures on the Press*, p. 78.
75 NUJ, NUJ Annual Report 1972–3, p. 49.
76 Wintour, *Pressures on the Press*, Chapters 7 and 8.
77 David Ross, "Staff Help to Shape a Paper", *The Journalist*, May 1973.
78 Smith, *British Press*, p. 302.
79 Free Communications Group, *In Place of Management, No 1*, pp. 6–15, quoted in Smith, *British Press*, pp. 290–4.

80 Wintour, *Pressures on the Press*, p. 88.
81 Humphreys, *Western Europe*, pp. 108–9.
82 Home Policy Committee, Communications, RD 324, April 1972, p. 6.
83 Viner, NUJ Policy, pp. 1–2.
84 Anon, "Our 'Special' Role in Industrial Democracy", *The Journalist*, August 1973.
85 Goodman, Quality, p. 3.
86 Communications Study Group, 4th Meeting, p. 3; Neal Ascherson, Internal Press Freedom: Notes on Democratic Control in the Newspaper Industry, March 1973; Curran interview. The award-winning journalist and author Neal Ascherson started as a reporter and leader writer for the *Manchester Guardian* before working for the *Scotsman* and then moving to *The Observer* in 1960. He was the Eastern European correspondent from 1968 to 1975 and a columnist and associate editor from 1985 to 1989. In 1990, he became a columnist on *The Independent on Sunday (Who's Who* (2002)).
87 Ascherson, Internal Press Freedom.
88 Labour Party, Conference 1972, pp. 348–9; Anon, "The Ethics of Circumstance", *Tribune* (1 October 1972); Linton, Policies, p. 1.
89 Benn, *Speeches*, pp. 173–5; Panitch and Leys, *Parliamentary Socialism*, pp. 59–60.
90 Communications Study Group, 4th Meeting, p. 3; Ascherson, Internal Press Freedom; Curran interview.
91 Labour Party, *Labour's Programme for Britain*, pp. 87–8.
92 Christopher Mayhew, Note on Draft Report, RD 961, December 1973, p. 1; Benn, *Against the Tide*, p. 98. Mayhew was a former junior defence minister who resigned from the Labour Party in 1974 to join the Liberal Party.
93 Communications Study Group, Minutes of the Second Home Policy Committee on Communications, 10 May 1973, pp. 1–2; Benn, *Against the Tide*, p. 31.
94 Labour Party, *Let Us Work Together*; Harrison, *Poor Men's Guardians*, pp. 242–3.
95 Labour Party, *People and the Media*, p. 3.
96 O'Malley, "Demanding Accountability", pp. 89–90.
97 Labour Party, *People and the Media*, pp. 5, 6; Communications Study Group, Communications: Draft Report, pp. 2–3.
98 Labour Party, *People and the Media*, pp. 16, 17; Communications Study Group, Communications, pp. 15, 16.
99 Labour Party, *People and the Media*, pp. 8, 12–13, 30; Allaun, *Spreading the News*, p. 86.
100 Labour Party, *People and the Media*, pp. 26–9, 31–2; Communications Study Group, Communications, pp. 28–9; Allaun, *Spreading the News*, pp. 85–6. See also O'Malley, "Demanding Accountability", pp. 89–90; 94; Curran, "Different Approaches", pp. 112–13.
101 Labour Party, *People and the Media*, pp. 29–32.
102 *Ibid.*, p. 6; Communications Study Group, Communications, pp. 2–3.
103 Labour Party, *People and the Media*, pp. 26–9, 31–2. See also Allaun, *Spreading the News*, pp. 85–6; O'Malley, "Demanding Accountability", pp. 89–90, 94; Curran, "Different Approaches", pp. 112–13.
104 Collins and Murroni, *New Policies*, pp. 4, 11.

105 Hamilton, *British Press*, pp. 15–16.
106 Curran interview; James Curran, "Different Approaches", p. 113.
107 Hayek et al., *Collectivist Economic Planning*; Wainwright, *New Left*, p. 50.
108 *Ibid.*
109 Tomlinson, *Hayek and the Market*, pp. 6–7, 112.
110 NEC and Cabinet, "Revised Outline of a Manifesto", RES 130: July 1974, p. 36. See also Freedman, *Television 2000*, p. 143.
111 Labour Party, *Britain Will Win*.
112 Grant, "Letter: Press Freedom", *The Times* (16 April 1975), also quoted in Freedman, *Television 2000*, p. 152; *Freedman, Television 2001*, p. 100. John Grant was a *Daily Express* journalist before becoming an MP in 1970. He left the Labour Party and joined the SDP before becoming the head of public relations for the controversial right-wing union the EEPTU (Edward Pearse, "Obituary: John Grant", *The Guardian* [4 October 2000]).
113 Allaun, *Spreading the News*, p. 85.
114 Communications Study Group, *Communications*, pp. 25–6

3   The Party, the Government, the Commission and its Minority: Labour from 1974 to 1979

1   The quotes are from Trade Minister Peter Shore, who was the minister overseeing the press industry, during a House of Commons debate on the press (HOC, Hansard, 14 May 1974, vol. 873, cols. 1135–7, 1140–41).
2   The chapter title of the book by Panitch and Leys is "The Labour New Left in government: Containment and Marginalisation" (Panitch and Leys, *Parliamentary Socialism*, Chapter 5.)
3   Callaghan, *Retreat*, pp. 46–7; Shaw, *1945*, pp. 122–5.
4   Shaw, *1945*, pp. 127–58; Callaghan, *Globalisation*, pp. 14–15; Coates, *Labour in Power?*, pp. 179–86.
5   For a debate on this see Radice and Radice, *Socialists in the Recession*; Coates, *Labour in Power?*, pp. 30–50, 83–4 and Clarke, *Keynesianism, Monetarism and the Crisis*, pp. 316–18.
6   Hatfield, *House*, pp. 173, 255–6; Labour Party, *Programme, 1973*, pp. 26–8; Labour Party, *Let Us Work Together*; Labour Party, *Britain Will Win*.
7   Panitch and Leys, *Parliamentary Socialism*, pp. 128–30.
8   Labour Party, *Conference 1975*, p. 330.
9   *Ibid.*, p. 332.
10 HOC, 2 May 1974, vol. 872, col. 1322.
11 Peter Shore was a political economist and former head of Labour's research department. He was PPS to Prime Minister Harold Wilson before becoming a minister under Wilson. He was made secretary of state for trade in 1974, before becoming an environment minister in 1976. He was a Shadow minister until 1984. He was raised to a peerage in 1997 (*Dod's* [2001], pp. 283).
12 HOC, 14 May 1974, vol. 873, cols. 1140–41.
13 He noted that there were "some who even say" that the proprietors threatened press freedom (HOC, 14 May 1974, vol. 873, col. 1232).
14 If a new position was taken "on high", "[w]hat happened was that no one bothered to write an article which was contrary to the newspaper's new line" (HOC, 14 May 1974, vol. 873, cols. 1233–4).
15 HOC, 14 May 1974, vol. 873, col. 1234.
16 Pimlott, *Wilson*, pp. 625–9, 631–2; Dorril and Ramsay, *Smear!*; Anon, "Comment", *Labour Weekly*, 12 April 1974.

17 HOC, 14 May 1974 vol. 873, col. 1234.

18 The member was Ioan Evans (HOC, 21 March 1974, vol. 870, cols. 1320–21). A similar point was made by him to the House in April (HOC, 11 April, vol. 831, cols. 632–3).

19 See HOC, 21 March 1974, vol. 870, col. 1321; HOC, 2 May 1974, vol. 872, cols. 1323 and 1329; HOC, 14 May 1974 vol. 873, cols. 1133–4.

20 HOC, 14 May 1974, vol. 873, col. 1234

21 Curran interview; Linton interview.

22 See Baistow, *Fourth-rate Estate*, p. 60.

23 Baistow, *Fourth-rate Estate*, p. 60; Curran interview; Linton interview.

24 HOC, 2 May 1974, vol. 872, cols. 1330–31.

25 Linton interview. The tension among Labour leaders is described by Curran thus: "So one part wanted to kick the press issue into touch and the royal commission was a nice way of doing that. But another part of them felt that something should be done and if there was a commission, this could build up a consensus for some kind of reform. And this would enable them to act without completely souring their relationship with the press" (Curran interview).

26 Wilson, Evidence to the Royal Commission; Dorril and Ramsay, *Smear!*, pp. 315–16.

27 Wilson, Evidence to the Royal Commission, p. 10.

28 Labour Party, Oral Evidence, 11 March 1976, pp. 7–10.

29 Labour Party, Evidence, 83 E1, April 1975, pp. 1, 4, 10.

30 *Ibid.*, pp. 6–7, 8–9; Labour Party, Oral Evidence, 11 March 1976, pp. 14–16.

31 Labour Party, Evidence, 83 E1, April 1975, p. 7.

32 *Ibid.*, pp. 11; Home Policy Committee, Royal Commission, p.1.

33 Royal Commission, *Final Report*, p. 118.

34 The association represented all the national press owners, with the exception, at the time, of the Mirror Group and the *Morning Star* (NPA, Evidence, p. 51).

35 *Ibid.*; Newspaper Editors' Guild, Evidence, p. 17; Speech by Edward Heath, HOC, 14 May 1974, vol. 873, col. 1129.

36 NPA, Evidence, pp. 46; Newspaper Editors' Guild, Evidence to the Royal Commission on the Press, 7 February 1975, p. 17.

37 NPA, Evidence, pp. 6, 44; NGA, Evidence; Newspaper Editors' Guild, Oral Evidence, p. 17.

38 NPA, Evidence, pp. 42–4.

39 Advertising Association, Evidence.

40 See Tunstall, *Newspaper Power*, pp. 12–14.

41 Nevertheless, it should be said, he still believes the flexible application of a revenue board scheme would have been more effective in broadening diversity (Curran interview). See also Royal Commission on the Press, *Final Report*, p. 121.

42 NPA, Evidence, p. 29.

43 *Ibid.*, p. 15.

44 NPA, Evidence, pp. 47–8; Advertising Association, Evidence, pp. 32–3.

45 Curran interview.

46 Labour Party, Oral Evidence.

47　Labour Party, Evidence, p. 9. For proposals on industrial democracy in other areas see Wickham-Jones, *Economic*, pp. 68–9.
48　As indicated at by the quote the start of the book from the NPA's chair, Lord Goodman (NPA, Evidence, pp. 14–15).
49　*Ibid.*
50　Wainwright, *New Left*, pp. 57–60.
51　The argument is that strengthening democratic participation in the newspapers themselves would provide an effective power base to protect the independence of newspapers from state interference.
52　See Gillmor, *We the Media*, pp. 16–17.
53　Lively, *Democracy*, p. 51.
54　Norbeto Bobbio discusses this question more generally in relation to industrial democracy (Bobbio, *Which Socialism?*, p. 84).
55　See, for instance, Bobbio, *Which Socialism?*, pp. 71–2; Garnham, "Public Sphere", p. 366.
56　Held, *Democracy and the Global Order*, pp. 280–81; Arblaster, *Democracy*.
57　HOC, 24 March 1974, vol. 871, cols. 393–5, 399–401.
58　Wickham-Jones, *Economic*, pp. 137–43.
59　Allaun, *Spreading the News*, pp. 51; Hodgman, "A New Paper is Born"; Stephen Kelly, "Outlook is Grim for the 'Miracle' Paper that Glasgow Workers Started", *Tribune* (17 October 1975).
60　Allaun, *Spreading the News*, p. 51; Hodgman, "A New Paper is Born"; Kelly, "Outlook".
61　Hodgman, "A New Paper is Born".
62　Wilson cancelled a last-ditch meeting with Benn to discuss the amount, said to be £40,000 (Benn, *Against the Tide*, pp. 335, 358); Kelly, "Outlook"; Interview with former *Scottish Daily News* employee and NUJ official Tim Gopsill, 1 October 2002.
63　Anon., "Why I Quit the SDN".
64　Neal Ascherson, "Newspapers and Internal Democracy", in Curran, *The British Press*, pp. 135–6; Tim Gopsill interview.
65　Gopsill interview.
66　Advertising Association, pp. 8–10.
67　Ascherson, "Internal Democracy", p. 135.
68　Barnes and Reid, *Governments and Trade Unions*, pp. 140–45, Ross, *TUC*, pp. 305.
69　Ross, *TUC*, pp. 305.
70　James Prior, HOC, 12 February 1975, vol. 886, col. 421.
71　HOC, 12 February 1975, vol. 886, cols. 439–536; Greenslade, *Press Gang*, p. 284. Although there is a difference between these two sorts of agreement, depending on whether union membership was demanded pre-entry or post-entry, I shall treat these two sorts of agreements as synonymous.
72　The headline of *The Journalist*, produced by the NUJ, may have been overstating the general picture, however (Anon, "Militants in Power").
73　NUJ union branches are known as chapels.
74　Newspaper Editors' Guild, Oral Evidence March, pp. 13; Newspaper Editors' Guild, Oral Evidence February, pp. 20–24. See also HOC, 12 February 1975, vol. 886, cols. 427–8, 432–3, 439, 493, 504–5.

75 HOC, 12 February 1975, vol. 886, cols. 442–3 and 464.

76 HOC, 20 November 1974 vol. 881, col. 1318.

77 Anon. "Freedom"; Anon, "Editors' Freedom"; Anon, "Cardiff Line"; Royal Commission on the Press, Final Report, p. 158.

78 Ascherson, "Internal Democracy", pp. 126–9.

79 NPA, Evidence, p. 24; Newspaper Editors' Guild, 25 March 1976, pp. 2, 16. Indeed, one key Conservative objector, along with a prominent editor, quoted a passage in The People and the Media on access of the public to the media back at Labour (HOC, 12 February 1975, vol. 886, cols. 430–1).

80 Newspaper Editors' Guild, Oral Evidence February, p. 17.

81 HOC, 12 February 1975, vol. 886, col. 507.

82 HOC, 12 February 1975, vol. 886, col. 436–48, 522–33.

83 Ron Knowles and Roger Protz, "NUJ, Editors and the Closed Shop", Journalist, July 1974.

84 HOC, 12 February 1975, vol. 886, col. 465. This was a view that the insider Curran considers weighed on Labour politicians in their deliberations (Curran interview).

85 See, for instance, Employment Minister Albert Booth (HOC, 12 February 1975, vol. 886, col. 437; and Foot, HOC, 12 February 1975, vol. 886, col. 533).

86 Anon. "Hetherington Calls for Staff Politics Probe", The Journalist, March 1975.

87 Royal Commission on the Press, Final Report, p. 158; Ken Morgan, "Editors Reject Charter", The Journalist, March 1975.

88 Royal Commission on the Press, Final Report, pp. 163, 232–3.

89 Ibid., p. 156.

90 Curran interview.

91 Its emphasis was that the existing number of national newspapers should be maintained. Yet it shied away from the party proposals, which, whatever their motivation, were also aimed at providing diversity (see, for instance, Royal Commission on the Press, Final Report, pp. 159–60; also cited in O. R. McGregor, "Royal Commission on the Press, 1974–7: A Note" in Bulmer, Research, p. 155; Jeremy Tunstall, "Research for the Royal Commission on the Press, 1974–7", in Bulmer, Research, p. 126).

92 Curran interview; Royal Commission on the Press, Final Report, pp. 120–2.

93 Basnett and Goodman, Minority Report, p. 1.

94 David Basnett was General Secretary of the General Municipal Workers' Union from 1973 and the General, Municipal, Boiler Makers and Allied Trades Union from 1982. He was a member of numerous committees of enquiry (Who's Who [1985], p. 112)

95 Basnett and Goodman, Minority Report, p. 3; Allaun, Spreading the News, p. 72.

96 Basnett and Goodman, Minority Report, p. 1; Curran interview. It is interesting, for instance, that a recent work emphasizes the Minority Report's attempt to provide balance in a biased press (Greenslade, Press Gang, p. 347).

97 Basnett and Goodman, Minority Report, pp. 11–13, 14–15; Benn, Free Press, p. 4; Allaun, Spreading the News, pp. 72–3; Curran, "Different Approaches", pp. 117, 133; Royal Commission on the Press, Final Report, pp. 121–2.

98 Goodman interview, 1 August 2001. Also, see the Royal Commission on the Press, Final Report, pp. 10, 11.

99 Basnett and Goodman, *Minority Report*, p. 5.
100 *Ibid.*, pp. 5–6, 11–12.
101 *Ibid.*, p. 1.
102 *Ibid.*, p. 17.
103 As the proprietors' representatives put it: "Who would qualify? Would bureaucracy consent to print *Socialist Worker* or *Private Eye*?" Royal Commission on the Press, *Final Report*, p. 122.
104 Goodman interview, 1 August 2001.
105 NGA, Evidence; Advertising Association, Evidence, pp. 14–15; Newspaper Editors' Guild, Oral Evidence, pp. 5–6.
106 O'Malley, "Demanding Accountability", p. 95
107 Goodman interview.
108 Callaghan private correspondence.
109 Donoughue private correspondence.
110 Callaghan private correspondence.
111 Royal Commission on the Press, pp. 135–7.
112 HOC, 4 December 1978, vol. 959, col. 480–1. An ex-university lecturer and former close ally of Tony Benn, Meacher was an industry minister under Benn and Health and Social Security Minister in the 1974 Labour government. He became a trade minister in 1976. From 1978 to 1983 he was the chair of the pro-activist Labour Coordinating Committee. After 1979 he was associated with activist backlash against the Callaghan government. He stood for deputy leader in lieu of the electorally defeated Tony Benn as the left candidate. Meacher was elected onto the Shadow Cabinet in 1983. He had split from what is now known as the "hard left" in 1985, developing a "soft-left" grouping in the Shadow Cabinet and subsequently held a number of shadow posts. He was Minister for the Environment from 1997 to 2003 (*Dod's* [2001], p. 623; Roth and Criddle, *Parliamentary Profiles*, pp. 1525–32).
113 Dale, *Labour Party Manifestos*, p. 181.
114 Seyd, *Labour Left*; Benn, *Arguments for Democracy*, p. 182.
115 Labour Party, *Labour's Programme 1976*, p. 105.
116 Bish, "The Manifesto", in Barratt-Brown and Coates, *What Went Wrong*, pp. 187–95; Seyd, *Labour Left*, p. 122, Benn, *Arguments for Democracy*, p. 182.
117 Bish, "The Manifesto" in Barratt-Brown and Coates, *What Went Wrong*, pp. 686–7.
118 Morgan, *Callaghan*, p. 687; Benn, *Arguments for Democracy*, p. 182; Benn, *Conflicts*, pp. 480–2.
119 Benn, *Arguments for Democracy*, p. 182.
120 Seyd, *Labour Left*, p. 122; *Arguments for Democracy*, p. 182.
121 Curran, "Press Reformism", p. 48.
122 Gospel and Palmer, *British Industrial Relations*, pp. 245–6; Kessler and Bayliss, *Contemporary British Industrial Relations*, p. 115.

4 Flow and Ebb: Labour from 1979 to 1983

1 Shaw, *1979*, p. 20; Hattersley, *Who Goes Home?*, p. 221.
2 Labour Party, *Conference 1979*, pp. 275, 455; Labour Party, *Special Conference 1981*, pp. 143–8; Labour Party, *Conference 1981*, pp. 206–12; Dale, *Labour Party Manifestos*, p. 4; Seyd, *Labour Left*, p. 123.
3 Kogan and Kogan, *Labour Party*, pp. 98–9.
4 Panitch and Leys, *Parliamentary Socialism*, p. 192. See also Kogan and Kogan, *Labour Party*; Benn, *The End*, p. 4.

5   Anon, New Consultation Procedure, RD 260, February 1980.

6   Shaw, *1979*, pp. 6–9.

7   Shaw, *Discipline*, p. 246, cited in Panitch and Leys, *Parliamentary Socialism*, p. 145, 167. See also Hollingsworth, *Political Dissent*, pp. 37–76.

8   Kogan and Kogan, *Labour Party*, pp. 107, 130–9, 153–4; Benn, *Conflicts*, pp. 530–1; Benn, *The End*, pp. 230–1, 247, 251; Hattersley, *Who Goes Home?*, pp. 235–6; Panitch and Leys, *Parliamentary Socialism*, pp. 199–203.

9   Shaw, *1979*, pp. 12–14.

10 Hattersley, *Who Goes Home?*, p. 238.

11 Shaw, *1979*, p. 26.

12 Labour Party, Conference 1979, pp. 383–5.

13 Anon, Media Study Group Programme of Work, RD 409, May 1980.

14 Stuart Holland was personal assistant to Harold Wilson as Prime Minister in 1967–8, and to Judith Hart when she was Overseas Development Minister, 1974–5. The university lecturer wrote a series of books on economic planning and was an MP between 1979 and 1989.

15 Philip Whitehead was a BBC producer and editor of Thames TV's *This Week* programme in the 1960s, before becoming an MP in 1970. After returning to television production, he became a MEP in 1994 (*Dod's* [1979], p. 514; Roth, *The MPs' Chart*). A former university lecturer and television journalist, Austin Mitchell was the treasurer of the right-wing pressure group Labour Solidarity from 1981 to 1984. A supporter of Kinnock and then Bryan Gould in the 1980s and 1990s, he was a presenter on BSkyB from 1989 to 1998. He joined the left-wing Socialist Campaign Group of MPs in 1999 (Roth and Criddle, *Parliamentary Profiles*, pp. 1557–64).

16 Chris Mullin was editor of *Tribune* between 1982 and 1984. He was a key activist in CLPD, penning the book *How to Select and Reselect Your MP* and editing two of Tony Benn's books. He became an MP in 1987. He has written a series of political novels including *A Very British Coup*, which was serialised on TV (Roth and Criddle, *Parliamentary Profiles*, pp. 1613–21; Benn, *The End*, p. 636). He was associated with the Campaign Group in the 1990s. He was an environment minister between 1999 and 2001.

17 Greenslade, *Press Gang*, pp. 359–61.

18 Benn, *Conflicts*, p. 600.

19 TUC, *Behind the Headlines*, pp. 5, 6, 8.

20 Curran, "Different Approaches", p. 99; Curran and Seaton, *Power Without Responsibility*, p. 338.

21 Curran, "Different Approaches", pp. 99–100; Curran and Seaton, *Power Without Responsibility*, p. 338; Curran, *Policy for the Press*, p. 13.

22 Philip Elliot, Notes on Media Policy, RD 1073.

23 Michael Meacher, Reform of the Press, RD 2222, March 1982, pp. 5–6.

24 Taaffe, *What we Stand For*. For a critical discussion, see Curran, *Policy for the Press*, pp. 14–15.

25 Media Study Group, Minutes of the 6th Meeting, 19 January 1981.

26 Habermas, *Transformation*; Street, *Mass Media*, p. 253.

27 Media Study Group, 6th Meeting; Media Study Group, Minutes of the 21st Meeting, 20 September 1982.

28 Labour Party, Conference 1979, pp. 385–9; Media Study Group, Media Study Group Programme of Work, RD 409, May 1980.

29   Media Study Group, Draft Consultative Paper, RD 498, July 1980.

30   TUC, Conference 1984, p. 346.

31   Evans, *Good Times*, p. 103.

32   HOC, 23 January 1981, col. 567. As is well known, the legislation had a loophole. It denied referral if the titles involved were not commercially viable and would close if an existing press firm did not buy them. The Labour leadership put its case for referral based on its assessment that *The Sunday Times* was profitable, at least (HOC, 27 January 1981, cols. 784–5).

33   The campaign's policy here was written by *The Times*' father of chapel, and CPF chair, Jake Ecclestone (CPF, National Committee Minutes, 3 February 1981).

34   From the right of the party, David Owen called for the commission to be brought in (HOC, 23 January 1981, col. 568).

35   HOC, 27 January 1981, cols. 810–13, 816.

36   James Curran, Socialist Plan for the Press, January 1983. He had put forward a similar proposal in Curran, *The British Press*.

37   Allaun, *Spreading the News*, pp. 87–8.

38   Labour Party, *People and the Media*, p. 21; Tom Baistow, Media Study Group Right of Reply Draft', RD 1027, April 1981; Home Policy Committee Press and Publicity Committee; "The Right of Reply Draft NEC statement", RD 1112, August 1981; "Home Policy Committee Draft NEC statement"; October 1981; Labour Party NEC, Statement by the National Executive Committee: The Right of Reply, March 1982; Labour Party, Conference 1982, pp. 240–2.

39   Curran, Socialist Plan for the Press, p. 3. See also Labour Research Department, *The Press*, p. 21.

40   Curran, Socialist Plan for the Press, pp. 1–3.

41   Although at the time he identified technical flaws with the operation of the scheme, more recently he has seen the problem was its ambition and that it lacked political support, although he considers it defensible (Curran, "Different Approaches", p. 113; Curran interview).

42   Media Study Group, Minutes of the 22nd Meeting, 18 January 1983.

43   Media Study Group, Minutes of the 23rd Meeting, 1 February 1983.

44   Media Study Group, 22nd Meeting.

45   Media Study Group, 23rd Meeting.

46   Media Study Group, Labour's Programme 1982 – Media Section, RD 2165, March 1982; Media Study Group, Labour's Programme 1982 – Media Section (2nd Draft), RD 2239, March 1982; Special Home Policy Committee, Labour's Programme 1982 – Media Section (As Agreed by the Media Study Group), RD 2288, April 1982; Media Study Group, Minutes of the 17th Meeting, 15 March 1982; NEC Media Study Group, Minutes of the 18th Meeting, 31 March 1982.

47   The conference explicitly demanded "the owners of the British daily press to adhere to a strict code of impartiality" (Labour Party, *Conference 1982*, pp. 239–40).

48   The IWC, as mentioned, promoted democratic self-management of industry. Members were involved in the battle for constitutional changes in the Labour Party.

49   Curran and Holland, "Public Intervention in the Press", pp. 3–4.
50   Labour Party, *Conference 1979*, p. 384.
51   TUC, *Behind the Headlines*, pp. 23, 28.
52   Harold Frayman and Donald Ross "A Labour Daily?", *Workers' Control Bulletin*, No. 3, 1979, pp. 6–8.
53   *Ibid.*, pp. 4–5.
54   See, for instance, Royden Harrison, "The Congress of Workers' Councils, Yugoslavia", in *New Reasoner*, 1957, no. 2 and Michael Barratt Brown, "Jugoslavia Revisited" in *New Left Review*, 1960, no. 1.
55   Harold Frayman, Democracy and the Press, November 1980, RD 591, p. 1.
56   Media Study Group, Minutes of the 4th Meeting of the Media Study Group, 20 November 1980.
57   Curran, A Socialist Plan for the Press.
58   Media Study Group, 22nd Meeting.
59   Media Study Group, 23nd Meeting.
60   Neal Ascherson, Correspondence with the author, 24 April 2001; Curran interview.
61   Philip Whitehead and Austin Mitchell, "Some Suggestions for Media Policy", RD 2115, n.d.
62   Allaun, *Spreading the News*, pp. 88–9.
63   Frayman, Democracy and the Press, p. 3.
64   Curran interview.
65   *Ibid.*
66   Curran interview; Media Study Group, 4th Meeting, 20 November 1980.
67   CPF, Right of Reply. See also O'Malley and Soley, Press, p. 129.
68   TUC, Conference 1981; Anon, "Labour Movement's 'Yes' to Campaign", *Free Press*, October 1980.
69   Media Study Group, Right of Reply, p. 2.
70   Curran interview, Curran, "Press Reformism", p. 49.
71   Anon, "£50,000 appeal boost", *Free Press*, May–June 1982.
72   Alan Richardson and Mike Power, "Media Freedom", in Curran, *Bending*, pp. 209–10.
73   John Jennings, CPF Secretary's Report to AGM 1982, April 1982, p. 5 (internal correspondence).
74   Labour Party, *Conference 1975*, pp. 362; Labour Party, *Conference 1979*, pp. 383–4.
75   O'Malley and Soley, *Press*, pp. 72–83.
76   Media Study Group, 10th Meeting, 22 June 1981.
77   HOC, 18 February 1983, pp. 573, 617–18.
78   CPBF, *Labour Daily?*, p. 106; O'Malley and Soley, *Press*, p. 80.
79   Media Study Group, 9th Meeting, 18 May 1981; Media Study Group, 10th Meeting.
80   TUC, *Other Side*, p. 21; Anon, "Does the 'Right of Reply' Campaign Go Far Enough?", *Free Press*, May–June 1982.
81   Media Study Group, 6th Meeting; Baistow, "The Right of Reply" and "The Rights of Reply/Media Study Group Right of Reply Draft"; CPBF, Labour Daily?, p. 106.
82   CPBF, *Labour Daily?*, p. 106.

83 Media Study Group, 7th Meeting, 16 February 1981 and 9th Meeting.

84 Dewall, *Press Ethics*, pp. 21, 37–8, 55, 63–4, 104.

85 Media Study Group, 9th Meeting; Freedman, *Television 2000*, p. 182.

86 Media Study Group, 12th Meeting, 19 October 1981.

87 NEC, Right of Reply: Amendments to Draft Statement, RD 1084; NEC, Statement on the Right of Reply, RD 1027.

88 Media Study Group, Amendment from the Media Study Group to RD 1027, RD 1092 October 1981; Allaun, *Spreading the News*, p. 104; Labour Party, *Conference 1982*, pp. 240–3; Dale, *Labour Party Manifestos*, p. 181.

89 HOC, vol. 37, 18 February 1983, cols. 527–636; O'Malley and Soley, *Press*, pp. 80–1.

90 *Ibid.*, cols. 602–3, 605–6, 637; CPBF, *Labour Daily?*, p. 106.

91 Freedman, *Television 2000*, p. 183.

92 Baistow, Media Study Group Right of Reply Draft; Press and Publicity Committee, The Right of Reply Draft NEC statement; Home Policy Committee, Draft NEC Statement; NEC, Statement on the Right of Reply. Michael Meacher also expressed a similar view in the debate on the Right of Reply Bill in 1983 (HOC, vol. 37, 18 February 1983, col. 616).

93 Allaun, *Spreading the News*, p. 49.

94 Labour Party, *Conference 1992*, pp. 214–15; Baistow Media Study Group Right of Reply Draft; NEC, *Statement on the Right of Reply*.

95 Paul Foot, "Paul Foot on Right of Reply", *Free Press*, November–December 1984; Mike Power, "What Are We Going To Do About Paul Foot?", *Free Press*, January–February 1985, quoted in O'Malley and Soley, *Press*, p. 84.

96 CPBF, *Labour Daily?*

97 HOC, vol. 37, 18 February 1983, cols. 609, 618–19.

98 The right used its press contacts to discredit the left by linking it with extremism: "hence the imagery of 'bully boys', the analogies with Eastern Europe and the accusations of intimidation and brutality" (Shaw, *Discipline*, p. 246, cited in Panitch and Leys, *Parliamentary Socialism*, p. 167; see also p. 145).

99 Wring, *Labour Party*.

100 Hattersley, *Press Gang*, pp. 61–3.

101 Curran, "Different Approaches", p. 94.

102 Hattersley, *Press Gang*, p. 9. Interestingly, the *Mail*'s staff were said not always to share such a resigned attitude. Greenslade recounts how the NUJ chapel agreed to call on the editor David English to "give the other parties [apart from the Conservatives] a fair crack of the whip". English refused (Greenslade, *Press Gang*, p. 452).

103 Labour Party, *Conference 1982*, pp. 239–40, 241.

104 Freedman, *Television 2000*, pp. 184–5; Curran, "Different Approaches", p. 129. See also Freedman, *Television 2001*, p. 126.

105 Dale, *Labour Party Manifestos*, p. 181; Curran, "Different Approaches", p. 133; Baistow, *Fourth-rate Estate*, pp. 97, 98–100.

106 Curran, "Different Approaches", p. 133.

107 Francis Cripps, "The British Crisis – Can the Left Win?" in *New Left Review*, no. 128, July–August 1981, pp. 96–7.

108 Interview with John Monks, then NALGO communications officer, later UNISON head of communications, 24 August 2001.

109 Panitch and Leys, *Parliamentary Socialism*, pp. 155, 157–60, 163; David Aldridge, "Labour Party Broadcast Attacks Bias", *Free Press*, November–December 1981.
110 Benn, *Conflicts*, p. 503.
111 Benn, *The End*, pp. 69, 151. See also Benn, *Conflicts*, pp. 494, 546, 507, 547; Anon, "ITN Offers Benn Five Minutes", *Free Press*, October 1980; Gaber, "Benn and ITN", *Free Press*, December 1980.
112 Richardson and Power, "Media Freedom", in Curran, *Bending*, p. 209.
113 Dale, *Labour Party Manifestos*, p. 181.
114 Freedman, *Television 2000*, p. 182; Freedman, *Television 2001*, pp. 123–4.
115 Freeman, *Benn Heresy*, esp. pp. 109–12.

5 Changes and Political Communications: Labour in the 1980s

 1 Neil Kinnock, Letter to the CPBF, 9 May 1984, Kinnock's Personal Papers.
 2 *Free Press* March–April 1985. See also Dennis MacShane, "Media Policy and the Left", in Curran, *Bending*, pp. 218, 230–2.
 3 Andrews, *Failure*, p. 6.
 4 Hughes and Wintour, *Labour Rebuilt*; Panitch and Leys, *Parliamentary Socialism*; Shaw, *1979*; Shaw, *1945*; Callaghan, *Retreat*; Heffernan and Marqusee, *Defeat*.
 5 One area where he did specify that more policy work was needed was on press regulation (Research Secretary, Policy Development: A Further Note, Home Policy Committee, RD 2902, November 1983; Shaw, "Wilderness", in Brivati and Heffernan, *Labour Party*, p. 119).
 6 Research Secretary, Policy Development: A Further Note, Home Policy Committee, RD 2902, November 1983; Shaw, "Wilderness" in Brivati and Heffernan, *Labour Party*, p. 119; CLPD, Newsletter, No. 46 (Conference Edition), September–October 1992.
 7 Shaw, "Wilderness", in Brivati and Heffernan, *Labour Party*, p. 119.
 8 Panitch and Leys, *Parliamentary Socialism*, pp. 178, 219; Heffernan and Marqusee, *Defeat*, pp. 109–10; Callaghan, *Retreat*, pp. 192–3.
 9 Shaw, *1979*, p. 112; Callaghan, *Retreat*, pp. 192–3.
10 Kinnock's chief of staff, Charles Clarke, interviewed by Philip Gould, in Gould, *Unfinished Revolution*, p. 42.
11 Heffernan and Marqusee, *Defeat*, pp. 68–70; Shaw, "Wilderness", in Brivati and Heffernan, *Labour Party*, p. 122.
12 The LCC had been formed in 1978, as what would now be termed a Bennite "think tank". But its politics had shifted. By 1983 it supported Kinnock's campaign for party leadership. After that, it championed the centre-left coalition around Kinnock (Heffernan and Marqusee, *Defeat*, pp. 68–70).
13 An influential book in Britain, which shared the critical but sympathetic view of Hayek and gained a non-specialist readership, was Nove, *Economics of Feasible Socialism*.
14 As the journal's former editor explained, the magazine made "much of the intellectual running for Labour's Kinnockite revolution" (Martin Jacques, "Requiem for a Revolution", *The Times* [12 September 1990]). The soft left started supporting leadership calls for the market mechanism's implementation, explicitly citing the Soviet bloc's failures (LCC, Mailing, June 1984, Kinnock's Personal Papers).

15 Two very politically different commentators, Ivor Crewe and Richard Heffernan, are among those who note Thatcher's influence on Labour's politics (Crewe, "The Thatcher Legacy" in King, *Britain at the Polls*, pp. 1–28; Heffernan, *New Labour and Thatcherism*).

16 Shaw, *1979*, pp. 12–13, 47–50.

17 Labour Party, *New Hope for Britain*; Labour Party, *Investing in People*; Labour Party, *Britain Will Win*.

18 Other areas where municipal socialism developed included Manchester and Sheffield (Wainwright, *Labour*, pp. 127–36).

19 Mulgan and Worpole, *Saturday Night*, p. 13. Geoff Mulgan worked for the GLEB before becoming a lecturer. He was co-founder and director of the think-tank Demos from 1993 to 1999 and member of the Prime Minister's policy unit from 1997 to 2000. In 2000 he became Director of the Performance and Innovation Unit at the Cabinet Office.

20 Mulgan and Worpole, *Saturday Night*.

21 In fact, adherents even saw a market controlled by "right-wing populist businessmen" would provide a more appetizing alternative to a Labour movement press, which had a "habit of talking down to their audience in a way that the right does not seem to" (Mulgan and Worpole, "Selling the Paper" in Curran, *Bending*, p. 139).

22 The Labour leadership shifted broadcasting policies more dramatically in a pro-market direction, as Freedman indicates (Freedman, *Television 2000*, p. 197).

23 For instance, Mulgan advocated solutions for newspaper advertising in line with previous interventionist policies when at the GLEB (Mulgan, "Advertising", GLC, *State of the Art*, pp. 93–4).

24 The 1983 conference saw a call come from thirty constituencies for Labour and the TUC jointly to set up a daily newspaper. Rather simplistically, this was seen as an answer to the election defeat (Labour Party, *Conference 1983*, pp. 203–4, 208–9; *Free Press*, November–December 1983).

25 Labour Party, *Conference 1983*, pp. 205–6, 211.

26 See Hollingsworth, *Political Dissent*, and Heffernan and Marqusee, *Defeat*. On *The Sun*'s treatment of Kinnock see Greenslade, *Press Gang*, pp. 608–10.

27 Kinnock's Personal Papers.

28 From then on, one Kinnock biographer considers that "small mistakes by Kinnock were magnified into huge errors while big mistakes by Thatcher were microscopized down into miniscule faux pas" (Drower, *Kinnock*, pp. 189–90).

29 Philip Gould, Communications Review, 22 December 1985, Kinnock's Personal Papers.

30 *Ibid.*

31 Curran et al., *Culture Wars*, Chapters 4, 5 and 6 and p. 194.

32 Chippindale and Horrie, *News on Sunday*, p. ix. See also Anon, "Radical Left Collapse Shock", *The Economist*, 30 April 1988.

33 Curran, *London Press Sector*.

34 Chippindale and Horrie, *News on Sunday*, pp. 15–20, 30–3.

35 The GLEB successfully pressed for there to be a controlling group, which would protect the paper from an outside takeover, which became the independent Founders' Trust that would check that the paper stayed true to its

original commitments. The Founders were to have a veto over key decisions (Chippindale and Horrie, *News on Sunday*, pp. 30–3, 53–4; Anon, "Control Systems", *Free Press*, February 1987).

36 Chippindale and Horrie, *News on Sunday*, especially p. 224.

37 John Pilger, "The Birth of a New *Sun?*", *New Statesman*, 2 January 1987.

38 Chippindale and Horrie, *News on Sunday*, p. 53.

39 The initial investors had agreed the remaining members and plans to rotate these people had been dropped. The newspaper ran not as a co-operative, but as a private limited company (Cook interview, Allaun, *Spreading the News*, p. 57).

40 Cook interview.

41 Williams and Gopsill interviews; *A Lot of Balls*.

42 As they indicate, not one member of the Founders, the management team or the board of management "had even earned a regular living from national print journalism" (Chippindale and Horrie, *News on Sunday*, p. 125).

43 Andrews, Failure; Allaun, *Spreading the News*, p. 62.

44 Curran, *London Press Sector*, pp. 56–8.

45 Cook interview.

46 Chippindale and Horrie, *News on Sunday*, pp. 182–3, 196.

47 Chippindale and Horrie, *News on Sunday*, pp. 183, 226; Andrews, *Failure*.

48 It failed to get City funding that other less left-wing titles, such as *Today* – launched around the same time – received, which affected the quality of the staff recruited and the product as a whole (Andrews, *Failure*; Curran and Seaton, *Power Without Responsibility*, p. 103; Chippindale and Horrie, *News on Sunday*, pp. 99–121).

49 Chippindale and Horrie, *News on Sunday*, pp. 58–9, 196.

50 Allaun, *Spreading the News*, p. 62.

51 Wring, *Politics of Marketing*, pp. 48–58; Wring, "Soundbites versus Socialism", pp. 59–68.

52 Wring, *Political Marketing*, pp. 1–12.

53 Wring, *Politics of Marketing*, pp. 76–80; Wring, *Labour Party*, pp. 144–5.

54 Curran, *Media and Power*, p. 49.

55 Labour Party, *Conference 1983*, p. 36, Shaw, *1979*, p. 54 and Wring, *Politics of Marketing*, pp. 83–4.

56 Wring, *Politics of Marketing*, p. 84.

57 Paul Convery, Letter to NEC Members, n.d., Neil Kinnock's Personal Papers.

58 Interview with Mike Smith, TUC head of secretariat and former head of its press and information department, 1 October 2002.

59 Wring, *Politics of Marketing*, pp. 82–3, 164.

60 Tunstall, *Newspaper Power*, pp. 136, 137.

61 Wring, *Politics of Marketing*.

62 Wring, *Politics of Marketing*, pp. 84–8; Hughes and Wintour, *Labour Rebuilt*, p. 53; McSmith, *Faces*, p. 255.

63 Panitch and Leys, *Parliamentary Socialism*, p. 221; Gould, *Unfinished Revolution*; Shaw, *1979*.

64 Interview with the Secretary to the Labour Party's Arts Committee, Tricia Sumner, 6 February 2002 and McSmith, *Faces*, p. 257. See also Wring, *Politics of Marketing*, pp. 84, 89. The SCA was developed and operated in secret in the

year before the NEC approved of it (Gould, *Unfinished Revolution*, pp. 56–7).

65 Wring, *Politics of Marketing*, p. 112.

66 Shaw, 1979, p. 62; Heffernan and Marqusee, *Defeat*, p. 212; Anderson and Mann, *Safety First*, p. 365–6; Gould, *Goodbye To All That*, p. 217; Hughes and Wintour, *Labour Rebuilt*, p. 183.

67 Leader, "The Package Has Come a Long Way", *The Guardian* (23 April 1986); Leader, "Labour Starts to Get its Act Together", *The Observer* (27 April 1986); Leader, "Mr Kinnock's New Party", *Financial Times* (23 April 1986); Leader, "Smile Please", *Evening Standard* (23 April 1986); Leader, *The Economist*, 26 April 1986. See also Shaw, *1979*, p. 71.

68 Gould, *Unfinished Revolution*, pp. 60–1; Hughes and Wintour, *Labour Rebuilt*, pp. 56–7.

69 Heffernan and Marqusee, *Defeat*, p. 207.

70 Shaw, *Discipline*, p. 259; Panitch and Leys, *Parliamentary Socialism*, p. 217.

71 Shaw, *1945*, pp. 174–5; Shaw, *Discipline*, pp. 259–90; Hughes and Wintour, *Labour Rebuilt*, pp. 9–10.

72 Gould, *Unfinished Revolution*, pp. 76, 77, 93, 144–5. When, for instance, the SCA internally justified the presidential course, polling was presented on Thatcher but not on Kinnock (Gould, Election Strategy Meeting, n.d., Neil Kinnock's Personal Papers).

73 For a more extensive discussion of this question see Tunney, Maxwell.

74 Indeed, Greenslade notes that the personal relations between Maxwell and the Kinnocks were not warm (Greenslade, *Maxwell*, pp. 186–7).

75 Answers to questions on the points raised by the Royal Commission on the Press, Mirror Group Newspapers Ltd, August 1975, p. 5.

76 Goodman interview, 2 January 2003.

77 Evidence to the Royal Commission on the Press submitted by Mirror Group Newspapers Ltd, April 1975, (1) 8, (1) 9.

78 Goodman interviews, 1 August 2001 and 2 January 2003.

79 Interview with Paul Foot, 6 January 2003.

80 Bower, *Final*, pp. 371–2.

81 Bower, *Outsider*, p. 288.

82 Patricia Hewitt, Letter to Neil Kinnock, 17 October 1983, Neil Kinnock's Personal Papers.

83 Neil Kinnock, Letter to the Editor of the *Daily Mirror*, 17 October 1983, Neil Kinnock's Personal Papers.

84 Paul Foot interview and Goodman interview, 2 January 2003.

85 Goodman interview, 2 January 2003 and interview with Mike Power, then of the CPBF, now TUC campaigns officer, 6 January 2003; Bower, *Final*, p. 364.

86 Patricia Hewitt, Notes of Meeting between Neil Kinnock and Tony Miles and Mike Molloy, 5 July 1984, Neil Kinnock's Personal Papers. Goodman interview, 2 January 2003. Patricia Hewitt was Kinnock's press secretary and then policy coordinator for the leader's office. She became Trade and Industry Minister in the Blair government, before being appointed Secretary of State for Health in May 2005.

87 Patricia Hewitt, Notes of Meeting between Neil Kinnock and Tony Miles and Mike Molloy, 5 July 1984, Neil Kinnock's Personal Papers.

88 HOC, 13 July 1984, col. 1468.
89 Neil Kinnock, Letter to the Editor of the *Daily Mirror*, 17 October 1983, Neil Kinnock's Personal Papers.
90 Bower, *Outsider*, p. 281.
91 Patricia Hewitt, "Notes of Meeting between Neil Kinnock and Tony Miles and Mike Molloy", 5 July 1984, Neil Kinnock's Personal Papers. As it happened, the fears of Maxwell having a Thatcherite agenda were largely unfounded (Thomas, "The 'Max Factor'", pp. 213–14).
92 Bower, *Final*, pp. 371–2; *Free Press*, November–December 1984; Greenslade, *Maxwell*, p. 63.
93 Robert Maxwell, Letter to Kinnock, 9 July, 1984, Neil Kinnock's Personal Papers.
94 Neil Kinnock's Office, Press Release, 9 July 1984, Neil Kinnock's Personal Papers.
95 Labour Party, *Conference 1991*, pp. 91–2.
96 Roy Hattersley, "Reflections on the Mirror", *Financial Times* (16 November 1991).
97 Foot interview.
98 Heffernan and Marqusee, *Defeat*, p. 123; Sumner interview; Frank Allaun, "A True Fighter for Press Freedom", *Free Press*, November–December 1990.
99 Benn, *The End*, pp. 488–90; Freedman, *Television 2000*, p. 204; Freedman, *Television 2001*, pp. 140–41; Heffernan and Marqusee, *Defeat*, pp. 123–4.
100 Freedman, *Television 2000*, p. 204; Freedman, *Television 2001*, p. 140.
101 Nevertheless, an indication that the matter was not resolved by Kinnock's intervention was that Labour went into the 1987 and 1992 elections still committed to creating a unified ministry of the media and arts (Dale, *Labour Party Manifesto*s, p. 308).
102 One exception in mentioning it is MacShane, "Media Policy", in Seaton and Pimlott, *British Politics*, pp. 215–35.
103 Labour Party, *Britain Will Win*, p. 14.
104 Neil Kinnock, Speech to the Wapping Rally at Wembley, n.d., Neil Kinnock's Personal Papers; Compaine, *Who Owns the Media?*, pp. 56, 312; Shawcross, *Murdoch*, pp. 92–4, 212–15.
105 So the NGA insisted on not using the Anglicized first name that Shah preferred, but emphasized his foreigner status by insisting on describing him by his original name, Selim Jehan Shah (see for instance, NGA (82), Second Briefing Conference for MPs Background Notes, November 1983 and MacArthur, *Eddy Shah*, p. 31; Neil, *Disclosure*, p. 94.)
106 TUC, *Conference 1986*, p. 636.
107 TUC, *Conference 1986*, p. 639. See also Anon, "What the TUC Decided in Brighton", *Tribune* (12 September 1986).
108 Labour Party, *Conference 1986*, p. 118.
109 Labour Party, *Agenda 1986*, p. 70; Interview with the CPBF's former *Free Press* editor Granville Williams, 14 June 2002.
110 According to Lord Corbett, the view was that "what this party ought to be about is 'sticking one up Murdoch' – a perfectly understandable, but not a wholly credible, policy" (Interview with Lord Corbett, 10 October 2002). "I have never forgotten Austin Mitchell wandering into the room when we were

discussing the whole ownership issue and he just sort of said: 'Oh let's just slap on that no foreigners can own media here.' I was saying that: 'This is going to catch minority publications, it's xenophobic.' He said: 'It doesn't matter, it will be popular and we will catch Murdoch now.' What worried me [was] it was so sort of simplistic and populist" (Jempson interview).

111 Labour Party, *Britain Will Win*, p. 14. The 1988 party conference reiterated the commitment (Labour Party, *Conference 1988*, p. 176).
112 Freedman, *Television 2000*, p. 207.
113 Seaton and Pimlott, *British Politics*, p. 300.
114 Labour Party, *Britain Will Win*.
115 Allaun, *Spreading the News*, p. 91.

6 Policy Reviewed: Neil Kinnock and John Smith

1 Ann Clwyd, "He's Used His Power to Evade Controls That Governments Might Place on Him", *Daily Mirror* (3 September 1993). The former BBC employee and Guardian journalist Ann Clwyd became an MP in 1984. She had been a member of the 1972–1974 Labour Party media study group. From 1987 until 1995, she was, variously, Labour's spokesperson on women, education, overseas development, Wales, media and national heritage, employment and foreign affairs (*Who's Who* [2001], p. 411). Under Blair, she has been a special envoy to Iraq and Chair of the Parliamentary Labour Party.
2 Robin Cook and Ann Clwyd, Cook and Clwyd Call for MMC Inquiry into Murdoch Ownership, Labour Party Press Release, 3 September 1993.
3 Labour Party, *Meet the Challenge*, p. 6; Driver and Martell, *New Labour*, pp. 17–18; Anderson and Mann, *Safety First*, pp. 71–2. Former diplomat, law lecturer and TV presenter, Bryan Gould was a member of the Shadow Cabinet from 1986 to 1992. He was Labour spokesman on trade and industry, on economy and party campaigns, and national heritage, which included press policy. He retired from British political life to become vice chancellor of Waikato University, New Zealand (*Who's Who* [2002], p. 836; *Dod's* [2001], p. 454).
4 MacShane, *French Lessons*, p. 5.
5 Labour Party, *Meet the Challenge*, p. 6.
6 Austin Mitchell, "The Party of Producers and Consumers", *The Independent* (24 July 1987); Minkin, *Contentious Alliance*, p. 472; Shaw, "Wilderness", in Brivati and Heffernan, *Labour Party*, p. 128.
7 Wring, *Politics of Marketing*, pp. 101–17; Shaw, "Wilderness", in Brivati and Heffernan, *Labour Party*, pp. 129–33; Heffernan and Marqusee, *Defeat*, pp. 166–84.
8 CLPD, Newsletter, No. 46 (Conference Edition), September–October 1992.
9 National Executive Committee. Policy Making; Labour Party, *Agenda for Change*, p. 28.
10 McKie, McKie, "'Fact is Free but Comment is Sacred'", in Crewe and Gosschalk, *Political Communications 1992*, pp. 121; Jones, *Kinnock*, pp. 189–90; Freedman, *Television 2001*, p. 157.
11 A term used in *Tribune* 10 July 1995 (Wring, *Politics of Marketing*, pp. 123, 207).
12 Wring, *Politics of Marketing*, pp. 123, 173. See also Curran et al., *Culture Wars*, p. 215.
13 Wring, *Politics of Marketing*, pp. 172–3.

14 Curran et al., *Culture Wars*, pp. 208–9.
15 Driver and Martell, *New Labour*, pp. 24–5. See also, for instance, McSmith, *Playing*, pp. 237–8, 240; McSmith, *John Smith*, pp. 298–301; Rentoul, *Blair*, pp. 238–242.
16 Wring, *Politics of Marketing*, p. 130.
17 Wring, *Politics of Marketing*, p 147.
18 Rentoul, *Blair*, pp. 267–8.
19 McSmith, *Playing*; Panitch and Leys, *Parliamentary Socialism*, p. 225; Fielding, *Labour Party*, p. 87; McSmith, *John Smith*, p. 331.
20 Ludlam, *Norms and Blocks*, pp. 232, 234; Shaw, *1945*, pp. 192–5. See also Fielding, *Labour Party*, pp. 85–7; McSmith, *Playing*, pp. 244–6.
21 Anderson and Mann, *Safety First*, pp. 95–6.
22 Fairclough, *New Labour*, pp. 23–34. For an example, see Blair, *New Britain*, pp. 89–90.
23 HOC, 18 December 1989, col. 49.
24 Shaw, "Wilderness", in Brivati and Heffernan, *Labour Party*, p. 125.
25 Curran et al., *Culture Wars*, pp. 272–3.
26 Taylor, *Labour's Renewal?*, p. 12.
27 Wring, *Political Marketing*, pp. 12–15, 17.
28 Wring, *Politics of Marketing*, pp. 120–1; Taylor, *Labour's Renewal?*, p. 12.
29 Ed Straw, Opposition into Government – A Strategic Framework, 26 June 1987; Leslie Butterfield et al., Towards a Communication Strategy for the Labour Party, n.d. Neil Kinnock Archives.
30 Gould, *Unfinished Revolution*, p. 77.
31 Gould, *Unfinished Revolution*.
32 Neil Kinnock, "Reforming the Labour Party", p. 544. Also cited in Panitch and Leys, *Parliamentary Socialism*, p. 320.
33 Bob Worcester interviewed in *Tribune*, 21 July 2000, quoted in Wring, *Politics of Marketing*, p.108. Shaw, *1979*, pp. 64, 148; Anderson and Mann, *Safety First*, p. 367.
34 Krueger, *Focus Group Results*, pp. 11, 34–38; Morgan, *Focus Group Guide*, p. 62.
35 Brook, *British Social Attitudes*, A-32; Seyd and Whiteley, *Labour's Grass Roots*, p. 54.
36 Seyd and Whiteley, *Labour's Grass Roots*; Brook, *British Social Attitudes*.
37 Labour Party, *Aims and Values*, p 6.
38 Labour Party, *Conference 1988*, p. 176, Anon, "Labour Launches Media Proposal", *Free Press* October 1988.
39 Labour Party NEC, "NEC Minutes at the 1989 Labour Party Conference".
40 Labour Party, *Conference 1989*, p. 173.
41 Labour Party, *Opportunity Britain*, p. 45; Labour Party, *Meet the Challenge*, pp. 59–60.
42 Labour Party, *Conference 1989*, p. 127.
43 Blunkett and Crick, *Aims and Values*.
44 Labour Party, *Democratic Socialist Aims and Values*, p. 6.
45 Labour Party, *Conference 1989*, p. 127.
46 Benn, *The End*, p. 565.
47 HOC, 3 February 1989, cols. 546–609; HOC, 21 April 1989, cols. 605–623; Allaun, *Spreading the News*, pp. 91–2.

48 Corbett interview.

49 NEC, "Dispute with News International", 29 January 1986.

50 Littleton, *Wapping*, p. 83

51 Neil Kinnock, "Letter to Chris Moncrieff", 29 January 1986, Chris Moncrieff, "Letter to Neil Kinnock", 29 January 1986, Neil Kinnock's Personal Papers; Benn, *The End*, p. 438; Jones, *Kinnock*, pp. 80–1; Littleton, *Wapping*, pp. 82–3.

52 Jones, *Kinnock*, pp. 80–81.

53 Office of the Leader of the Opposition, "15.45: Meeting with unions re Fulham", n.d., Neil Kinnock's Personal Papers.

54 Interview with Philip Gould in Gould, *Unfinished Revolution*, p. 214.

55 Neil, *Disclosure*, p. 161.

56 Rentoul, *Blair*, pp. 183, 185, 191.

57 Gould, *Unfinished Revolution*, p. 112.

58 For the US see Bagdikian, *Media Monopoly*; McChesney, *Rich Media*; Herman and Chomsky, *Global Media*.

59 Freedman, *Television 2001*.

60 Shawcross, *Murdoch*, p. 302; Neil, *Disclosure*, p. 374.

61 HOC, 19 May 1989, cols. 630–3; HOC, 18 December 1989, col. 42.

62 HOC, 19 May 1989, col. 597.

63 HOC, 18 December 1989, col. 53.

64 Quoted in Georgina Henry, "Satellite Merger Escapes Scrutiny", *The Guardian* (19 December 1990).

65 Labour Party, *Conference 1988*; Anon, "Labour Launches Media Proposal", *Free Press*, October 1988; Labour Party, *Meet the Challenge*, p. 59.

66 Wring, *Politics of Marketing*, p. 103.

67 HOC, 9 May 1990, cols. 241–2.

68 Hughes and Wintour, *Labour Rebuilt*, pp. 166–175; Wring, *Politics of Marketing*, pp. 107–11, 119–20; Shaw, *1979*, p. 112. See also Taylor, *Labour's Renewal?*, pp. 57–8, 103.

69 Gould, *Unfinished Revolution*, pp. 108–10.

70 *Ibid.*, pp. 101–14; Heffernan and Marqusee, *Defeat*, pp. 227–9, 231.

71 For example, the inner circle latterly concentrated on proportional representation. However, how important it became seems to have been a case more of accident than design (Gould, *Unfinished Revolution*, pp. 150–1).

72 Gould, *Unfinished Revolution*, p. 109. See also Heffernan and Marqusee, *Defeat*, p. 315.

73 Hattersley, *Who Goes Home?*, p. 305.

74 Gould, *Unfinished Revolution*, p. 109; David Blunkett, "Letter to NEC members", 16 June 1992 and "Letter to Larry Whitty", 28 March 1992, Neil Kinnock Personal Papers.

75 Cook, "The Labour Campaign" in Crewe and Gosschalk, *Political Communications 1992*, p. 15; Gould, *Unfinished Revolution*, pp. 130–41.

76 Corbett interview.

77 *Ibid.*

78 George Jones, "Free Press at Risk from Labour, says Wakeham", *Daily Telegraph* (29 February 1992).

79 Dale, *Labour Party Manifestos*, p. 308. See also Shawcross, *Murdoch*, p. 542;

David Owen, "Hattersley Promise on Incomes", *Financial Times* (16 March 1992); Steve Thompson, "Comment Hits Media Stock", *Financial Times* (24 March 1992).

80 HOC, 24 April 1991, col. 1172.

81 A similar point is made by Freedman, *Television 2000*, p. 207.

82 Austin Mitchell, HOC, 24 April 1991, col. 1171.

83 David Owen, "Hattersley Promise on Incomes", *Financial Times* (16 March 1992); Steve Thompson, "Comment Hits Media Stock", *Financial Times* (24 March 1992).

84 Shawcross, *Murdoch*, p. 542.

85 Routledge, *Mandy*, pp. 139, 140, 146; Macintyre, *Mandelson*, pp. 236, 246, 248–9; Gould, *Unfinished Revolution*, pp. 161–2.

86 Wring, *Politics of Marketing*, p. 126.

87 He was said to have described Mandelson's then associate, Derek Draper, as "that little bastard" (Routledge, *Mandy*, pp. 137, 147). See also McSmith, *John Smith*, p. 205.

88 Jempson interview.

89 Gould, *Unfinished Revolution*, p. 105; also cited in Macintyre, *Mandelson*, p. 241.

90 According to his director of communications David Hill, who would later provide a similar role to Blair (Macintyre, *Mandelson*, p. 241).

91 These more traditional social democrats had John Prescott as a leading figure (McSmith, *Playing*, pp. 241–2, 246; McSmith, *John Smith*, pp. 302–3). A more bizarre aspect was the personalised public spat with Mandelson, which reached its apogee when Prescott conducted a "conversation" with a crab he christened "Peter" at a photo call with reporters.

92 See Wring, *Politics of Marketing*, p. 126.

93 McSmith, *John Smith*, pp. 302–3.

94 Williams interview; Jempson interview; *Freedman, Television 2001*, p. 160.

95 HOC, 22 February 1993, col. 668; Anon, "Brooke Rejects Media Complaint", *Financial Times* (23 February 1993).

96 HOC, 10 June 1993, col. 474; Ivor Owen, "Labour Pledge on Press Ownership", *Financial Times* (11 June 1993).

97 Andrew Culf, "Murdoch Claims His Technology Will Conquer National Media Laws", *The Guardian* (13 October 1993) and "Clwyd Attacks Tory Line on Broadcasting", *The Guardian* (27 September 1993). See also Freedman, *Television 2001*, p. 161.

98 Michael Jones, "Labour in a Silly Spin over Satellite Success", *Sunday Times* (5 September 1993).

99 HOC, 8 July 1993, col. 568.

100 Corbett interview.

101 Gould, *Unfinished Revolution*, p. 202.

102 Corbett interview.

103 *Ibid.*

104 Jempson interview.

105 Corbett interview.

106 Fairclough, *New Language*.

107 Patricia Wynn Davies, "Labour Attacked Over TV 'Sell-out'", *The Independent* (26 November 1993).

108 Goodwin, *Television*, p. 143.

109 HOC, 24 April 1991.

110 Doyle, *Media Ownership*, pp. 94–5. The BMIG included the Pearson Group (involved with the *Financial Times*), Associated Newspapers (*The Daily Mail* and *Mail on Sunday*), the Guardian Media Group and the *Telegraph* newspapers.

111 Goodwin has effectively dismissed the BMIG's claims that its demands for increased cross-ownership were a response to a new multimedia environment (Goodwin, *Television*). Nor was it clear that their members' financial survival was threatened (Maggie Brown and Michael Leapman, "Let the Feeding Frenzy Commence", *The Independent* (12 January 1994); TUC, *Conference 1994*, p. 301).

112 Freedman, *Television 2001*, pp. 161–2.

113 Maggie Brown, "Giant Media Groups on the Way", *The Independent* (4 January 1993); Raymond Snoddy, "Media Review Aims to Boost UK Ownership Overseas", *Financial Times* (4 January 1993).

114 Marjorie Mowlam, "Labour's Watching Brief", *The Independent* (12 January 1994).

115 Williams interview; Goodwin, *Television*, p. 146; Freedman, *Television 2001*, p. 163.

116 Although it should be pointed out that Corbett did approve of listening to business lobbyists (Corbett interview).

117 Mo Mowlam, questioned by the author at the launch meeting for her book, *Momentum*, in Brighton on 6 May 2002.

118 Maggie Brown, "Rule Change Urged on Media Ownership", *The Independent* (14 July 1994).

119 Georgina Henry, "Balancing Act on a See-saw", *The Guardian* (27 June 1994). See also TUC, Conference 1994, p. 389; O'Malley and Soley, *Press*, p. 94.

120 Georgina Henry, "Balancing Act on a See-saw", *The Guardian* (27 June 1994).

121 Mowlam in Brighton.

122 See, for instance, Steven Barnett, "Bill Throws Broadcast Up In Air", *The Observer* (5 May 2002) and Jamie Doward, "How Far Can Blair Go Before Murdoch Hits Back?", *The Observer* (5 May 2002).

123 See, for instance, Leader, "A Place in the Sun for Blair?", *The Independent* (10 August 1994).

124 Jempson interview, Freedman, *Television 2000*, p. 230.

125 Jempson interview, Corbett interview.

126 TUC, Conference 1994, pp. 389–91; Freedman, *Television 2000*, pp. 230, 232–4.

127 HOC, 11 January 1995, cols. 153–6. See also Humphreys, "New Labour", p. 228.

128 Roland Rudd, "Tougher Line on Media Urged", *Financial Times* (8 October 1994).

7 Living with the Enemy: Press Policy under Tony Blair

1 Robin Cook and Ann Clwyd, Cook and Clwyd call for MMC Inquiry into Murdoch Ownership, Labour Party Press Release, 3 September 1993.

2 DTI/DCMS, *Draft Communications Bill*; DTI/DCMS, *Draft Communications Bill Regulatory Impact Assessment*.

3 Martin J. Smith, "The Transition to New Labour", in Brivati and Heffernan, *Labour Party*, pp. 146–7.

4 Wring, *Politics of Marketing*, p. 155.

5 Ludlam, *Norms and Blocks*, p. 232.

6 NEC, *Partnership in Power*.

7 Patrick Wintour and Sarah Hall, "Labour Inquest on Membership Loss", *The Guardian* (29 January 2002); Patrick Wintour, "Labour Membership Halved", *The Guardian* (3 August, 2004).

8 Wring, *Politics of Marketing*, p. 143.

9 Driver and Martell, *New Labour*, p. 40.

10 Labour Party, *Labour's Business Manifesto 1997*, pp. 5, 9, 15–16, 29; Labour Party, *Labour's Business Manifesto 2001*, p. 1.

11 Labour Party, *Rulebook*, p. 4.

12 Labour Party, *Labour's Business Manifesto 1997*, p. 1; Labour Party, *Vision for Growth*, p. 12.

13 Paul Webster, "Britain Sank Jospin's EU Jobs Scheme", *The Guardian* (21 June 1997). See also David Marquand, "After Euphoria", p. 336; Anderson and Mann, *Safety First*, pp. 114–15.

14 Driver and Martell, *New Labour*, pp. 172–3.

15 Gould, *Unfinished Revolution*, p. 212.

16 Heffernan, *New Labour and Thatcherism*.

17 Leader, "The Vision Thing", *The Economist*, 27 September 1997.

18 Labour Party, *Vision for Growth*, p. 12, Blair, *New Britain*, pp. 23, 89–90.

19 Fairclough, *New Language*, p. 28.

20 Peter Mandelson, "There's Plenty of Life in the 'New' Third Way Yet", *The Times* (19 June 2002).

21 For one thing, a core within the party still did not share these New Labour values.

22 Driver and Martell, *New Labour*, pp. 118–20, 130–2; Anderson and Mann, *Safety First*, pp. 243–8. For the link between the Clinton, the communitarians and New Labour, see Gould, *Unfinished Revolution*, pp. 233–4. For the argument that this rejected Thatcherite neo-liberal individualism in favour of conservatism see Driver and Martell, *New Labour*, pp. 28–9, 167, 169.

23 See, for instance, Gordon Brown, "Introduction", in Blair, *New Britain*, p. 2.

24 Driver and Martell, *New Labour*, p. 2.

25 Heffernan, *New Labour and Thatcherism*.

26 Hills, *Inequality and the State*, p. 37.

27 Held, *Global Transformations*, pp. 7, 3–10.

28 Fairclough, *New Language*, p. 27 and Blair, *New Britain*, p. 204.

29 Lance Price, Newsnight BBC Two, 26 September 2005.

30 Bryan Gould, "The Long Retreat from Principle", *New Statesman*, 29 January 1999.

31 Jones interview.

32 Jones interview.

33 Linton, *Was it The Sun?*, esp. pp. 29–31.

34 Peter Mandelson, Lecture at the London School of Economics, 25 February

2003; Jones interview; Oborne, *Campbell*, pp. 140–1, 194; Roy Greenslade, "Nice One Sun, says Tony", *The Guardian* (19 May 1997).

35 Jones interview. See also Price, *Diary*, p. 318.

36 Wring, *Politics of Marketing*; Jones, *Sultans of Spin* and *Control Freaks*.

37 McNair, *Journalism and Democracy*, pp. 149–50; Linton interview.

38 For examples, see NUJ magazine *The Journalist*.

39 Seymour-Ure, "Editorial Opinion", p. 84.

40 Richard Brooks, "Love, Marriage and the Real Rupert Murdoch", *The Observer* (8 November 1998); Neil, *Disclosure*; Wyatt, *Diaries*.

41 *Ibid.*

42 Wyatt, *Diaries*, p. 442, see also 105, 324–5, 443. See also Neil, *Disclosure*, p. 569.

43 Quoted in McKie, "Clingers", in Crewe et al., *Political Communications 1997*, p. 117.

44 Junor, *Major*, p. 216, 202.

45 Wyatt, Diaries, p.163. We now know that Major had conducted an affair with a Conservative colleague in the 1980s (Edwina Currie, "I Chose My Lover Too Well", *The Times* [30 September 2002]).

46 Wyatt, *Diaries*, p. 514.

47 *Ibid.*, p. 162.

48 Curran and Seaton, *Power Without Responsibility*.

49 Wyatt, *Diaries*, p. 481. See also pp. 511 and 602.

50 Wyatt, *Diaries*, pp. 536, 550, 553, 514, 582, 684, 720, 722. Donald Macintyre, "The Odd Couple on Honeymoon in the Sun", *The Independent* (18 July 1995).

51 Cohen, *Cruel Britannia*, p. 234.

52 McKie, "Clingers", p. 117 in Crewe et al., *Political Communications 1997*; Bruce Page, *Murdoch Archipelago*, p. 447; Matthew Parris, "How Murdoch Interferes Less Than Other Proprietors", *New Statesman*, 14 March 1998.

53 Frank, *One Market*, pp. 29–31, 43, 56, 55, 93, 169, 179–80, 203–4, 347–8; Mulgan, *Politics*, p. 127; Charles Leadbetter and Geoff Mulgan, "Lean Democracy and the Leadership Vacuum", in Mulgan, *Life*, p. 256; Andrew Adonis, and Geoff Mulgan, "Back to Greece" in Mulgan, *Life*, p. 232.

54 Frank, *One Market*, pp. 86–7, 97, 93, 366–9.

55 Charles Leadbetter and Geoff Mulgan, "Lean Democracy and the Leadership Vacuum", in Mulgan, *Life*, p. 256; Ian Traynor, "Peter's Passions", *The Guardian* (16 March 1998); Gould, *Unfinished Revolution*, pp. 297–8, 328.

56 Mair, "Partyless Democracy", pp. 21–35; Barnett, "Corporate Populism and Partyless Democracy", pp. 81–9.

57 Wring, *Politics of Marketing*, pp. 176–7.

58 Brind, *The Labour Video Project*.

59 Franklin, *Tough on Soundbites*.

60 *The Century of the Self*, Part Four, RDF Media, BBC Two.

61 Franklin, *Tough on Soundbites*.

62 Department of National Heritage, *Media Ownership* esp., pp. 7, 15; Collins and Murroni, *New Policies*, p. 70; Goodwin, *Television*, pp. 147–8, Steven Barnett, "More Noise, Fewer Voices", *The Independent* (27 March 1995).

63 Wyatt, *Diaries*, pp. 511, 582; Andrew Culf, "Murdoch Dismisses 'Paranoid'

Critics", *The Guardian* (22 May 1995). See also Oborne, *Campbell*, p. 142.

64 Wyatt, *Diaries*, pp. 536, 550, 553, 514, 582, 684, 720, 722.

65 Neil, *Disclosure*, pp. xxii–xxiii, 209–10; Wyatt, *Diaries*. See also Oborne, *Campbell*, pp. 141–2 and Greenslade, *Press Gang*, p. 621.

66 Schultz, *Fourth Estate*.

67 Bruce Manners, "Blair Learns From Down-underWorldWhere Left is Right", *Sunday Telegraph* (31 December 1995); John Pilger, "TheVery Best of Mates", *The GuardianWeekend* (23 July 1994); John Pilger, "Murdoch's Love for New Labour", *Free Press*, September–October 1995.

68 Blair, *New Britain*, pp. 204–5; John Pilger, "Murdoch's Love for New Labour", *Free Press*, No. 88, September–October 1995.

69 Linton interview.

70 Lance Price, Newsnight BBC Two, 26 September 2005. See also Price, *Diary*.

71 Neil, *Disclosure*, p. xxv.

72 Linton interview.

73 Jones interview.

74 Price, *Diary*, pp. 45, 95, Wring, *Politics of Marketing*, p. 153.

75 Kevin Brown, "Labour Backs Off in Threat to Murdoch", *Financial Times* (24 March 1995).

76 Patricia Wynn Davies and Matthew Horsman, "Prescott Slaps Down Complaint over BSkyB", *The Independent* (21 November 1995).

77 Goodwin, *Television*, pp. 152–3; Freedman, *Television 2000*, pp. 233–4; Freedman, *Television 2001*, p. 165. For an analysis of the 1996 Broadcasting Act, see Doyle, *Media Ownership*, Chapters 6 and 7 and Goodwin, *Television*.

78 Freedman suggests a similar path was taken with regard to broadcasting policy (Freedman, *Television 2000*, p. 236; Freedman, *Television 2001*, p. 165).

79 Department of National Heritage, pp. 7, 20–1.

80 HOC, 2 July 1996, cols. 843–4; Maggie Brown, "Gloves Off in the Free for All", *The Guardian* (15 April 1996).

81 HOC, 2 July 1996, cols. 843–4. See also Paul Foot, "Sour Note, Moonie Tune", *The Guardian* (15 April 1996); Leader, "Mirror, Mirror on the Screen" *The Guardian* (17 April 1996) and Doyle, *Media Ownership*, p. 110.

82 News International, *Response to the White Paper, A New Future for Communications*, p. 4, <www.communicationswhitepaper.gov.uk>, quoted in Doyle, *Media Ownership*, p. 135.

83 Goodwin, *Television*, pp. 152–3; Patrick Wintour, "Government Facing Defeat", *The Guardian* (16 May 1996); Rebecca Smithers and Patrick Wintour, "Tory MPs Quit After Media Bill Revolt", *The Guardian* (22 May 1996).

84 Paul Foot, "Sour Note, Moonie Tune", *The Guardian* (15 April 1996). See also Freedman, *Television 2000*, p. 234; Freedman, *Television 2001*, p. 166.

85 Freedman, *Television 2000*, pp. 233–4; Freedman, *Television 2001*, p. 166.

86 The opposition included those not associated with the left, such as Giles Radice (HOC, 2 July 1996, cols. 833–4, 835–7).

87 HOC, 2 July 1996, cols. 835–7.

88 HOC, 2 July 1996, cols. 835, 838 and 840.

89 HOC, 2 July 1996, cols. 843–850, Tim Gopsill, "Meanwhile back on the benches. . .", *Free Press,* No. 93, July–August 1996; Humphreys, "New Labour", p. 229.

90 Jones interview; Jones, *Control Freaks*, esp. pp. 198–206; Oborne, *Campbell*, esp. pp. 174–6.

91 Wring, *Politics of Marketing*, p. 151.

92 Interview with Roy Greenslade, "Nice One Sun, Says Tony", *The Guardian* (19 May 1997).

93 Andy McSmith and John Arlidge, "Sun Chiefs Tried to Defy Murdoch", *The Observer* (23 March 1997); Neil, *Disclosure*, p. xxiv.

94 Interview with Lindsay Baker, "Made in England", *The Guardian* (28 June 1997).

95 *The Sun, Mirror* and *Daily Star* were positioned on the same side as *The Guardian, The Independent* and the *Financial Times*.

96 Franklin, *Packaging Politics* (2004), p. 143.

97 Roy Greenslade, "Taming Paper Tigers, But for How Long?", *The Guardian* (1 May 1997).

98 Alex Bellos, "Daily Mail Proprietor Gives New Hint of Election Backing for Blair", *The Guardian* (15 April 1996).

99 Wyatt, *Diaries*, pp. 720, 722.

100 Seymour-Ure, "Editorial Opinion", p. 79.

101 Interview with Roy Greenslade, "Nice One Sun, Says Tony", *The Guardian* (19 May 1997).

102 Emily Bell, "Rivals Sniff at Cut-price Tactics", *The Observer* (5 September 1993); Anon, "The Multi-media Monopoly Machine", *Daily Mirror* (3 September 1993).

103 OFT, *Press Release: Newspaper Pricing: News International Gives Assurances*, 21 May 1999.

104 Humphreys, "New Labour", p. 125.

105 House of Lords Hansard for 13 Nov 1997, cols. 309–313.

106 Lords Hansard text for 9 February 1998, cols. 913–23.

107 HOC, 8 July 1998, cols. 1136–52; Price, Diary, p. 13.

108 HOC, 8 July 1998, col. 1155.

109 House of Lords Hansard Debates for 20 October 1998, cols. 1347–60.

110 Humphreys, "New Labour", p. 232.

111 OFT, *Press Release: Scottish Newspaper Group Fined for Predatory Pricing*, 16 July 2001.

112 OFT, *Press Release: Newspaper pricing: News International Gives Assurances*, 21 May 1999.

113 Williams interview.

114 HOC, 8 Jul 1998, col. 1152.

115 Labour Party, *New Labour*, p. 31. See also Freedman, *Television 2000*, p. 239.

116 DCMS/DTI, *Regulating Communications*, p. 32.

117 *Ibid.*, p. 16.

118 *Ibid.*, p. 174.

119 *Ibid.*, sections 1.13, 2.11 and 3.11.

120 See AHRB Centre for British Film and Television Studies, Sheffield Hallam University, "Broadcasting, Citizen Rights and Social Cohesion", Section 5, Sheffield Hallam University; Doyle, *Media Ownership*, pp. 130–1.

121 DCMS/DTI, *New Future*, Chapter 4.

122 *Ibid.*, p. 19.

123 Price, *Diary*, pp. 270, 286.
124 Rebecca Allison, "Times Backs Labour For the First Time", *The Guardian* (5 June 2001); Anon, "Times Gives Backing to Blair", *The Independent* (5 June 2001).
125 Franklin, *Packaging Politics* (2004), pp. 144–5.
126 *Ibid.*, pp. 143–4.
127 Curran and Seaton, *Power Without Responsibility* (2003), pp. 75–6.
128 Philip Robinson, "Back-Seat Role for Lord Stevens", *Daily Telegraph* (14 November 1996); Neil Bennett, "The Odd Couple", *Sunday Telegraph* (28 November 1999). See also Cohen, *Cruel Britannia*, pp. 145–6.
129 Business Comment, "View Looks Good from Lord Hollick's Chair", *The Independent* (11 September 1997). See also Freedman, *Television 2000*, p. 267.
130 Richard Addis, "A Red Rose Blooms in Blackfriars", *The Independent* (9 June 1997).
131 Interview with a former Daily Express reporter, 12 November 2000; Chris Blackhurst, "Bad Days at Blackfriars" (*The Guardian*, 29 January, 2001).
132 Bill Hagerty, "Cap'n Spin Does Lose His Rag!", *British Journalism Review*, vol. 11, no. 2, 2000; Katherine Viner, "Window Dressing", *The Guardian* (5 October 1998); Roy Greenslade, "Boycott Sacks Platell", *The Guardian* (25 January, 1999); John Gapper and David Wighton, "Sunday Express Chiefs Quit in Mandelson Row", *Financial Times* (20 January 1999).
133 Peter Cole, "Lesson Number One: Don't Sack Your Readers, *The Independent* (May 18, 1998).
134 Chris Blackhurst, "Bad Days at Blackfriars", *The Guardian* (29 January, 2001). See also Bill Hagerty, "Citizen Clive, pp. 19–28.
135 Bill Hagerty, "Citizen Clive", pp. 19–28.
136 Chris Blackhurst, "Bad Days at Blackfriars", *The Guardian* (29 January, 2001). See also Greenslade, *Press Gang*, p. 666.
137 Interview with a former *Daily Express* reporter, 12 November 2000.
138 Stephen Glover, "It Was a Dreadful Picture; But It Spoke for Humanity", *Spectator*, 14 October 2000.
139 Kevin Maguire, "Byers Urged to Block Express Buyout", *The Guardian* (23 December 2000); The Monopoly and Mergers Commission, Mr David Sullivan and the Bristol Evening Post PLC.
140 Kamal Ahmed and Antony Barnett, "The Deal That Put a Porn Baron In Favour With No 10", *The Observer* (12 May 2002); Jessica Hodgson, "Blair Contacted Desmond Minutes After Express Takeover", *The Guardian* (13 May, 2002).
141 NUJ, *Communications Bill 2002*.
142 DCMS/DTI, Consultation on Media Ownership Rules, sections 6.4.15 and 6.5.12.
143 News International, *Response to Consultation on Media Ownership Rules*, DCMS <www.culture.gov.uk>; Campaign For Press and Broadcasting Freedom, *Response to Consultation on Media Ownership Rules By DCMS and DTI* (November 2001).
144 John Cassy, "Murdoch on Blair, Britain and Babies. And Those Whiners at ITV As Well", *The Guardian* (3 November 2001); George Trefgarne, "BSkyB Boss Threatens to Turn Titles Anti-Labour", *Daily Telegraph* (3 November 2001).

145 Page, *Murdoch Archipelago*, p. 444.
146 See DTI/DCMS, *Policy Narrative;* DTI/DCMS, *Regulatory Impact Assessment.*
147 In a tired rehash of Bad Godesberg, Jowell argued that there was a need to get "rid of regulation where possible but to keep them where necessary" (Tessa Jowell, Voice of the Listeners and Viewers Meeting at the House of Commons, 14 May 2002).
148 News International, *Response to Consultation on Media Ownership Rules*, DCMS, <www.culture.gov.uk>, 2002, p. 4.
149 DTI/DCMS, *Regulatory Impact Assessment*, pp. 65–7.
150 DCMS/DTI, *New Future.*
151 Tessa Jowell, Guardian Online chat, 10 May 2002, <talk.guardian.co.uk>.
152 It was promoted as a pro-business measure: "The removal of rules that stipulate public interest tests will remove the significant risk for businesses of spending a great deal of time and resource putting together merger proposals that are subsequently rejected" (DTI/DCMS, *Regulatory Impact Assessment*, pp. 65–7).
153 *Ibid.*, pp. 61–3.
154 DTI/DCMS, *Communications Bill*, pp. 411–16; Anon, "Local Radio Ownership Proposals in Full", *The Guardian* (14 November 2002).
155 DTI/DCMS, *Regulatory Impact Assessment*, p. 65.
156 Steven Barnett, "One Man, One Media?", *The Guardian* (8 May 2002).
157 Private information.
158 NUJ, *Communications 2002.*
159 Joint Committee on the Draft Communications Bill, *Draft Communications Bill*, HMSO, July 2002.
160 Joint Committee on the Draft Communications Bill, *Proceedings of the Committee Relating to the Report*, 25 July 2002, <www.publications.parliament.uk/pa/jt200102/jtselect/jtcom>.
161 John Cassy and Patrick Wintour, "Blair faces fight on TV controls", *The Guardian* (29 July 2002); David Rose, "Blair will force Lords to accept US buyers", *Broadcast*, 4 October 2002.
162 Curran and Seaton, *Power Without Responsibility* (2003), p. 360.
163 Mike Smith interview.
164 Williams interview; Gopsill interview.
165 Williams interview.
166 Gopsill interview,
167 TUC, *Conference 1996*, pp. 27–8; TUC, *Conference 1998*, pp. 90–2; Anon, "Murdoch Should Mark His Words", *The Journalist*, October–November 1998.
168 TUC, Conference 1998, pp. 91, 92.
169 Williams interview.
170 Mike Smith interview.
171 Personal information.
172 Gopsill interview.
173 TUC, General Purposes Committee Report to Congress 2002, p. 23. Tony Dubbins, "Fighting Against Media Monopoly", *Morning Star* (1 October 2002), Personal information.

174 Labour Party, *Democracy*.

8 Epilogue and Concluding Remarks: How Did We Get Here?

1 Frank Kane, "How We Won the Telegraph – By the Barclays", *The Observer* (27 June 2004).

2 DTI/DCMS, *Communications Bill*, HMSO, 2002, esp. pp. 6 and 287–8.

3 Lord Puttnam, Hard Talk, BBC News 24, 4 October 2002.

4 Humphreys, "New Labour", p. 222.

5 For such a report see Neil Armstrong, "When will the Americans Land?" *Mediaweek*, 4 October 2002.

6 HM Government, *Communications Act 2003*, sections 373–9; News International, Response to Consultation on Media Ownership Rules, DCMS, <www.culture.gov.uk>.

7 DTI/DCMS, *Draft Communications Bill Regulatory Impact Assessment*, p. 62.

8 DCMS/DTI, *New Future*, Section 9.4.7, DTI/DCMS, *Draft Communications Bill Regulatory Impact Assessment*, p. 62.

9 Doyle, *Media Ownership*, pp. 130–1.

10 DTI, Enterprise Act 2002, Section 23, <www.dti.gov.uk>. Competition Commission, Merger References: Competition Commission Guidelines, June 2003, <www.competition-commission.org.uk>.

11 DTI, Public Interest Intervention, col. 2.6, <www.dti.gov.uk>.

12 House of Lords, Hansard, 23 June 2003, cols. 11–23.

13 DTI, Public Interest Intervention, Executive Summary, <www.dti.gov.uk>.

14 *Ibid.*, cols. 2.4–5.

15 *Ibid.*, cols. 2.6, 3.5–6, 5.3.

16 *Ibid.* See for instance the very useful diagram in Annex A.

17 *Ibid.*, col. 9.4, <www.dti.gov.uk>; OFCOM, OFCOM Guidance for the Public Interest Test for Media Mergers, cols. 74–5, <www.ofcom.org.uk>; Roy Greenslade, "Shouldn't This Man Be Worried?", *The Guardian* (12 January 2004).

18 DTI, *Public Interest Intervention*, May 2004, cols. 5.6–5.7, <www.dti.gov.uk>.

19 Roy Greenslade, "Shouldn't This Man Be Worried?", *The Guardian* (12 January 2004).

20 <www.ofcom.org.uk>; <www.dti.gov.uk>.

21 News International, *News International Ltd's Response to the Consultation on OFCOM Guidance for the Public Interest Test for Media Mergers*, <www.dti.gov.uk>.

22 Trinity Mirror, *Trinity Mirror Plc's Response to the Document "Consultation on OFCOM Guidance on the Public Interest Test for Media Mergers"*, <www.dti.gov.uk>.

23 Dan Milmo, "Ex Editors Will Vet Telegraph Bids to Advise on Public Interest", *The Guardian* (8 May 2004); Tom Leonard, "Telegraph Sale May Face Test", *Daily Telegraph* (8 May 2004).

24 Frank Kane, "How We Won the Telegraph – By the Barclays", *The Observer* (27 June 2004).

25 <www.guardian.co.uk/freedom>.

26 Tessa Jowell, Letter to Les Hinton, 30 May 2003, <www.guardian.co.uk/freedom>.

27 Raymond Snoddy, "Lord Puttnam – 'I Should Have Been Smarter'", *The Independent* (9 May 2005).

28 David Currie, *The Newspaper Society Annual Lunch*, 17 May 2005, <www.ofcom.org.uk>.

29 Freedman, *How Level is the Playing Field?*, Goldsmiths College and the ESRC, 2005.

30 Curran, "Press Reformism".

31 Freedman, *Television 2000*.

32 However, even here, it is important to note there has been discussion of recent implementation of similar demands in other countries. Some US states have said to have implemented an advertising tax, including on parts of the media (Richard Tomkins, "Let's Ban Advertising. Only Joking, Let's Tax It", *Financial Times* [16 May 2003]).

33 Collins and Murroni, *New Policies*, pp. 3–4. See also Freedman, *Television 2001*, p. 2.

34 Panitch and Leys, *Parliamentary Socialism*. The link is reflected and acknowledged in the title of the book. A more critical reading of the new left legacy, influenced by Panitch and Leys, has been provided more recently by Wickham-Jones (Wickham-Jones, "New Left" in Plant, *Soul*).

35 As Seymour-Ure says, a government press subsidy would have kept Conservative-supporting titles running, possibly at a cost to the Labour-backing *Daily Mirror* (Seymour-Ure, *British Press and Broadcasting*, p. 215).

36 Davis, *Public Relations Democracy*, pp. 114–15, 125–49.

37 Lukes, *Power*.

38 Curran, "Different Approaches", pp. 89–135; Curran, *Policy for the Press*. (Such an assessment is not withstanding the fact that the lottery as it exists has problems of equitable distribution and the funds needed for new publications are substantial.)

39 Curran, "Different Approaches", pp. 89–135, 119.

40 O'Neil, "Practices of Toleration", in Lichtenberg, *Democracy and the Mass Media*, pp. 155–85.

41 *Ibid.*, p. 173.

42 See, for instance, Giddens, *The Third Way*, pp. 85–8.

43 O'Neil, "Practices of Toleration", p. 178.

44 O'Malley, "Demanding Accountability", p. 89.

45 Allaun, *Spreading the News*, p. 93.

46 Freedman, *Television 2000*, p. 183.

47 Seymour-Ure, *British Press and Broadcasting*, p. 242. See also O'Malley and Soley, *Press*.

48 DTI/DCMS, *Policy Narrative*, DTI/DCMS, *Draft Communications Bill*.

49 Wring, *Politics of Marketing*, pp. 178–9.

50 Doyle, *Media Ownership*, pp. 31–2, 150, Chapter 10; Doyle, *Understanding*, p. 169. See also Humphreys, "New Labour", p. 231.

51 Hewitt and Jowell, *A Summary of Our Proposals*, HMSO, 2002.

52 DTI/DCMS, *Draft Communications Bill*.

53 Ambler, *French Socialist Experiment*, pp. 8, 10, 17, 208–10; Halimi, "Less Exceptionalism than Meets the Eye", in Daley, *The Mitterrand Era*, pp. 86, 91.

54 Seymour-Ure, "National Press", pp. 265–6.

55 Callaghan, *Retreat.*
56 DTI/DCMS, *Draft Communications Bill Regulatory Impact Assessment,* p. 62.
57 Harrison, *Poor Men's Guardians,* p. 221.
58 Linton interview.
59 For a debate on this see Pippa Norris, "Political Communications in Post-Industrial Democracies", in Keith Dowding et al., *Challenges to Democracy,* pp. 100–17, 103; Jones, *Soundbites and Spin Doctors*; Jones, *Sultans* and *Control Freaks* and Franklin, *Packaging Politics* (2004).
60 MORI poll, July 23 2000, conducted for the *Mail on Sunday,* <www.mori.com>.
61 MORI, The Bubble Bursts, June 2000, <www.mori.com>.
62 Anthony King, "Labour Viewed as 'Sleazy and Disreputable'", *Daily Telegraph* (20 June 2002).
63 Wring, *Politics of Marketing,* pp. 158–9.
64 Dominic Wring, "The Labour Campaign", in Norris and Wlezien, eds., *Parliamentary Affairs,* special issue on 2005 British general election.
65 Linton interview.
66 De Bens and Østbye, "The European Newspaper Market" in McQuail and Siune, *Media Policy,* pp. 7–22, 14.
67 Seymour-Ure, *British Press and Broadcasting,* p. 273.
68 Curran interview.
69 Hall, *Change.*

Bibliography

Books, Pamphlets, Articles and Television Programmes

Anon. 1979. *Who's Who*. London: A. & C. Black.

Anon. 1985. *Who's Who*. London: A. & C. Black.

Anon. 2002. *Who's Who*. London: A. & C. Black.

Anon. 1983. *Dod's Parliamentary Companion*. London: Dod's Parliamentary Companion Ltd.

Anon. 2000. *Dod's Parliamentary Companion*. London: Dod's Parliamentary Companion Ltd.

Anon. 1972. "Case for a Labour Press: Where the Dream is a Reality", *Labour Weekly* (30 June 1972).

Anon. 1972. "Briginshaw Bashes Trade Union Bashers", *Labour Weekly* (11 August 1972).

Anon. 1972. "The Ethics of Circumstance", *Tribune* (1 October 1972).

Anon. 1973. "Our 'Special' Role in Industrial Democracy", *The Journalist*, August 1973.

Anon. 1974. "Comment", *Labour Weekly* (12 April 1974).

Anon. 1975. "Hetherington Calls for Staff Politics Probe", *The Journalist*, March 1975.

Anon. 1980. "Labour Movement's 'Yes' to Campaign", *Free Press*, October 1980.

Anon. 1980. "ITN Offers Benn Five Minutes", *Free Press*, October 1980.

Anon. 1982. "Does the 'Right of Reply' Campaign Go Far Enough?", *Free Press*, May–June 1982.

Anon. 1982. "£50,000 appeal boost", *Free Press*, May–June 1982.

Anon. 1986. "What the TUC Decided in Brighton", *Tribune* (12 September 1986).

Anon. 1988. "Labour Launches Media Proposal", *Free Press*, October 1988.

Anon. 1988. "Radical Left Collapse Shock", *The Economist*, 30 April 1988.

Anon. 2001. "Times Gives Backing to Blair" *The Independent* (5 June 2001).

Addis, Richard. 1997. "A Red Rose Blooms in Blackfriars", *The Independent* (9 June 1997).

Ahmed, Kamal and Antony Barnett. 2002. "The Deal That Put a Porn Baron in Favour with No 10", *The Observer* (12 May 2002).

Aldridge, David. 1981. "Labour Party Broadcast Attacks Bias", *Free Press*, November–December 1981.

Allaun, Frank. 1988. *Spreading the News*. Nottingham: Spokesman.

Allaun, Frank. 1990. "A True Fighter for Press Freedom", *Free Press*, November–December 1990.

Allison, Rebecca. 2001. "Times Backs Labour for the First Time", *The Guardian* (5 June 2001).

Ambler, John. 1985. *The French Socialist Experiment*, Philadelphia: Institute for the Study of Human Issues.

Anderson, Perry. 1980. *Arguments within English Marxism*. London: Verso.

Anderson, Paul, and Nyta Mann. 1997. *Safety First*. London: Granta.

Arblaster, Anthony. 1987. *Democracy*. Milton Keynes: Open University Press.

Armstrong, Neil. 2002. "When will the Americans Land?" *Mediaweek*, 4 October 2002.

ABC. 2005. *Audit Bureau of Circulation, National Newspapers – Audit Period December 2005*, <www.abc.org.uk>.

Ayerst, David. 1971. *Guardian: Biography of a Newspaper*. London: Collins.

Bagdikian, Ben. 1992. *The Media Monopoly*. Boston: Beacon Press.

Bagdikian, Ben. 2004. *The New Media Monopoly*. Boston: Beacon Press.

Baistow, Tom. 1985. *Fourth-rate Estate*. London: Comedia.

Barnes, Denis and Eileen Reid. 1982. *Governments and Trade Unions*. London: Heinemann Educational Books.

Barnett, Anthony. 2000. "Corporate Populism and Partyless Democracy." *New Left Review*. May–June 2000.

Barnett, Steven. 1995. "More Noise, Fewer Voices", *The Independent* (27 March 1995).

Barnett, Steven. 2002. "Bill Throws Broadcast Up In Air", *The Observer* (5 May 2002).

Barnett, Steven. 2002. "One Man, One Media?", *The Guardian* (8 May 2002).

Barratt Brown, Michael. 1960. "Jugoslavia Revisited" in *New Left Review*, no. 1.

Barratt Brown, Michael and Ken Coates. 1979. *What Went Wrong*. Nottingham: Spokesman.

Basnett, David and Geoffrey Goodman. 1977. *Royal Commission on the Press: Minority Report*, London: Labour Party.

Bell, Emily. 1993. "Rivals Sniff at Cut-price Tactics", *The Observer* (5 September 1993).

Benn, Tony. 1974. *Speeches by Tony Benn*. Nottingham: Spokesman.

Benn, Tony. 1979. *The Need for a Free Press*. Nottingham: Institute for Workers' Control.

Benn, Tony. 1990. *Against the Tide*. London: Arrow Books.

Benn, Tony. 1991. *Conflicts of Interest*. London: Arrow Books.

Benn, Tony, and Chris Mullin. 1982. *Arguments for Democracy*. Harmondsworth: Penguin.

Benn, Tony, and Ruth Winstone. 1992. *The End of an Era*. London: Hutchinson.

Bennett, Neil. 1999. "The Odd Couple", *Sunday Telegraph* (28 November 1999).

Bellos, Alex. "Daily Mail Proprietor Gives New Hint of Election Backing for Blair", *The Guardian* (15 April 1996).

Blackhurst, Chris. 2001. "Bad Days at Blackfriars", *The Guardian* (29 January, 2001).

Blair, Tony. 1996. *New Britain*. London: Fourth Estate.

Blunkett, David and Bernard Crick. 1998. *The Labour Party's Aims and Values: An Unofficial Statement*, Nottingham: Spokesman.

Bobbio, Norberto. 1987. *Which Socialism?* Cambridge: Polity.

Bower, Tom. 1991. *Maxwell: The Outsider*. London: Mandarin.

Bower, Tom. 1996. *Maxwell: The Final Verdict*. London: HarperCollins.

Brind, Don. 2002. *The Labour Video Project*, Presentation Given to the Bournemouth University/London School of Economics Promotional Practices and Political Participation Conference, 22 November 2002.

Brivati, Brian and Richard Heffernan. 2000. *The Labour Party: A Centenary History*. Basingstoke: Macmillan.

Brooks, Richard. 1998. "Love, Marriage and the Real Rupert Murdoch", *The Observer* (8 November 1998).

Brown, Kevin. 1994. "Labour Backs Off in Threat to Murdoch", *Financial Times* (24 March 1995).

Brown, Maggie. 1993. "Giant Media Groups on the Way", *The Independent* (4 January 1993).

Brown, Maggie and Michael Leapman, Maggie Brown and Michael Leapman, "Let the Feeding Frenzy Commence", *The Independent* (12 January 1994).

Brown, Maggie. 1994. "Rule Change Urged on Media Ownership", *The Independent* (14 July 1994).

Brown, Maggie. 1996. "Gloves Off in the Free For All", *The Guardian* (15 April 1996).

Bulmer, Martin. 1980. *Social Research and Royal Commissions*. London: G. Allen & Unwin.

Burnham, James. 1942. *The Managerial Revolution*. London: Putnam.

Byrne, Ciar. 2002. "Mirror Sales Hit All-time Low", *The Guardian* (6 September 2002).

Callaghan, John. 2000. *The Retreat of Social Democracy*. Manchester: Manchester University Press.

Callaghan, John. 2002. *Globalisation: The End of Social Democracy?*, Essex: Essex Papers.

CPF. 1981. *The Right of Reply*. Hadleigh: Campaign for Press Freedom.

CPBF. 1984. *Labour Daily?* London: CPBF.

CLPD. 1992. Newsletter, No. 46 (Conference Edition), September–October 1992.

Campbell, Alastair. 2006. The Internet as Seen by the Technophobe, <http://discuss.aol.co.uk>.

Cassy, John. 2001. "Murdoch on Blair, Britain and Babies. And Those Whiners at ITV As Well", *The Guardian* (3 November 2001).

Cassy, John and Patrick Wintour. 2002. "Blair faces fight on TV controls", *The Guardian* (29 July 2002).

The Century of the Self, Part Four, RDF Media, BBC Two.

Chippindale, Peter, and Chris Horrie. 1988. *Disaster!: The Rise and Fall of News on Sunday*. London: Sphere.

Clarke, Simon. 1988. *Keynesianism, Monetarism and the Crisis of the State*. Aldershot: Edward Elgar.

Clwyd, Ann. 1993. "He's Used His Power to Evade Controls That Governments Might Place On Him", *Daily Mirror* (3 September 1993).

Coates, David. 1980. *Labour in Power?* London: Longman.

Cohen, Nick. 2000. *Cruel Britannia*. London: Verso.

Cole, Peter. 1998. "Lesson Number One: Don't Sack Your Readers", *The Independent* (18 May 1998).

Cole, Peter. 2002. "Have the 20p Tabloids Shot Themselves in the Foot?", *The Guardian* (19 May 2002).

Collins, Richard, and Cristina Murroni. 1996. *New Media, New Policies*. Cambridge: Polity.

Compaine, Benjamin and Douglas Gomery. 2000. *Who Owns the Media?*, Mahwah, N.J.: Lawrence Erlbaum Associates.

Competition Commission. 2003. Merger References: Competition Commission Guidelines, <www.competition-commission.org.uk>.

Cook, Robin and Clwyd, Ann. 1993. Cook and Clwyd Call for MMC Inquiry into Murdoch Ownership, Labour Party Press Release, 3 September 1993.

Crewe, Ivor and Martin Harrop. 1986. *Political Communications: the General Election Campaign of 1983*. Cambridge: Cambridge University Press.

Crewe, Ivor and Martin Harrop. 1989. *Political Communications: the General Election Campaign of 1987*. Cambridge: Cambridge University Press.

Crewe, Ivor, and Brian Gosschalk. 1995. *Political Communications: the General Election Campaign of 1992*. Cambridge: Cambridge University Press.

Crewe, Ivor et al., 1998. *Political Communications: Why Labour Won the General Election of 1997*. London: Frank Cass.

Crosland, Anthony. 1957. *The Future of Socialism*. New York: Macmillan.

Culf, Andrew. 1993. "Murdoch Claims His Technology Will Conquer National Media Laws", *The Guardian* (13 October 1993).

Culf, Andrew. 1993. "Clwyd Attacks Tory Line on Broadcasting", *The Guardian* (27 September 1993).

Culf, Andrew. 1993. "Murdoch Dismisses 'Paranoid' Critics", *The Guardian* (22 May 1995).

Curran, James. 1978. *The British Press: a Manifesto*. London: Macmillan.

Curran, James. 1983. *Report on the London Press Sector*. London: Greater London Enterprise Board.

Curran, James. ed. 1986. *Bending Reality*. London: Pluto.

Curran, James. 1991. "Rethinking the Media as a Public Sphere", in Peter Dahlgren and Colin Sparks, eds., *Communication and Citizenship*. London: Routledge.

Curran, James. 1995. *Policy for the Press*. London: IPPR.

Curran, James. 1996. "Mass Media and Democracy Revisted", in James Curran and Michael Gurevitch, eds., *Mass Media and Society*. London: Arnold.

Curran, James. 2000. "Press Reformism 1918-98: A Study in Failure", in *Media Power, Professionals and Policies*, edited by Howard Tumber. London: Routledge.

Curran, James. 2000. "Rethinking Media and Democracy", in Curran, James, and Michael Gurevitch, eds., *Mass Media and Society*. London: Arnold.

Curran, James. 2002. *Media and Power*, London: Routledge.

Curran, James and Stuart Holland, "Public Intervention in the Press", *Workers' Control Bulletin*, No. 3, 1979.

Curran, James, and Jean Seaton. 1997/2003. *Power Without Responsibility*. London: Routledge.

Curran, James, Ivor Gaber and Julian Petley. 2005. *Culture Wars*. Edinburgh: Edinburgh University Press.

Currie, Edwina. 2002. "I Chose My Lover Too Well", *The Times* (30 September 2002).

Currie, David. 2005. The Newspaper Society Annual Lunch, 17 May 2005, <www.ofcom.org.uk>.

Dale, Iain, and Labour Party. 2000. *Labour Party General Election Manifestos, 1900-1997*. London: Politico's.

Daley, Anthony. 1996. *The Mitterrand Era*. Basingstoke: Macmillan.

Davies, Patricia Wynn. 1993. "Labour Attacked Over TV 'Sell-out'", *The Independent* (26 November 1993).

Davies, Patricia Wynn and Matthew Horsman. 1995. "Prescott Slaps Down Complaint over BSkyB", *The Independent* (21 November 1995).

Davis, Aeron. 2002. *Public Relations Democracy*. Manchester: Manchester University Press.

Department of National Heritage. 1995. *Media Ownership*. London: HMSO.

DCMS/DTI. 1998. *Regulating Communications*. London: HMSO.

DCMS/DTI. 2000. *A New Future for Communications*. London: HMSO.

DCMS/DTI. 2002. *Draft Communications Bill*. London: HMSO.

DCMS/DTI. 2002. *Communications Bill*. London: HMSO.

DTI. 2000. *A New Future for Communications: Summary of Proposals*. London: DTI.

DTI. 2002. *Enterprise Act 2002*, <www.dti.gov.uk>.

DTI. 2004. *Enterprise Act 2002: Public Interest Intervention in Media Mergers*, <www.dti.gov.uk>.

Dewall Gustaf, von. 1997. *Press Ethics*. Dusseldorf: European Institute for the Media.

Dorril, Stephen and Robin Ramsay. 1992. *Smear!: Wilson and the secret state*. London: Grafton Books.

Doward, Jamie. 2002. "How Far Can Blair Go Before Murdoch Hits Back?", *The Observer* (5 May 2002).

Dowding et al. 2001. *Challenges to Democracy*. Basingstoke: Palgrave.

Doyle, Gillian. 2002. *Media Ownership*. London: Sage.

Doyle, Gillian. 2002. *Understanding Media Economics*. London: Sage Publications.

Driver, Stephen, and Luke Martell. 1998. *New Labour: Politics after Thatcherism*. Cambridge: Polity.

Dubbins, Tony. 2002. "Fighting Against Media Monopoly", *Morning Star* (1 October 2002).

Leader. 1986. *The Economist*, 26 April 1986.

Leader. 1997. "The Vision Thing", *The Economist*, 27 September 1997.

Entman, Robert. 1989. *Democracy Without Citizens*. New York: Oxford University Press.

Evans, Harold. 1983. *Good Times, Bad Times*. London: Weidenfeld & Nicolson.

Leader. 1986. "Smile Please", *Evening Standard* (23 April 1986).

Fairclough, Norman. 2000. *New Labour, New Language?* London: Routledge.

Fielding, Steven. 1997. *The Labour Party*. Manchester: Manchester University Press.

Leader. 1986. "Mr Kinnock's New Party", *Financial Times* (23 April 1986).

Foot, Paul. 1996. "Sour Note, Moonie Tune", *The Guardian* (15 April 1996).

Foot, Paul. 2000. *Articles of Resistance*. London: Bookmarks, 2000.

Frank, Thomas. 2002. *One Market under God*. London: Vintage.

Franklin, Bob. 1998. *Tough on Soundbites, Tough on the Causes of Soundbites*. London: Catalyst Trust.

Franklin, Bob. 1994/2004. *Packaging Politics*. London: Hodder Arnold.

Frayman, Harold and Donald Ross. 1979. "A Labour Daily?", *Workers' Control Bulletin*, No. 3, 1979.

Freedman, Des. 2000. *The Television Policies of the British Labour Party: 1951-2000*: University of Westminster.

Freedman, Des. 2003. *Television Policies of the Labour Party: 1951-2001*: London: Frank Cass.

Freedman, Des. 2005. *How Level is the Playing Field?*, London: Goldsmiths College and the ESRC.

Freeman, Alan. 1982. *The Benn Heresy*. London: Pluto.

Garnham, Nicholas. 1992. "The Media and the Public Sphere", in Craig Calhoun, *Habermas and the Public Sphere*. Cambridge, Mass.: MIT Press.

Gaber, Ivor. 1980. "Benn and ITN", *Free Press*, December 1980.

Gapper, John and David Wighton. 1999. "Sunday Express Chiefs Quit in Mandelson Row", *Financial Times* (20 January 1999).

Gillmor, Dan. 2004. *We the Media*. Sebastopol: O'Reilly Media.

Giddens, Anthony. 2000. *The Third Way and its Critics*. Malden: Polity.

Glover, Stephen. 2000. "It Was a Dreadful Picture; But It Spoke for Humanity", *Spectator*, 14 October 2000.

Goodwin, Peter. 1998. *Television under the Tories*. London: BFI Publishing.

Gopsill, Tim. 1996. "Meanwhile Back on the Benches...", *Free Press*, July-August 1996.

Gospel, Howard and Gill Palmer. 1993. *British Industrial Relations*. London: Routledge.

Gould, Bryan. 1999. "The Long Retreat from Principle", *New Statesman*, 29 January 1999.

Gould, Philip. 1998. *The Unfinished Revolution*. London: Little Brown.

Grant, John. 1975. "Letter: Press Freedom", *The Times* (16 April 1975).

Greenslade, Roy. 1992. *Maxwell's Fall*. London: Simon & Schuster.

Greenslade, Roy. 1997. "Nice One Sun, says Tony", *The Guardian* (19 May 1997).

Greenslade, Roy. 1997. "Taming Paper Tigers, But for How Long?", *The Guardian* (1 May 1997).

Greenslade, Roy. 1999. "Boycott sacks Platell", *The Guardian* (25 January, 1999).

Greenslade, Roy. 2003. *Press Gang*. Basingstoke: Macmillan.

Roy Greenslade, "Shouldn't This Man Be Worried?", *The Guardian* (12 January 2004).

Leader. 1986. "The Package Has Come a Long Way", *The Guardian* (23 April 1986).

Leader. 1996. "Mirror, Mirror on the Screen", *The Guardian* (17 April 1996).

Habermas, Jurgen. 1989. *The Structural Transformation of the Public Sphere*. Cambridge: Polity.

Hagerty, Bill. 1999. "Citizen Clive. Interview with Lord Hollick", *British Journalism Review*, vol. 10, no. 1, 1999.

Hagerty, Bill. 2000. "Cap'n Spin Does Lose his Rag!", *British Journalism Review*, vol. 11, no. 2, 2000.

Hall, Phoebe. 1986. *Change, Choice and Conflict in Social Policy*. Aldershot: Gower.

Hamilton, Dennis. 1976. *Who is to Own the British Press?* London: Birkbeck College.

Hansen, Bjorn. 1972. "Where Labour Has a Good Press", *Labour Weekly* (9 June 1972).

Harrison, Stanley. 1974. *Poor Men's Guardians*. London: Lawrence and Wishart.

Hastings, Max. 2002. *Editor*. London: Macmillan.

Hatfield, Michael. 1978. *The House the Left Built*. London: Gollancz.

Hattersley, Roy. 1983. *Press Gang*. London: Robson Books.

Hattersley, Roy. 1991. "Reflections on the Mirror", *Financial Times*, (16 November 1991).

Hattersley, Roy. 1995. *Who Goes Home?* London: Little Brown & Co.

Heffernan, Richard. 2001. *New Labour and Thatcherism*. Basingstoke: Palgrave.

Heffernan, Richard, and Mike Marqusee. 1992. *Defeat From the Jaws of Victory*. London: Verso.

Held, David. 1987. *Models of Democracy*. Cambridge: Polity.

Held, David. 1995. *Democracy and the Global Order*. Cambridge: Polity Press.

Held, David. 1999. *Global Transformations*. Stanford: Stanford University Press.

Henry, Georgina. 1990. "Satellite Merger Escapes Scrutiny", *The Guardian* (19 December 1990).

Henry, Georgina. 1994. "Balancing Act on a See-saw", *The Guardian* (27 June 1994).

Herman, Edward, and Robert McChesney. 1997. *The Global Media*. London: Cassell.

Hewitt, Patricia and Tessa Jowell. 2002. *A Summary of our Proposals*. London: HMSO.

Hills, John. 2004. *Inequality and the State*. Oxford: Oxford University Press.

Hodgson, Jessica. 2002. "Blair Contacted Desmond Minutes After Express Takeover", *The Guardian* (13 May, 2002).

Hodgman, John. 1975. "A New Paper is Born", *Journalist*, April 1975.

Hollingsworth, Mark. 1986. *The Press and Political Dissent*. London: Pluto.

Høst, Sigurd. 1991. "The Norwegian Newspaper System: Structure and Development" in *Media and Communication*, edited by Helge Ronning and Knut Lundby. Oslo: Norwegian University Press.

Hughes, Colin and Patrick Wintour. 1990. *Labour Rebuilt*. London: Fourth Estate.

Humphreys, Peter. 1996. *Mass Media and Media Policy in Western Europe*. Manchester: Manchester University Press.

Humphreys, Peter. 2000. "New Labour Policies for the Media and the Arts", in *New Labour in Power*, edited by David Coates and Peter Lawler. Manchester: Manchester University Press.

Leader. 1994. "A Place in the Sun for Blair?", *The Independent* (10 August 1994).

Business Comment, "View Looks Good from Lord Hollick's Chair", *The Independent* (11 September 1997).

Jacques, Martin. 1990. "Requiem for a Revolution", *The Times* (12 September 1990).

Jones, Eileen. 1994. *Neil Kinnock*. London: Robert Hale.

Jones, George. 1992. "Free Press at Risk from Labour, says Wakeham", *Daily Telegraph* (29 February 1992).

Jones, Michael. 1993. "Labour in a Silly Spin over Satellite Success", *Sunday Times* (5 September 1993).

Jones, Nicholas, *Personal Notes*.

Jones, Nicholas. 1995. *Soundbites and Spin Doctors*. London: Cassell.

Jones, Nicholas. 2000. *Sultans of Spin*. London: Orion.

Jones, Nicholas. 2001. *The Control Freaks*. London: Politico's.

Brook, Lindsay et al. 1992. *British Social Attitudes Cumulative Sourcebook*, Aldershot: Gower.

Jowell, Tessa. 2002. Guardian Online chat, May 10, <talk.guardian.co.uk>.

Jowell, Tessa. 2003. Letter to Les Hinton, <www.guardian.co.uk/freedom>.

Junor, Penny. 1993. *The Major Enigma*. London: Michael Joseph.

Kane, Frank. 2004. "How We Won the Telegraph - By the Barclays" (*Observer*, 27 June 2004).

Keane, John. 1991. *The Media and Democracy*. Cambridge, MA: Polity.

Kelly, Stephen. 1975. "Outlook is Grim for the "Miracle" Paper that Glasgow Workers Started", *Tribune* (17 October 1975).

Kenny, Michael. 1995. *The First New Left*. London: Lawrence & Wishart.

King, Anthony. "Labour Viewed as 'Sleazy and Disreputable'", *Daily Telegraph* (20 June 2002).

King, Anthony, ed. 1998. *New Labour Triumphs: Britain at the Polls*, Chatham, N.J.: Chatham House.

Kinnock, Neil. 1994. "Reforming the Labour Party", *Contemporary History Record* 8:3.

Knowles, Ron and Roger Protz. 1974. "NUJ, Editors and the Closed Shop", *The Journalist*, July 1974.

Kogan, David, and Maurice Kogan. 1982. *The Battle for the Labour Party*. London: Kogan Page.

Koss, Stephen. 1984. *The Rise and Fall of the Political Press in Britain*. London: Hamilton.

Krueger, Richard. 1998. *Analyzing and Reporting Focus Group Results*. Thousand Oaks: Sage.

Labour Party. 1974. *Let Us Work Together*. London: Labour Party.

Labour Party. 1974. *The People and the Media*. London: Labour Party.

Labour Party. 1976. *Labour's Programme for Britain*. London: Labour Party.

Labour Party. 1984. *Rulebook of the Labour Party*: London: Labour Party.

Labour Party. 1987. *Britain Will Win*. London: Labour Party.

Labour Party. 1988. *Democratic Socialist Aims and Values*, London: Labour Party

Labour Party. 1989. *Meet the Challenge, Make the Change*, London: Labour Party

Labour Party. 1991. *Opportunity Britain*, London: Labour Party

Labour Party. 1992. *Agenda for Change*. London: Labour Party.

Labour Party. 1996. *Vision for Growth*. London: Labour Party.

Labour Party. 1997. *Labour's Business Manifesto*. London: Labour Party.

Labour Party. 1997. *New Labour: Because Britain Deserves Better*. London: Labour Party.

Labour Party. 2001. *Labour's Business Manifesto*. London: Labour Party.

Labour Party. 2002. *Democracy and Citizenship*. London: Labour Party.

Labour Party NEC. 1997. *Partnership in Power*. London: Labour Party.

Labour Research Department. 1922. *The Press*: London: Labour Research.

Lefties: A Lot of Balls, BBC Four.

Leonard, Tom. 2004. "Telegraph Sale May Face Test", *Daily Telegraph* (8 May 2004).

Levy, Phillip. 1967. *The Press Council*. London: Macmillan.

Lichtenberg, Judith ed. 1990. *Democracy and the Mass Media*. Cambridge: Cambridge University Press.

Linton, Martin. 1972. "The Case for a Labour Press", Labour Weekly (9 June 1972).

Linton, Martin. 1995. *Was It The Sun Wot Won It?* Oxford: Nuffield College, 1995.

Lively, Jack. 1975. *Democracy*. Oxford: Basil Blackwell.

Lukes, Steven. 1974. *Power: A Radical View*. Basingstoke: Macmillan.

MacBride, Sean. 1980. *Many Voices One World*. London: Kogan Page.

Macintyre, Donald. 1995. "The Odd Couple on Honeymoon in the Sun", *The Independent* (18 July 1995).

Macintyre, Donald. 1999. *Mandelson*. London: HarperCollins.

MacShane, Denis. 1986. *French Lessons for Labour*. London: Fabian Society, 1986.

Maguire, Kevin. 2000. "Byers Urged to Block Express Buyout", *The Guardian* (23 December 2000).

Mair, Peter. 2000. "Partyless Democracy: Solving the Paradox of New Labour?", *New Left Review*, March–April 2000.

Mandelson, Peter. 2003. *Lecture at the London School of Economics*, February 25 2003.

Mandelson, Peter. 2002. "There's Plenty of Life in the 'New' Third Way Yet", *The Times* (19 June, 2002).

Manners, Bruce. 1995. "Blair Learns From Down-under World Where Left is Right", *Sunday Telegraph* (31 December 1995).

Marquand, David. 1997. "After Euphoria: The Dilemmas of New Labour", *The Political Quarterly*, no. 4, 1997.

Mattick, Paul. 1971. *Marx and Keynes*. London: Merlin Press.

McCann, Gerald. 1997. *Theory and History*. Aldershot: Ashgate.

McChesney, Robert. 1997. *Corporate Media and the Threat to Democracy*. New York: Seven Stories Press.

McChesney, Robert. 2000. *Rich Media, Poor Democracy*. Urbana: University of Illinois Press.

McNair, Brian. 1999. *Journalism and Democracy*. London: Routledge.

McNair, Brian. 1999. *News and Journalism in the UK*. London: Routledge.

McQuail, Denis et al. 1998. *Media Policy*. London: Sage Publications.

McSmith, Andy. 1993. *John Smith: Playing the Long Game*. London: Verso.

McSmith, Andy. 1994. *John Smith: A Life, 1938–1994*. London, Mandarin.

McSmith, Andy. 1996. *Faces of Labour*. London: Verso.

McSmith, Andy and John Arlidge, "Sun Chiefs Tried to Defy Murdoch", *The Observer* (23 March 1997).

Miller, William. 1991. *Media and Voters*. Oxford: Oxford University Press.

Milmo, Dan. 2004. "Ex Editors Will Vet Telegraph Bids to Advise on Public Interest", *The Guardian* (8 May 2004).

Minkin, Lewis. 1980. *The Labour Party Conference*. Manchester: Manchester University Press.

Minkin, Lewis. 1991. *The Contentious Alliance*. Edinburgh: Edinburgh University Press.

Mitchell, Austin. 1987. "The Party of Producers and Consumers", *The Independent* (24 July 1987).

The Monopoly and Mergers Commission. 1990. *Mr David Sullivan and the Bristol Evening Post PLC*. London: MMC.

Morgan David, 1998. *The Focus Group Guide Book*. Thousand Oaks: Sage.

Moonman, Eric. 1972. "Future of the Press – Does Anyone Care?", *Labour Weekly* (9 June 1972).

Morgan, Ken. 1975. "Editors Reject Charter", *The Journalist*, March 1975.

Morgan, Kenneth 1997. *Callaghan: A Life*. Oxford: Oxford University Press.

Mowlam, Marjorie. 1994. "Labour's Watching Brief", *The Independent* (12 January 1994).

Mulgan, Geoff and Ken Worpole. 1986. *Saturday Night or Sunday Morning?* London: Comedia.

Mulgan, Geoff. 1994. *Politics in an Antipolitical Age.* Cambridge: Polity.

Mulgan, Geoff, ed. 1997. *Life after Politics,* London: Fontana.

Murschetz, Paul. 1998. "State Support for the Daily Press in Europe: A Critical Appraisal", *European Journal of Communication* 13.

Murschetz, Paul. 1997. *State Support for the Press.* Dusseldorf: European Institute for the Media.

NGA (82). 1983. "Second Briefing Conference for MPs Background Notes", November 1983.

NUJ. 2002. *Communications Bill 2002: The NUJ's Response: Briefing for Members of Parliament.*

Negrine, Ralph. 1989. *Politics and the Mass Media in Britain.* London: Routledge.

News International. 2002. Response to Consultation on Media Ownership Rules, <www.culture.gov.uk/creative/index.html>.

Neil, Andrew. 1997. *Full Disclosure.* London: Pan Books.

Oborne, Peter. 1999. *Alastair Campbell.* London: Aurum.

Leader. 1986. "Labour Starts to Get its Act Together", *The Observer* (27 April 1986).

OFCOM. 2004. *OFCOM Guidance for the Public Interest Test for Media Mergers.*

OFT. 1999. *Press Release: Newspaper Pricing: News International Gives Assurances,* 21 May 1999.

OFT. 2001. *Press Release: Scottish Newspaper Group Fined for Predatory Pricing,* 16 July 2001.

O'Malley, Tom. 1998. "Demanding Accountability: The Press, the Royal Commissions and the Pressure for Reform, 1945–77", in Michael Bromley and Hugh Stephenson. 1998. *Sex, Lies and Democracy.* New York: Longman.

O'Malley, Tom and Clive Soley. 2000. *Regulating the Press.* London: Pluto.

Østbye, Helge. 1997. "Norway", in *The Media in Western Europe,* edited by Stubbe Ostergaard Bernt. London: Sage.

Owen, David. 1992. "Hattersley Promise on Incomes", *Financial Times* (16 March 1992).

Panitch, Leo, and Colin Leys. 1997. *The End of Parliamentary Socialism: from new left to New Labour.* London: Verso.

Parris, Matthew. 1998. "How Murdoch Interferes Less Than Other Proprietors", *New Statesman,* 14 March 1998.

Pateman, Carole. 1970. *Participation and Democratic Theory.* Cambridge: Cambridge University Press.

Pearse, Edward. 2000. "Obituary: John Grant", *The Guardian* (4 October 2000).

Pilger, John. 1987. "The Birth of a New *Sun?*", *New Statesman,* 2 January 1987.

Pilger, John. 1994. "The Very Best of Mates", *The Guardian Weekend* (23 July 1994).

Pilger, John. 1994. "Murdoch's Love for New Labour", *Free Press,* September–October 1995.

Pimlott, Ben. 1993. *Harold Wilson.* London: HarperCollins.

Plant, Raymond et al., eds. 2004. *The Struggle for Labour's Soul.* London: Routledge.

Porter, Henry. 1994. "Murdoch: The Wooing Game", *The Guardian* (26 September 1994).

Power, Mike. 1985. "What Are We Going To Do About Paul Foot?", *Free Press,* January–February 1985.

Puttnam, David. 2002. *Hard Talk*, BBC News 24, 4 October 2002.

Radice, Giles, and Lisanne Radice. 1986. *Socialists in the Recession*. London: Macmillan.

Rentoul, John. 1995. *Tony Blair*. London: Little Brown and Co.

Richards, Huw. 1997. *The Bloody Circus*. London: Pluto.

Robertson, Geoffrey. 1983. *People against the Press*. London: Quartet.

Robinson, Philip. 1996. "Back-Seat Role for Lord Stevens", *Daily Telegraph* (14 November 1996).

Rose, David. 2002. "Blair will force Lords to accept US buyers", *Broadcast*, 4 October 2002.

Rose, Richard. 1993. *Lesson-Drawing in Public Policy*. Chatham, N.J.: Chatham House.

Ross, David. 1973. "Staff Help to Shape a Paper", *The Journalist*, May 1973.

Roth, Andrew, and Byron Criddle. 2000. *1997-2002 Parliamentary Profiles*. London: Parliamentary Profiles.

Roth, Andrew. 1979. *The MP's Chart*. London: Parliamentary Profiles.

Routledge, Paul. 1999. *Mandy*. London: Simon & Schuster.

Royal Commission on the Press. 1977. *Royal Commission on the Press. Final Report*. London: HMSO.

Harrison, Royden. 1957. "The Congress of Workers' Councils, Yugoslavia", in *New Reasoner*, no. 2.

Rudd, Roland. 1994. "Tougher Line on Media Urged", *Financial Times* (8 October 1994).

Sanchez-Tabernero, Alfonso, and Alison Denton. 1993. *Media Concentration in Europe*. Manchester: European Institute for the Media.

Scannell, Paddy. 1989. "Public Service Broadcasting and Modern Life", *Media, Culture and Society* 11.

Schultz, Julianne. 1998. *Reviving the Fourth Estate*. Cambridge: Cambridge University Press, 1998.

Scott, John. 1985. *Corporations, Classes and Capitalism*. London: Hutchinson.

Seaton, Jean. 1978. "Government Policy and the Mass Media", in *The British Press: A Manifesto*, edited by James Curran and Acton Society Press Group. London: Macmillan.

Seaton, Jean, and Ben Pimlott, eds. 1987. *The Media in British Politics*. Aldershot: Dartmouth.

Seyd, Patrick. 1987. *The Rise and Fall of the Labour Left*. Basingstoke: Macmillan Education.

Seyd, Patrick, and Paul Whiteley. 1992. *Labour's Grass Roots*. Oxford: Clarendon Press.

Seymour-Ure, Colin. 1994. "Who Owns the National Press?", *Contemporary Record* 8.

Seymour-Ure, Colin. 1996. *The British Press and Broadcasting since 1945*. Oxford: Blackwell.

Seymour-Ure, Colin. 1997. "Editorial Opinion in the National Press", in *Britain Votes 1997*, edited by Pippa Norris and T. Gavin Neil. Oxford: Oxford University Press.

Shaw, Eric. 1988. *Discipline and Discord in the Labour Party*. Manchester: Manchester University Press.

Shaw, Eric. 1994. *The Labour Party Since 1979*. London: Routledge.

Shaw, Eric. 1996. *The Labour Party Since 1945*. Oxford: Blackwell.

Shawcross, William. 1993. *Rupert Murdoch*. London: Pan.

Skogerbø, Eli. 1997. "The Press Subsidy System in Norway: Controversial Past – Unpredictable Future?" *European Journal of Communication* 12.

Smith, Anthony. 1974. *The British Press Since the War*. Totowa, N.J.: Rowman and Littlefield.

Smith, Anthony, ed. 1980. *Newspapers and Democracy*. London: MIT Press.

Smithers, Rebecca and Patrick Wintour. 1996. "Tory MPs Quit After Media Bill Revolt" (*The Guardian*, 22 May 1996).

Snoddy, Raymond. 1993. "Media Review Aims to Boost UK Ownership Overseas", *Financial Times* (January 4 1993).

Snoddy, Raymond. 2005. "Lord Puttnam – 'I Should Have Been Smarter'", *The Independent* (9 May 2005).

Sparks, Colin. 1995. "Concentration in the UK National Press", *European Journal of Communication*, 10.

Sparks, Colin. 1999. "The Press", in *The Media in Britain*, edited by Jane Stokes and Anna Reading. Basingstoke: Macmillan.

Street, John. 2001. *Mass Media, Politics, and Democracy*. Basingstoke: Palgrave.

Swedish Press Subsidies Council, <www.presstodsnamnden.se/english.htm>.

Taaffe, Peter. 1981. *What We Stand For*. London: Militant.

Taylor Gerald, R. 1997. *Labour's Renewal?* Basingstoke: Macmillan.

Thomas, Harford. 1967. *Newspaper Crisis*. Zurich: International Press Institute.

Thomas, James. 2000. "The 'Max Factor' - a Mirror Image? Robert Maxwell and the *Daily Mirror* Tradition", in *Northcliffe's Legacy*, edited by Colin Seymour-Ure et al. Basingstoke: Macmillan.

Thompson, Noel. 1996. *Political Economy and the Labour Party*. London: UCL Press.

Thompson, Steve. 1992. "Comment Hits Media Stock", *Financial Times* (24 March 1992).

Tomkins, Richard. 2003. "Let's Ban Advertising. Only Joking, Let's Tax It", *Financial Times* (16 May 2003).

Tomlinson, Jim. 1990. *Hayek and the Market*. London: Pluto.

Tracey, Michael. 1998. *The Decline and Fall of Public Service Broadcasting*. Oxford: Oxford University Press.

TUC. 1980. *Behind the Headlines*. London: TUC.

TUC. 1983. *The Other Side of the Story*. London: TUC.

Traynor, Ian. 1998. "Peter's Passions", *The Guardian* (16 March 1998).

Trefgarne, George. 2001. "BSkyB Boss Threatens to Turn Titles Anti-Labour", *Daily Telegraph* (3 November 2001).

Tulloch, John. 1998. "Managing the Press in a Medium Sized European Power", in Michael Bromley and Hugh Stephenson. 1998. *Sex, Lies and Democracy*. New York: Longman.

Tunney, Sean. 2004. "Neil Kinnock and Robert Maxwell", in *Media History*, 10.

Tunstall, Jeremy. 1983. *The Media in Britain*. London: Constable.

Tunstall, Jeremy. 1995. *Newspaper Power*. Oxford: Oxford University Press.

Viner, Katherine. 1998. "Window Dressing", *The Guardian* (5 October 1998).

Wainwright, Hilary. 1987. *Labour: A Tale of Two Parties*. London: Hogarth.

Wainwright, Hilary. 1994. *Arguments for a New Left*. Cambridge, Mass.: Blackwell.

Wasko, Janet and Vincent Mosco, eds. 1992. *Democratic Communications in the Information Age*. Toronto: Garamond Press.

Webster, Paul. 1997. "Britain Sank Jospin's EU Jobs Scheme", *The Guardian* (21 June 1997).

Wickham-Jones, Mark. 1996. *Economic Strategy and the Labour Party*. New York: St. Martin's Press.

Widgery, David. 1976. "The Double Exposure: Suez and Hungary, in *The Left In Britain 1956-68*, edited by David Widgery. Harmondsworth: Penguin.

Williams, Kevin. 1998. *Get Me a Murder a Day!* London: Arnold.

Williams, Raymond. 1966. *Communications*. London: Chatto & Windus.

Wintour, Charles. 1972. *Pressures on the Press*. London: André Deutsch.

Wintour, Patrick. 1996. "Government Facing Defeat", *The Guardian* (16 May 1996).

Wintour, Patrick. 2004. "Labour Membership Halved", *The Guardian* (3 August 2004).

Wintour, Patrick and Sarah Hall. 2002. "Labour Inquest on Membership Loss", *The Guardian* (29 January 2002).

Wring, Dominic. 1995. "Soundbites versus Socialism: The Changing Campaign Philosophy of the British Labour Party," *Javnost* 4.

Wring, Dominic. 1995. *Political Marketing and Organisational Development*. Cambridge: Judge Institute of Management Studies, University of Cambridge.

Wring, Dominic. 1997. *Political Marketing and the Labour Party*. Cambridge: University of Cambridge.

Wring, Dominic. 2005. *The Politics of Marketing the Labour Party*. Basingstoke: Palgrave Macmillan.

Wring, Dominic. 2005. "The Labour Campaign", in Pippa Norris and Christopher Wlezien, eds., *Parliamentary Affairs* special issue on 2005 British General Election.

Wyatt, Woodrow, and Sarah Curtis. 2000. *The Journals of Woodrow Wyatt, Volume 3*. London: Macmillan.

Reports

House of Commons Hansard Debates (HOC)
House of Lords Hansard Debates
HM Government Consultations
Labour Party Conference Reports
TUC Congress Reports

Archives

Kinnock, Neil. 1983-1994. *Personal Papers*, Churchill Archive.

Labour Party, *Shadow Cabinet, NEC and Joint Trade Union and Study Group Minutes*, Labour Party Archive, National Museum of Labour History.

Royal Commission on the Press. 1977. *Reports, Submissions and Evidence*, City University.

Campaign for Press Broadcasting Freedom, *Minutes, Correspondence and Internal Papers*.

TUC Archives, *NUJ and TUC papers*. London Metropolitan University.

Journals

Free Press
Labour Weekly
The Journalist
New Left Review
New Socialist
New Statesman
Tribune

Index

WITHDRAWN from STIRLING UNIVERSITY LIBRARY